Maurice Nicoll: A Portrait

MAURICE NICOLL
A Portrait

By Beryl Pogson

'Those born of the Spirit are unpredictable'

FOURTH WAY BOOKS
NEW YORK

ISBN 0-936385-24-3
LIBRARY OF CONGRESS CATALOG CARD NO. 87-082275

10 9 8 7 6 5 4 3 2 1
MANUFACTURED IN THE UNITED STATES

Contents

List of Illustrations		viii
Biographical Table		ix
Acknowledgements		xi
Introduction		xiii
I	EARLY YEARS (1884-1912)	1
II	DECISIVE INFLUENCES	19
III	THE 1914 WAR – ACTIVE SERVICE IN GALLIPOLI AND MESOPOTAMIA (1914-1917)	30
IV	EMPIRE HOSPITAL (1917-1918)	50
V	MARRIAGE – MEETING WITH OUSPENSKY AND GURDJIEFF – TRAINING AT THE CHÂTEAU DU PRIEURÉ (1920-1923)	67
VI	RELATIONSHIP WITH OUSPENSKY (1923-1931)	93
VII	GROUP WORK IN LONDON AND ESSEX (1931-1939)	110
VIII	1939 WAR – BIRDLIP (1940-1941)	131
IX	EXTRACTS FROM WAR DIARY	149
X	BIRDLIP 1942	198
XI	BIRDLIP 1943-1944	215
XII	QUAREMEAD (1945-1946)	226
XIII	GREAT AMWELL HOUSE (1946-1951)	237
XIV	PUBLICATIONS	256
XV	LAST YEARS AT GREAT AMWELL HOUSE (1951-1953)	268
Index		285

List of Illustrations

1. About 1890   *facing page*   18

2. 1899 (Aldenham)   19

3. Medical Student, Bart's   34

4. R.A.M.C. 1914, with Constance, his sister   35

5. Marriage, 1920   66

6. Catherine Nicoll, 1920   67

7. P. D. Ouspensky at Alley Cottage   82

8. Carpenter's Shop, Prieuré   83

9. After Fontainebleau, with Jane   146

10. The Old Manse, Lumsden   147

11. Bay Tree Lodge   147

12. Château du Prieuré   162

13. Tyeponds   162

14. Alley Cottage   162

15. Great Amwell House   163

16. With the author, 1949   258

17. In his study, Great Amwell House   259

18. In the 'George IV'   259

19. 1953   274

Biographical Table

'The ideal biography should begin with a very clear chronological table, shewing at a glance how the life was divided. For want of this we misconceive – we do not see how events are spread about or crowded together in a space of years.' W. ROBERTSON NICOLL: *Letters on Life.*

1884   Born at the Manse, Kelso, 19th July.

1886   Father retired from Ministry.

1889   Family removed to Bay Tree Lodge, Hampstead. Entered University College Preparatory School.

1891   Death of Grandfather, Rev. Harry Nicoll.

1894   Death of Mother.

1897   Father's marriage to Miss Catherine Pollard. Entered Aldenham School.

1904   Entered Gonville and Caius College, Cambridge.

1906   B.A. Cantab – 1st Class Honours. Entered Bart's Hospital.

1909   Father received knighthood.

1910   Qualified in Medicine. Joint publication with his sister of *Lord Richard in the Pantry*.

1912   Studied Psychology in Vienna and Zürich.

1913   In practice in Golders Green. Partnership with Dr Crichton Miller.

1914   Received Commission in R.A.M.C.

1917   Work in Empire Hospital on shell shock.

1920   Marriage to Miss Catherine Champion Jones.

1921   Father awarded C.H. Birth of daughter. Meeting with Ouspensky.

1922   Meeting with Gurdjieff. Gave up London practice – went to Institute.

1923   Death of Father.

1924 Resumed practice in Harley Street.

1931 Received authority from Ouspensky to teach the System.

1939 Retired from Harley Street practice.

1940 Moved to The Knapp, Birdlip.

1945 Moved to Quaremead, Ugley.

1946 Moved to Great Amwell House, Ware.

1948 Birth of granddaughter.

1949 Private publication of three volumes of *Commentaries on the Teaching of Gurdjieff and Ouspensky*.

1950 Publication of *The New Man*.

1951 Serious operation.

1952 Publication of three volumes of *Commentaries on the Teaching of Gurdjieff and Ouspensky*. Publication of *Living Time*.

1953 Death.

Acknowledgements

I SHOULD like to thank Maurice Nicoll's family for the appreciation and encouragement which they have never failed to give me during the writing of this book. I was particularly grateful to the late Lady Robertson Nicoll for her clear recollections of his childhood, and for the loan of letters and photographs and for permission to quote from her private publication, *Under the Bay Tree*. I was very thankful that she was able to read the book in manuscript before she died and to express her approval of it. My thanks are due also to Mrs Elystan Miles, Mrs Grange Kirkcaldy and Mrs John Mounsey for letters, photographs and reminiscences and to Lady Syfret, Mrs Mayor, Miss Moxon, Mrs Ronald Jeans, Mr Kenneth Walker, Mr Thomas Casswell, Mr Cyril Parfit, Mr David Squire, Mr Harold Rubinstein and Mr Michael Rubinstein for valuable material and photographs. I am grateful to Mrs Humphrey Butler for helpful suggestions in the early stages of the writing and I owe much to Miss Edith Saunders for her expert advice in the arrangement of the manuscript at a time when I had become discouraged. Further, my thanks are due to Mrs Hodder for secretarial help, and to Miss Rosanne McCullagh for the final typing of the text, to Mr Lewis Creed for his drawing of Bay Tree Lodge from a reproduction of an original drawing, to Mr E. C. Macinnes Begg, Mrs Janet Hagon, Mr T. Marriner, Rear-Admiral R. W. Oldham and Mr Harold Rubinstein for proof-reading, and to those members of my group who have assisted in the compilation of the Index.

Introduction

'Every man's life may be best written by himself.'
SAMUEL JOHNSON

On 2nd October, 1953, about a month after Dr Nicoll died, Mrs Nicoll asked me if I would write his biography. This was seven years ago. At first I tried to write an orthodox biography, but eventually abandoned the attempt.

This book is a portrait of Maurice Nicoll sketched against the background of his life as he himself remembered it. I have recorded what he himself told us of his experiences. When he gathered the threads of his life together during his last years he emphasized that certain periods were unimportant, but that memory selected those events, moments, experiences which were nodes in the pattern of the whole. The Time-Body of his life was ever present to him. He could see the way in which he was prepared during his early life for his destiny.

His professional life, in which he won some distinction, no longer remained in detail in his memory. He regarded it simply as useful in qualifying him to understand those who later became his pupils – thus he rarely spoke of it. The years before he met Gurdjieff and Ouspensky counted for him only as a necessary period of preparation for his work as a transmitter of the teaching that he received from them.

I was Dr Nicoll's pupil for nineteen years and his secretary for fourteen years during which period I was one of the small group who lived with him.

In the later chapters of this book I have described our way of life. Dr Nicoll was one-pointed in his aim – everything else was subordinated to it. It was always understood that I should one day write about his external daily life. What I have not written of in this volume is the private teaching which he gave to those of us who were close to him, which included his interpretation of our dreams and his sharing with us some of his own inner life. The real teaching is always oral and secret.

CHAPTER ONE

Early Years

THE PRIVACY OF CHILDHOOD

Now I am on the road alone
Without companion save my soul.
Ah, blessed intake of Nature!
I can idle at a fence or wander
Down a little stream or sit
On what I like.
No pretence is necessary.
I do not have to be like
Anything save myself.
And all at once there come
The old feelings of freedom
That I have forgotten,
Of the old, tranquil, long,
Unhurried life,
The feelings of boyhood
Before I committed the sin
Of naming everything
And thinking I knew,
Yes, before I ate
Of the tree of knowledge
And pretended I knew,
Before I became a botanist
And a lover of the country,
Or wrote things down in books;
When I saw things as they are
And stared at birds
And grass and trees
And felt the turf and heard
Everything speaking,
And came home with wonder,
Drenched with air and pleasure
That I would never share
With anyone
Because it was my own delight,
My very life, and not pretence.
And people said 'What did you do
This afternoon, dear,
And where were you?'
Ah, 'where were you?'

MAURICE NICOLL

Ah, where was I, I thought
And I sat up and said something,
Something quite untrue – a lie:
'I went to Parson's Farm
And then turned up the lane
Leading to Deep End,'
And sat in silence.
'That's good,' they said,
'It will keep you fit.'
Fit for what, I wondered.

Maurice Nicoll

Henry Maurice Dunlop Nicoll was born half an hour after midnight on 19th July 1884 at the Free Church Manse, Kelso, Scotland, where his father, the Rev. William Robertson Nicoll (later Sir William Robertson Nicoll) was Minister. He remembered little of his birthplace as eighteen months after his birth his father was obliged to resign his charge at Kelso owing to a serious illness. Dr Robertson Nicoll went first to Dawlish, where he was able to recuperate, and then to Upper Norwood. This was an important turning-point, for it was through having to give up the Ministry, owing to his failing health, that he took up a literary career. He had for some time worked for the publishers, Messrs Hodder and Stoughton, and, with their cordial co-operations, founded *The British Weekly* (in 1886), later editing *The Expositor* and *The Bookman* and eventually becoming one of the most famous men of letters of his day. In 1889 Bay Tree Lodge in Frognal, Hampstead, became the home of the Nicoll family, and it was here that Dr Nicoll spent his childhood, boyhood and youth, living his own private life in this gracious house with its pleasant garden, against a background of all the social, political and literary activity that his father's career demanded.

Dr Nicoll's impressions of his childhood were sometimes given in informal conversations to those of us who knew him well in his later life. He never failed to remind us of the inadequacy and inaccuracy of our memory of our past life. His most vivid recollection of his very early days was of his delight in going off by himself to fish in the Scottish burns when he stayed in the summer at the Old Manse at Lumsden. Memories of long days of freedom among the heather-covered moors, fishing for trout, were to him an unfailing source of joy. He remembered the endlessness of time on such days. This recollection is the theme of his poem, 'The Privacy of Childhood'.

He told us how interested he had been in the sundew plant that eats flies and is found in the peat-bogs. He used to draw it, paint it, study it together with some mosses and asphodel, as he said, all for his own private love of them. The memory of the pleasure that this gave him thus remained with him because the experience belonged to the real part of himself. Another memory which remained was that of a certain velvet suit he wore which pleased him very much, and of some scratchy woollen stockings which annoyed him.

He remembered too his first disillusionment, experienced at an early age while living at Bay Tree Lodge. He had lent a much prized steam-engine to the boy next door and this was never returned. He asked for it back but the boy pretended that he had never had it. It was the first incident which caused him to lose faith in others. It was a great shock, so great that he could not speak to his parents about it. It was characteristic of him that he accepted this event as inevitable and took no steps to recover his property from his dishonest neighbour. All through his life he was to lose his possessions continually, and to accept each loss without taking action.

Of the University College Preparatory School which he attended in Hampstead he had little to tell, but what was unforgettable was the handicap of his stammer which caused him to spend long periods during the Latin lessons, for example, in hoping he would not be called on to read or construe. He remembered also the first question that was addressed to him by the Head Master of his school on his first entry into his Latin class. 'What is sex?' he had thundered. This terrific question was a surprise to the shy new boy and he had no idea of the answer, not realizing that it was asked in connection with gender and grammar. Dr Nicoll told us that he thought that the Head Master had seen into his young, dark and secret soul, and the moment of awe always remained in his mind. Recovering from his surprise and terror, he managed to say slowly: 'I don't know, sir.' No one knew what an effort it cost him to speak so calmly. Some of the boys giggled, but from that time he was 'somebody' to them.

Sunday was the day that he liked least, for on that day the brougham would come to the door and all the family would drive to St John's Wood Presbyterian Church, where they sat in the gallery. The drive there and back took a long time, the service was tedious and altogether these Sunday mornings seem to have been for a small boy an ordeal which had the effect of making him look back on Sunday as a dreary day. He found the sermons particularly wearying and apparently avoided the hearing of sermons for ever afterwards.

His mother, formerly Miss Isa Dunlop of Kelso, the only daughter of Peter Dunlop of Skaithmuir near Coldstream, was very dear to him, and he used to tell us of her beauty and gentleness. She was a fine musician who taught him to play the violin and he owed his love of music to her. The day when he was told of her death stood out vividly in his memory, and it is characteristic of his inner sincerity and powers of self-observation even at that early age, that he observed at the same time the sudden thought that came to him: 'that will be something to tell the boys at school tomorrow.' He was ten years old at this time. He and his elder sister, Constance (now Mrs Elystan Miles), missed their mother very much, especially during the period before their father remarried. During this interim period a cousin of their mother's, a Miss Maclagan, came to take charge of the household, and later a Miss Pierpoint. The children were by then absorbed in the life of their day schools. Maurice had his own little den on the ground floor of Bay Tree Lodge, where he was mysteriously occupied in his free time. He used to conduct electrical and chemical experiments there – a hobby which still entertained him in his later years.

In 1897 his father married Miss Catherine Pollard and from that moment Bay Tree Lodge became transformed. I quote her own description of her arrival home after a honeymoon in Paris:

> I entered my new home, at Hampstead, on the evening of Ascension Day, 27th May 1897. Bay Tree Lodge, in Frognal, was a Queen Anne house, with later additions, standing back in a garden, with a little lodge at the gates and stables and a cottage at the back. A verandah, covered with wistaria and

clematis, made a sort of porch. My sister Nellie was staying
in the house, having come up from High Down some days
before to arrange my own furniture in my boudoir and also
to be with my two stepchildren when the housekeeper, Miss
Pierpoint, left. Connie and Maurice stood with my sister in
the doorway to receive us and to give me a piece of short-
bread to break and eat as I crossed the threshold. Maurice, a
handsome little boy of nearly thirteen, had insisted on wearing his best suit in my honour – a fawn cloth. . . . The new
housemaid was awaiting me in my bedroom – Julia: gentle
and calm, a true East Anglian. . . . I remember unpacking,
Maurice helping me and receiving delightedly the chocolates
and presents we had brought for him and Connie.

Dr Nicoll used often to talk to us about his stepmother, to whom
he felt much indebted and with whom he always had a very good
relationship. He admired her tremendously and loved her very
much. In a recent letter Lady Robertson Nicoll describes her impressions of him during the period immediately after her marriage:

When I married W. R. N. in May 1897, Maurice was a
handsome, smiling friendly boy, small for his age, and not
overstrong. Before our marriage my husband had described
the two children to me. 'Connie' (aged 15) was 'very clever,
a real booklover – taking all the prizes at school'. 'Maurice
was stupid, and slow at his lessons, but a dear boy, and so
honourable. If you told him he might bicycle alone to a
certain spot you knew he would turn exactly at that spot.'
I found him a bright happy boy – always ready to do anything I asked. Getting him off to school was a business! His
cap could never be found, having been flung off just anywhere on returning home the previous day. He never knew
what the Prep was – till I requested his form master to send
me daily a list of what should be done – and I would see that
the work was carried out. We got on very happily. I do not
remember him being in the least lazy or unwilling. Most of
his spare time was spent in making electric toys and putting
electric bells about the house, a comparatively new idea in
1897. This I would say proved he was clever and ingenious

and not stupid. One of his greatest successes was a clockwork bogey – to alarm Connie. She had a schoolgirl horror and nervousness of all spiders and daddy-long-legs. At midnight, a light suddenly appeared on the ceiling of Connie's bedroom with the shadow of a giant spider. This was truly alarming and was not encouraged a second night. But it won my admiration.

This latter incident is interesting in view of the fact that Dr Nicoll always described his sister Connie as a great tease. Apparently not all the teasing was on one side. And as for his obedience in never bicycling beyond a certain spot, he often spoke of this and said how much better it would have been if he had ventured further. His real life began when he stepped over the boundary. He apparently respected his stepmother's very sensible and matter of fact treatment of him. She told him for instance that he was a nuisance to everyone when he was ill. This was a most salutary remark which gave him a new point of view.

The most unusual room at Bay Tree Lodge was the library which Sir William built on to the top of the house shortly before his marriage. It was 40 feet long and eventually contained about 25,000 books, arranged on the plan of Mr Gladstone's library at Hawarden. It was in this library, with its view (on a clear day) of the Surrey hills, that Sir William received his guests. His wife's boudoir was opposite, also on the top floor. Guests and secretaries and messengers from his office were continually making their way up to the library where he worked indefatigably, his paper the *British Weekly* being then at the height of its fame. The guests and secretaries would stay to luncheon at two o'clock, the children having already had their luncheon in their own room at one. At five, Sir William, after an afternoon's writing, would join his family at tea, when the children would have arrived home from school. The life of an important literary editor and critic was of necessity very highly organized and each day had its own routine, described thus by his wife:

On Monday evening the 'Claudius Clear' letter was always dictated (the three-column article contributed every week to the *British Weekly* under the heading 'Correspondence of

Claudius Clear'). Tuesday was the most exacting of all my husband's days and the evening was devoted to his leader – to which he used to say he gave the greatest thought and pains. On Wednesday at 11.0. he went off to his printers in the City to 'see the paper through'. He lunched with his publishers and went later to the Bath Club and dined there, joined by two or three special friends. This was the day when any upheaval of the house could be undertaken as he would not be back until late evening. For this reason I arranged that my At Home day should be Wednesday – in the days when At Homes were the fashion. On Thursday he took his rest and no assistants came. He would stay in bed until early afternoon and then walk with me on the Heath. On Friday he went again to town, to meet at his Club literary people of all kinds, usually visiting bookshops and bookmen on his way home. On Saturday the morning was spent working in bed and in the afternoon he would walk again on the Heath.

Against such a background Maurice lived his own private life absorbed in his hobbies. The terrific figure of his father dominated the household, and, indeed, all his boyhood and youth. But what it most pleased him to recall to us was the scene in his father's bedroom every morning where he used to dictate to his secretaries while still in bed surrounded by newspapers and by his much loved cats. These cats had Biblical names, Aaron, Moses and Solomon – all blue Persians. There was also a half-Persian, Samuel, with a rich black and yellow coat, which excelled the Persians in beauty but not in intellect. To the outsider it must have appeared a scene of great confusion, but from it emerged the lucid thinking of 'Claudius Clear' which stimulated the *British Weekly* readers week by week.

Among the cats Sir William would read the newspapers and smoke innumerable cigarettes, each necessitating an incredible number of matches; but his wife's fears of a resulting fire proved needless. His method of reading amazed his friends. Each journal would be glanced at and immediately thrown on the floor and yet in that brief instant the essential in each paper had been seen and grasped. Every day he read all the London dailies and many

7

of the Scottish and provincial papers and also the evening papers, not to speak of all the English and some American weeklies. All newspapers were kept for a fortnight in case they should be needed for reference. The piles were so big that they were known to the household as 'the haystacks'.

The summer holidays were spent in Scotland, and I quote Lady Robertson Nicoll's description of the Old Manse which is now her home.

When the children's summer holidays came they went up to Lumsden, the Aberdeenshire home, with one housemaid, Agnes, leaving Julia with us. My husband could only spare a fortnight in August, a few days of which we spent at Lumsden with the children. . . . The Old Manse had been the Free Church manse of my husband's father, the Rev. Harry Nicoll. I had heard much from my husband about the Old Manse and about his father, a remarkable scholar and book-man, for whom he had a real love and deep veneration – he admired his character and his learning. When his father retired my husband had bought the house for him, and after the father's death it became his own summer holiday home. I found a tiny cosy-looking house. Mr Nicoll when he first entered it in 1848 had described it as 'a most comfortable and commodious residence. Thanks be to God'. My husband had kept it as it had always been. On one side of the little entrance hall was a dining-room, on the other a study abso-lutely lined with bookshelves, not only all round the room from floor to ceiling, but above the fireplace and the doorway also. Beyond these rooms were two others, also with many books and periodicals, and at the end of the house a large pleasant kitchen with big open hearth. My husband often said that no roast fowls were so good as those roasted by the good old servant Mary over that open fire when he was a little boy. Upstairs was another room entirely devoted to books. This had been the father's sanctum which none but a sacred few – bookmen – might enter. The Rev. Harry Nicoll had arranged in it what appeared to me to be a Hampton Court maze of bookshelves about five feet high, and between

8

these only a slender figure like his own could move. I was told that after his death some hundreds of the 17,000 books had been given to various libraries, but the house even then seemed to have books everywhere. Later on, when he added a new wing to the house, my husband arranged a library on the ground floor and the books from the sanctum were brought down to it, giving another much needed bedroom.

One of the children's holiday delights at Lumsden was the opportunity of serving in the village shop. Lady Robertson Nicoll writes in *Under the Bay Tree*:

> The shop was an intense joy for our children of different periods, for they were allowed to serve behind the counter regardless of the muddle and delay they must have caused. Connie, Maurice and my nephews have all gloried in playing shopmen and I have rejoiced in knowing that a wet day was of no moment since the children were happily and safely employed.

Holidays were also spent with the Pollard family at High Down in Hertfordshire, an old Tudor Manor House built by Sir Thomas Dowcra, Grand Prior of the Knights of St John of Jerusalem. Here 'Aunt Minnie' taught Maurice to ride and fish, for which he spoke of her often with gratitude. He was much impressed also at that time by 'Aunt Nellie's' playing of the harp and used to tell us how he admired her beautiful arms while she was playing. He spoke with great affection of his stepmother's father, Mr Joseph Pollard, and of his two uncles.

When Maurice was thirteen, it was decided that he should go to Aldenham. This school was recommended by Mr Joseph Pollard. It was chosen partly because it was within driving distance of Hampstead, and indeed his father and stepmother drove out on several occasions along the peaceful Hertfordshire lanes to spend the afternoon with him. At Aldenham he enjoyed singing in the choir and was one of four soloists who sang in St Albans' Cathedral. We knew his voice as a tenor, very true. As an alto it must have been delightful. Often he used to imitate for us the manner in which these choir boys behaved. They accepted their singing

duties with the utmost simplicity, being always ready to eat
sweets or exchange pet frogs when there was an opportunity
during the services (or even when there was not) and the next
moment soaring to their top notes like angels. It was at Aldenham
that in the sixth form he had his second disillusionment. He
describes it thus:

> When I heard the New Testament I could not understand
> what the parables meant, and no one seemed to know or care
> what they meant. But once, in the Greek New Testament
> class on Sundays, taken by the Head Master, I dared to ask,
> in spite of my stammering, what some parable meant. The
> answer was so confused that I actually experienced my first
> moment of consciousness – that is, I suddenly realized that
> *no one knew anything. . . .* From that moment I began to think
> for myself or rather knew that I could. . . . I remember so
> clearly the class room, the high windows constructed so that
> we could not see out of them, the desks, the platform on
> which the Head Master sat, his scholarly, thin face, his nervous
> habits of twitching his mouth and jerking his hands – and
> suddenly this inner revelation of *knowing that he knew nothing*
> – nothing, that is, about anything that really mattered. This
> was my first liberation from the power of external life.

It was in the School Chapel one Easter time that Maurice had
his first moment of real religious feeling. He was moved by a great
love for Christ and when the story of Peter's denial was read in
the Gospel, he said to himself: 'I would never do that – I would
never do that.' The memory of this moment remained with him
– it was the beginning of an awareness of a dedicated affection for
the being of Christ, apart from any formatory dogma.

Lady Robertson Nicoll relates that when a baby sister, Mildred,
was born, both Connie and Maurice were charming to her.
Maurice, who was an extremely clever photographer, took her
first photograph when she was four weeks old. He gave her her
first teddy bear and mended her toys. 'When the journey to
Lumsden was discussed for the one-year-old baby girl and the
long night journeys, he devised a hammock for her, to be swung
from the luggage rack, a most ingenious and intricate affair.' The

following extract from a letter from Lady Robertson Nicoll to his father from Lumsden heralds the future:

> Baby is very well, and proves her good health by being very good and happy. This morning two dolls had two arms out of their sockets. I suggested mending them. Maurice heard us, and called that he had some glue and would do it for us. So we carried the dolls and their arms to his little room, and he very nicely and neatly mended each. Then Baby said most sedately: 'Thank you, Mr Doctor,' and we carried them downstairs very gently and put them to bed and Baby said: 'Now they will be so better they will dance about.'

Maurice was at Aldenham from 1898 until 1903 when he gained a Scholarship and entered Gonville and Caius College, Cambridge, on the advice of Mr Joseph Pollard, whose sons had been there. It is interesting to learn that Medicine was not his first choice of a career. At one time he thought he would like to be an engineer, and indeed he would have excelled in the field of electrical engineering. His anxious father, however, sought the best possible advice about the state of the engineering world and the result was that after consulting with various notable heads of engineering firms, he was of the opinion that such a career did not offer great possibilities at that time.

Kenneth Walker, who also lived in Frognal with his parents, had already been up at Caius for two years when Maurice entered. He recalls an interview with Dr Robertson Nicoll in his library, when, plied with champagne, and impressed by his surroundings, he was exhorted by his host to keep an eye on his son. He found that this was not very easy and soon gave it up as Maurice quickly chose his own friends, not those whom Mr Walker would have chosen for him, but those who could give him the gay companionship which was a necessity for him all his life. Thus it came about that his Cambridge friends were neither the intellectuals nor those who had the most brilliant personalities, but such men as Bill Adams, Basil Atkins, and Gordon Moore who were possessed of a certain gaiety and could toss life up with a sense of humour. Basil Atkins was destined for the Indian Army and joined the 11th Rajputs. He was a particularly charming man with a great gift for faithful and unselfish friendship. All the family loved him, and when he was on leave he stayed in turn at Bay Tree, the Old Manse and High Down. Mrs Kirkcaldy recalls that Gordon Moore and Kenneth Walker often came to Bay Tree and both stayed at the Old Manse and that one summer Kenneth and Maurice had a riding tour in Aberdeenshire, accompanying members of the family who drove in a large landau. They both had great understanding of children – and patience with them – and encouraged the small Mildred to edit a paper named *The Jolly Wobbler* to which they both contributed. When Kenneth Walker wrote his famous children's book, *The Log of the Ark*, he included the imaginary family of Clidders who originally belonged to Mildred and her sister. He recently recalled a week-end visit to Basil Atkins' home at Devizes, on which he accompanied Maurice, and said that Atkins was a simple, jovial type, fond of drinking and laughter, with whom Maurice felt at ease.

He was a member of the Boat Club and rowed in one of the Caius Boats. It is recorded in *The Caian* that as a member of the Science and Arts Society he once read a paper on 'How to use Science for sordid ends', which seems to foreshadow his later method of satirizing the scientist. *The Caian* further records that as a member of 'C' Coy of the O.T.C. he took part in a Field Day on the Gogs: 'a great success, the notable feature of the day being an exhibition by Pte. Nicoll on "How to retire coolly under fire".'

In the summer of 1906 Maurice was awarded a First in the Natural Science Tripos. He became Senior Soph. Prizeman and was elected to a Foundation Scholarship which, however, he did not take up. Mrs Elystan Miles recalls the day when the Final Results were to be posted in College:

> Maurice was having a bath (on purpose probably) and dispatched his great friend Gordon Moore to get the news. How well I remember being in the garden at Hampstead waiting for the telegram Maurice had promised to send. My father, who was deeply anxious for good news, kept on repeating as we paced the garden together that we must not hope for too much. The sympathetic presence of my step-mother helped as we waited. Up the long path came at last

the telegraph boy, and the wire told us that Maurice had indeed done as well as possible. My father was full of joy. He expected great things from us both.

Mr Joseph Pollard, who followed Maurice's career with the greatest interest and sympathy, was no less delighted, and in a letter of congratulation to Dr Robertson Nicoll expressed his great satisfaction that, in addition to his brilliant successes, the boy had throughout his university life been so steady and reliable. 'It is a cause for true thankfulness,' he wrote, 'that he has escaped the dangers attendant upon youthful life'.

Steady and reliable Maurice certainly was; but at the same time he was exceptionally lively and high-spirited – more so, perhaps, than good Mr Pollard realized. Mrs Elystan Miles, who used to visit him in May Week, recalls the gaiety of his life at Cambridge, in which work, at least to an onlooker, seemed to occupy a very small place indeed while social life and the society of congenial friends loomed very large. 'What I would chiefly like to emphasize,' she writes, 'is the high merriment of his mood in that delightful place. Full of gusto, he conducted at one time a correspondence in *The Times*, supposed to be from two residents, one pro the bell ringing in the city and the other against it as an interruption to the student. Nobody, I think, knew that the letters were from the same lively pen.'

Those who were with him were witnesses of the amusing time he was having, while sober friends and relatives of an older generation continued to receive gratifying news of his attainments. 'Maurice has got a prize from Caius College for an essay,' wrote Dr Robertson Nicoll to his wife in the course of the year 1908; 'so he is now Scholar and Prizeman of his College, which is satisfactory.'

Dr Nicoll did not tell us very much about his life at Caius, but he used to talk about the new steam car which he acquired which took him to the Newmarket races or to London for a dance at Bay Tree Lodge from which he would return to Cambridge at dawn. It was an extraordinary machine, terrifying alike to driver, passengers and onlookers. Though he said little about this period of his life, he remained devoted to the memory of his Cambridge days, and while we were living at Ugley in 1945 and 1946, a favourite expedition was a drive with him to Cambridge so that he could visit his tailor and we could all look through the ground floor windows at his old rooms in Caius.

From 1906 until 1910 Maurice studied Medicine at Bart's, where Kenneth Walker was again two years senior to him. During this period Gordon Moore shared rooms with him in Willow Road, Hampstead, a few minutes' walk from Bay Tree Lodge where they would join the family on Sundays. All accounts given to us of the medical studies at Bart's resemble nothing so much as chapters from the recently published *Doctor in the House*, particularly the gynaecological practical experience in the East End, where the medical students at last were brought face to face with some of the stark realities of life. Perhaps Dr Nicoll's most interesting comment on his medical training is expressed in a letter, which I quote below, written to Mrs Elystan Miles many years later to congratulate her on the success of her son who was also studying Medicine.

146 Harley Street, W.1.

Dearest C,   *Xmas 1937.*

I was very pleased to hear that Basil has got so far in his exams. It is a nightmare, and leaves a man usually without a mind – one needs to be able to see through and not accept blindly all that is said and claimed. Life and matter are greater mysteries than ever, and I hope he knows and feels this because with the sense of mystery always fresh, life continually remains itself and its real chemistry is maintained.

Very best of things to you and yours,

Yours,

M.

On 25th June 1909, Sir William received his knighthood for public services.

Although deeply engrossed in the study of medicine, Dr Nicoll's versatile mind could never limit itself to one field alone. He and his sister had edited a family newspaper from their nursery days, containing stories and the current home news, and he himself had written various stories about local life while on holiday at Lumsden. His love of writing led him at this time to pass some of his leisure moments in collaborating with his sister in writing a novel which, although they tossed it off lightly with no thought apart from amusing themselves, was destined to become a best-seller. The book was *Lord Richard in the Pantry*. Mrs Elystan Miles describes the way in which it came to be written:

After I had had an exhausting illness in the summer of 1910, my mother-in-law, who was herself going away, offered me the use of her pleasant house in Boscombe. I was told that I might have guests. My brother came down, with the idea, I think, of cheering me up. I remember being in a bath-chair wheeled down to the beach when we suddenly thought of writing a novel together. We soon found a plot, and would write in the long evenings, allotting to each other, by mutual planning, a chapter each at a time. I recall my somewhat literal-minded hospital nurse sitting reading in the same parlour while we were scribbling away. It was very quickly written, as my brother had a very rapid way of getting things on paper. The work took me quite out of my illness. We used to read snatches of the story aloud to one another as we went along, and often dissolved in laughter. The nurse would have to listen, and did so with a stern undiscriminating look. Maurice and I both felt we should like the novel, when finished, to find a publisher other than my father's firm, Hodder and Stoughton. We kept the matter quiet and sent the manuscript on its rounds. We wrote under the pseudonym of Martin Swayne. Finally Messrs Methuen said they would accept it, provided we put up a small amount of money which we might recover in royalties. My father was quite taken aback when the book was placed in his hands, but I think he was very pleased that we were so independent. Edition followed edition and finally we sold the dramatic rights, and the weekly cheque of £10 each, while the play flourished at the Criterion, was very welcome. However, we should have preferred it to remain as a light comedy and that it should not have been converted, however skilfully, into broad farce....

Sir William, on holiday at Cannes shortly after the publication of the novel, was heard to enquire at the Scotch Church Library there for a copy of it.

Dr Nicoll spoke of the novel later as 'a little gaiety in this near-dark age'. Indeed, its chief quality is best described as a kind of irrepressible, spontaneous gaiety. It is overflowing with high spirits and lifts the reader into a better place in himself. The story of a man of noble birth masquerading as a butler and falling in love with his mistress is a very old plot, but rarely can it have been treated with more delicacy and humour. In 1949, thirty-nine years after its publication, when we were living at Great Amwell House, Dr Nicoll was delighted to receive a letter from a school-boy who wrote to tell him how much pleasure the book had given him while he was ill in the sanatorium at his school in Yorkshire.

The question arose in 1910 of having a dramatic version of *Lord Richard* made for the stage. It was while the dramatization of the novel was being discussed, soon after the book's publication, that Dr Nicoll met Miss Maud Hoffman, an American, a Shake-spearean actress with some literary talent. He had been advised to discuss the possibility with her. Miss Hoffman was at that time sharing a flat in South London with Miss Mabel Collins. The dramatic version for which she was later responsible was not used, but Dr Nicoll's first meeting with Miss Hoffman was the initial link in a chain of interesting and important connections in his life and the beginning of a long friendship.

Eventually the novel was dramatized by other hands and pro-duced on the West End stage with Cyril Maude in the leading part. The delicate comedy had degenerated into farce but the play proved very popular. It ran for three years and was revived several times. Very small sums, representing royalties on the dramatic version of the novel, as a result of its performance by amateur dramatic societies, used to arrive by post at intervals during the whole of the period when I worked with Dr Nicoll. These varied from ten and six to two or three pounds after several deductions had been made. He used to send the cheque up to his wife and would then fling away the statement that accompanied it. The disappearance of these statements caused a recurring difficulty when they were required for Income Tax Returns as several were always missing and, year after year, Messrs A. P. Watt, his literary agents, had to be applied to for duplicates. Eventually I managed to secure the statements in time to prevent their loss. The continued performance of the play by amateurs certainly seemed to be proof of its vitality.

As soon as Dr Nicoll had qualified he went out to Buenos Aires as Ship's Surgeon. He had some startling reminiscences of this trip to tell us. He did not apparently have much scope during the inward and outward voyages for the exercise of his newly acquired medical skill, but attained a considerable proficiency in poker. It was the custom for some of the ship's officers to play nightly in the Captain's cabin with certain of the passengers, and the young officers were safeguarded from losing more than they could afford.

Mr Kenneth Walker was at that time Resident Medical Officer at the British Hospital in Buenos Aires. His sister had married a rich Argentinian and Dr Nicoll visited their ranch before his return voyage.

Dr Nicoll apparently enjoyed persuading his friend to eat some of the amusing and unusual dishes that appeared on the menu in the restaurants in Buenos Aires, such as roast armadillo, but he himself was reluctant to experiment.

On his return to London Dr Nicoll asked his father to allow him a year abroad studying new forms of psychology. He went first to Paris, then to Berlin and Vienna, and eventually to Zürich. He often talked of his stay in Vienna, lightly waving away all reference to his studies but delighting his hearers with accounts of his painful experiences during the riding lessons at the Spanish School, which he was fortunate enough to attend, and of his gay German lessons with his beloved teacher known to us as Georgette, with whom he passed many happy hours. She remained in his memory as a most romantic figure until the war years in Birdlip when the cold hand of reality dispelled some of the glamour which had surrounded her. One day a letter arrived from Vienna. To our delight it was from Georgette, and, what was more it was a begging letter, telling of the scarcity of clothes in Vienna, even giving her husband's measurements which, oddly enough, corresponded with Dr Nicoll's own, and from that time, at intervals, some of us had the task of making up gigantic parcels on the floor of his room for Georgette, containing his old tweed suits. This necessitated filling in various forms in triplicate, which was my particular task. Dr Nicoll himself would direct the operations with much vivacity and each parcel went off with the warmest feelings from us all.

In Vienna Dr Nicoll studied the Freudian System of psychology although he never met Freud himself. From Vienna he went to Zürich where his contact with Dr Jung was, he told us, the first important event in his life – an event which changed the direction of his career completely. His visit to Zürich marked the end of his youth. He acknowledged a debt to Dr Jung, a priceless gift, in that, through the impact of his teaching, he came into his own thinking, and when he returned to England he had a new confidence in himself, and an inner certainty of what he must do.

1. About 1890

2. 1899 (Aldenham)

CHAPTER TWO

Decisive Influences

Dr Nicoll always looked back with great appreciation on his father's generosity in allowing him his year abroad to study psychology after he had qualified in medicine. At that period this new subject was regarded rather doubtfully by the older generation and by orthodox medicine, and the generosity in this case cannot have been only financial. When he considered his life in retrospect Dr Nicoll emphasized that this year was of paramount importance in shaping the pattern of his future, for his contact with Dr Jung during his first visit to Zürich led to a mental turning-point, which did not become outwardly apparent for some time. However, one very striking physical manifestation resulted from this period of psychological study. Dr Jung gave him confidence in himself and his own thinking so that he lost his stammer. The hesitancy in his speech which had handicapped him during lessons at school and on other occasions was attributed by Dr Jung to the fear and lack of confidence that he had always felt in his father's presence, which had imposed on him a kind of inner restraint.

Dr Nicoll's relationship with his father, whom he admired very greatly but feared for many years, was one of the most important influences in his life. He must have resembled him in many ways although he himself denied this. Physically he came to resemble him more as he grew older, and towards the end of his life when he was acting in a charade, his wife remarked on the fact that he was suddenly transformed into 'the image of his father'. He used to tell us that his father treated him too harshly when he was a boy, he was too dominating, too overpowering, and indeed, too famous. He declared that it was a very great handicap to be the son of a famous father. At the same time he was exceedingly proud of him, and his sisters are agreed that his father loved him and took great pride in him. Dr Nicoll had always admired his father's courage in the face of his serious lung trouble. After his illness at Kelso a specialist had warned him that he had no chance of life if he stayed in England, but he refused to be daunted by this

verdict and crossed to the other side of the road where Sir Andrew
Clark was more reassuring, and his patient without further delay
founded the *British Weekly* and entered upon his literary career.
Dr Nicoll considered this a supreme example of the power of the
mind over the body.

Dr Nicoll fully agreed with Jung in attributing the lack of
confidence which lasted all through his boyhood to his father's
domination which made him unsure of himself, and in the
psychological talks that he gave us, he warned all parents to leave
their children free from parental tyranny. His own daughter he
left in complete freedom. In such an active household, it must
have been difficult to be himself, in spite of the never-failing
kindness and courtesy of his stepmother of which he often reminded us. I have found it interesting in reading Mr T. H.
Darlow's *Life and Letters of William Robertson Nicoll* to discover
where Dr Nicoll's description of his father corresponds with that
of his father's biographer, and where it differs. He always described himself as the antithesis of his father! Yet they seem to have
had a great deal in common.

Dr Nicoll often spoke of his mingled ancestry, saying that his
mother was a Dunlop and his father half a Lowlander, but that
Celtic blood came through his grandmother who was Miss Jane
Robertson, a Robertson of Struan. Dr Nicoll said that he thought
a fine Scots intellect was a wonderful endowment, and that his
father owed his mental equipment to his Lowland blood, saying
that the East Side of Scotland produced outstanding examples of
the logical mind, but that the intuitive mind was derived for the
most part from the Celtic strain. Both he and his father were
capable of violent anger and of passionate devotion to any cause
they held dear. Both were deeply religious in the true sense of the
word, in that the spiritual world was ever present to them. Sir
William was aware of the reality of Man's inner nature, although
it was invisible, and it was this mystery which became Dr Nicoll's
lifelong study.

Although Dr Nicoll was already thinking of a future vastly
different from that which Sir William had in mind for him, he
accepted the arrangement that was now made on his return from
abroad to set him up in private practice. His father had bought

him a house in Golders Green, in the new Garden Suburb where it was possible to put up a plate, and Dr Nicoll obviously felt that the least that he could do in return for his year abroad was to start his career as his father had planned. Thus he moved into the Golders Green house, where Mrs Elystan Miles helped with the decoration and the choice of furniture. She recalls how her brother insisted on having a frieze of Noah's Ark and the animals around the top of the walls of the consulting room. Dr Gordon Moore came into partnership with him, and they enjoyed one another's companionship but neither partner found the idea of general practice congenial and both were thankful when external circumstances released them from it.

Living nearby at that time was Mr Claud Mullins, who recalls evenings spent with Dr Nicoll, who talked to him of psychology. 'I cannot remember any of his words,' Mr Mullins said recently, 'except that he once asked me: "When you meet a stranger, who usually speaks first, you or he?" I said that I thought I did. He replied that I must be a dominant character.'

Dr Nicoll diverted himself by continuing to write short stories. While in Vienna he had begun to contribute to the *Strand Magazine* which an older generation will remember in its best period before the 1914 War. He told us that he felt afterwards that he had missed an opportunity in not using the Viennese background for his stories to which he had given a London setting. They were condensed, very effective in plot, with curious surprising twists in them. They were written in such a way that the unusual sounded normal. During the war years in Birdlip (1940) we collected the old bound volumes containing these stories, and enjoyed reading them. The Martin Swayne stories were 'Sir Clifford's Gorilla', 'The Alabaster Jar', 'The Corot Landscape', and there was one, whose title I forget, which had for its climax a fight with a puma in a dark dungeon into which a passer-by was beguiled so that certain scenes for a film might be shot. Other contributors to the *Strand* of those days were Arnold Bennett, Conan Doyle, Rider Haggard, Talbot Mundy, and H. A. Vachell.

The demands of the Golders Green practice were so light that Dr Nicoll was able to join Dr Crichton Miller in his work at

Bowden House, Harrow, and at 114a Harley Street. In his practice as consultant he was able to begin to use his knowledge of psychology, thus feeling his way towards his future work. Quite soon he became aware that the hypnotic method of treatment practised at Bowden House was not the line for him. In the summer of 1914 he returned to Zürich for a holiday of some weeks. The following letter to his parents written shortly before he left London, throws light on his state of mind:

114a Harley Street, W.1.
1914.

My dearest Parents,

I am typing you a letter of thanks in order that you may not have the difficulty of deciphering my writing. I am very much touched by your kindness in sending me a cheque for holiday purposes and it is needless to say it will help me greatly. But you must not take too high a view of the motives which lead me to holiday in Zürich. It is altogether a sense of my inadequacy to meet with my work, and the feeling that in order to keep my brass-plate bright I must get a better grip of things. And I think this is only possible by going through the process oneself that one is constantly putting others through.

I have not the slightest doubt of the value of this line of work that I am in. In fact, it is such a very extraordinary thing, so completely remarkable and curious that one finds it difficult to talk about and quite impossible to explain. It is an experience and not a teachable thing. For it ever to be accepted, either generally or popularly, would mean a complete social turnabout. But to me it seems a thing well worth devoting one's life to, whatever comment is made about the work. And I believe privately that it holds in some way that one cannot clearly see yet the key to the solution of a host of troubles that we comfortably think 'will be always with us'. I mean that out of it will arise that impulse that will give a universal newness as the impulse of Christianity gave a universal newness. And it is precisely because it is the last place that a man would look for such an impulse, because it is exactly where one would pour scorn and ridicule on such a possibility, that I feel confidence in the significance of it. So much for my confession of faith.

As I have said, I am greatly indebted to you for the present, and also for your support and confidence in what must be very puzzling to you. To make people look at things they do not want to look at is not a joyous task for life but a very necessary one. The meaning of 'Know thyself' is our motto, but what a shock it is! I am very happy and content, and doubly so because things are going so well with you.

Much love,
Maurice.

The above letter, in which Dr Nicoll dwells on the possibilities of Jung's psychological system, which had already displaced that of Freud in his mind, was followed by another from Zürich to Lady Robertson Nicoll:

Zürich,
Sunday 12th July 1914.

Dearest Mater,

Thank you for your long letter. I do not think I will be back before the 20th as Miller writes to say he does not leave for his holiday until the 23rd and says there is no reason why I should not stay on. I may travel a little en route home, but I am too lazy to make plans yet. My time continues to be very interesting, and I have now, in the dream, an instrument that is of comforting value in the direction of one's own affairs as well as of my patients, It is very hot here. I go up the Rigi tomorrow to do some sight-seeing; and dine with two English patients of Jung's on Tuesday. I am not looking forward to Harrow very much. A third partner is to be taken in, and with my approval 'and sanction'. I think it is necessary for various reasons, one being that it is perfectly clear to me that hypnotism is not my line. It is too exhausting, and too much working blindly in the dark for satisfaction and I wish to concentrate more in other more illuminating directions. Also I am not constituted to run a sanatorium. I see my line of work clearly: there is plenty of scope in it, plenty of future. For a year or two I must just work quietly, and then I will begin perhaps pushing out feelers in the journals and reading papers before outside societies. Jung has been helpful in this direction, and has given good advice. I was delighted to see the Pater in the *Sphere*. I have just rowed for an hour on the lake.

Best love,
Maurice.

Dr Nicoll had by now accepted the importance of Jung's work on dreams, which he was from that time to use extensively in his own psychological work, and it was at this point that he abandoned the use of hypnotism.

Dr Nicoll's contact with Dr Jung had been the beginning of a new relationship which was the strongest influence in his life for the ten years that followed. He often used to recreate for us the presence of this Nordic giant to whom he owed his understanding of dreams and who gave him his first awareness that his destiny was to be concerned not with the cure of physical illness but with the treatment of the condition of inner disharmony that lay at the root of all physical symptoms. Dr Nicoll studied the Jung method of dream interpretation and used to give us in later days an example of a dream in which his father appeared to be in possession of a rifle and a bullet marked with his son's name, which aroused anger in the dreamer. Jung's interpretation of this dream that remained permanently in Dr Nicoll's memory was this:

> This dream shews that you do not understand your father. You have to get free from the mechanical influence of your father. You must begin to understand all the difficulties that your father had in bringing you up. And (this was added slyly and maliciously, Dr Nicoll told us) how would you have liked to be your father with yourself as your son? How would you have liked to bring up yourself?

From that time Dr Nicoll began to look on his father in a new light and to appreciate some of the difficulties that he himself must have caused him in the past. He gave us many talks in later days about the relationship of parents and children, illuminated by the understanding that had come to him through his own study of the past in which he reversed the positions of father and son, and warned us of the possible wrong development that resulted from reaction to parents or imitation of them.

In 1939 Dr Nicoll wrote in *Pelican Hotel*, an unpublished, unfinished novel:

> My father had always taken life very seriously and it often happens that a child brought up in a serious and oppressive atmosphere reacts against it secretly or openly. I had certainly reacted in opposition to most of the factors that influenced my early life.

The chief way in which Dr Nicoll seemed to have reacted to the serious atmosphere which surrounded him in his boyhood and youth was in taking life on the surface lightly with jest and laughter. All through the years when he was teaching us he never failed to impress upon us that one of the secrets of transforming situations was to receive them with humour, and comment on them with wit. Beautifully printed on the wall where we had our meetings at Great Amwell House was the saying of a philosopher of the 5th century B.C.: 'Serious things can only be understood through laughable things.'

As a schoolboy among his father's guests, for the most part men of literary fame or men holding high office in the affairs of state, Dr Nicoll had been silent, oppressed by his stammer and the ignorance of his youth, unable in any case to get a word in, and petrified if a question were addressed to him. He had been a shy spectator and listener when the brilliant coterie, including Mr Lloyd George, Lord Riddell, Mr Asquith (as he then was), even sometimes the young Mr Winston Churchill, were discussing national affairs. But although he had been too young, and in his father's presence too diffident, to take part in the conversation (from his own account), among his own friends he had been quite different. At Cambridge he had become the centre of a circle who enjoyed life to the full and were sometimes addicted to practical jokes. I think it was a member of this circle who succeeded in digging up a large chunk of the roadway in Piccadilly without being interfered with for a long time. And it must have been the same practical joker who asked a passer-by to hold a tape for him while he measured something and then gave the other end of the tape to another pedestrian round the corner and went away leaving them to investigate the situation. This was the kind of practical joke that Dr Nicoll really enjoyed.

Dr Nicoll attributed to the restraint under which his father put him at home his longing for independence and the opportunity to follow a line quite different from that of politics or journalism. It was interesting that the two subjects in which he shewed great ability at an early age, electrical work and science, were closed books to his father, who could not bear even to know how his watch worked. Dr Nicoll felt that his father despised these subjects and held them of little account. He told us that it was through his stepmother's influence that he went up to Cambridge, and he thanked her for this repeatedly in later life. He felt that his father thought little of his ability, and he found it impossible to have a reasonable or an intimate conversation with him. This belief that his father thought little of him is not borne out by the testimony of his stepmother and sisters. Mrs Elystan Miles, who had had an excellent relationship with her father and shared his literary tastes, maintains that he adored his son. But obviously he was unable to express his affection, as he had all the Scot's reserve.

An aunt who stayed often at Bay Tree Lodge, on being asked what she remembered of Dr Nicoll said recently that what stood out most clearly in her memory was his skill in smoothing over any difficulties in the household. 'If Sir William were irritated, it was always Maurice who could bring him back into good humour.'

Dr Nicoll gained his father's respect through his brilliant success in all his examinations, and this made a closer link with him. He was very pleased to have been able to win honours in a field unexplored by his father. His aim had been to avoid any form of imitation. At the same time he shared his father's gift for writing and in the development of this it was important for him to follow a line of his own. In his early novels he was reacting against the serious background of his home in the expression of his character-istic gaiety and humour. The independence of the co-authors of *Lord Richard in the Pantry* in finding their own publisher instead of falling back on Hodder and Stoughton won Sir William's admiration.

Dr Nicoll shared his father's love of books, and love of writing. He preferred dogs to cats, and was not so much of an indoor man. He did not really like working in bed as his father did. Apparently Sir William dictated his articles from his bed in the morning 'amid a medley of newspapers and books and pipes and cigarette ash'. Dr Nicoll would reflect and ponder in the early morning, record his dreams and make pencil notes in his notebooks, which were material to be put into literary form later. If he dictated at all it would be later in the day, striding up and down the room. He dictated his psychological papers which were for reading aloud to his groups, but his literary work was written with an execrable pen, generally at his desk in almost illegible writing with many insertions enclosed in balloons all over the page. He talked more fluently than he wrote and his literary work was hard labour, although at times he produced his psychological papers very rapidly.

His father was known to have agreed with Leigh Hunt, Mr Darlow tells us, as to the advantage of people in bed over people who are up, but Dr Nicoll put the matter differently. He said that in a horizontal position a man was more passive and open to spiritual influences than when he was in the upright position.

A dislike of gardening was common to both. Like his father, Dr Nicoll rarely carried a watch, and hated to be interrupted by being reminded of the time. Dr Nicoll and his father shared the same favourite book – Boswell's *Life of Johnson*. Sir William maintained that a man ought to have three kinds of books which he described as 'lover, friend and acquaintance'. He wrote:

> Certain books you love, and they are the special books, the books you want to read every year, the books you would not be without, the books which you bind in morocco, the books you would keep at all costs. Find the books that you love and then find your friends among books. By friends I mean excellent books, though not the books that appeal most immediately and sharply. I love Boswell's *Life of Johnson*. Lockhart's *Life of Scott* is my friend. Your mental life will be determined by your lovers and your friends, but if you have lovers and friends, there is no reason why you should not

have a great number of acquaintances ... one may certainly know 4,000 books. (*People and Books* by W. Robertson Nicoll: Hodder and Stoughton.)

Sir William himself, possessing 4,000 biographical works, declared that biography was his favourite form of reading and considered that Boswell had written the first and possibly the last good biography of a man of letters. He wrote:

> After all, the only bits of biography that will survive are the Boswellian passages – all the rest goes – the letters, the philosophy, the criticism, the ponderous parts of life. A few characteristic incidents, a few saline sayings. (*People and Books* by W. Robertson Nicoll: Hodder and Stoughton.)

It was the characteristic incidents in Boswell's *Life of Johnson* that delighted Dr Nicoll, when we knew him, and he enjoyed reading or quoting to us the memorable saline sayings. Like his father Dr Nicoll used to be surrounded by a number of books that he was reading at the same time. He would have endorsed the views expressed by Sir William in the following passage which I quote:

> Sound bookmen always have three or four books on hand at a time. The idea that you should read one book at a time is the idea of those people who think you should dine upon one dish. You go up to your study after dinner and commence reading. There should be at least three books, four are better, awaiting you on the rug. You might begin with a little bit of biography or criticism. Then you should proceed to the book that is really furnishing you with thoughts, of whatever kind it may be. Then you should have in reserve a book of fiction, with which you may close the evening pleasantly. I like, for my part, every night to read, as a last thing, some poetry. (*People and Books* by W. Robertson Nicoll: Hodder and Stoughton.)

During the years when I knew him, Dr Nicoll would have many more than four books strewn about on the rug, or the table, or on his bed. He might well begin his evening-reading with biography, or possibly travel, his second love. He read few novels but would turn to a good detective story for relaxation, preferably one by Conan Doyle. This would serve the purpose of occupying part of his mind, leaving the deeper part free to continue thinking.

The differences between Dr Nicoll and his father are interesting; whereas Sir William, we are told, had no taste for mechanism and never attempted to gain any knowledge about science, Dr Nicoll was not only a distinguished scientist, but had a touch of genius in dealing with anything mechanical. Mr Darlow records that Sir William was very absent-minded, having been known to return from functions in a hat, or an overcoat, or even shoes that were not his own. I cannot recall that we ever saw Dr Nicoll returning home in a strange hat. We should have been most delighted if he had! Dr Nicoll loved painting and music and had considerable talent in both, but his father had little appreciation of either. Indeed, Dr Nicoll had capacities in all directions and had an exceptionally wide range of interests. Even the inner conflict with his brilliant and dominant father eventually added to his understanding and became useful to him. But it was typical of him that his mind so worked throughout life as to transform difficulties and handicaps, to learn from them and use them to his profit and in the guiding of others.

CHAPTER THREE

The 1914 War — Active Service

'I never met anyone who was sentimental in Mesopotamia.'
M. N. *In Mesopotamia*

It actually comes very suddenly, like an earthquake. Of course, many people even now think it is possible that it does not sound its unmistakable and terrible note until the last moment for the vast majority of us. It comes like a bolt from the blue, suddenly war – and then cheering crowds and suspense and that curious feeling of elation, which ushers in war in this period and makes it possible. Bands play and people go mad with excitement. Everyone feels a sort of release. They embrace each other in the streets, the bars are crowded and mad excitement sweeps over the country: work slows down, Buckingham Palace is surrounded by dense, cheering mobs. No one knows what it will mean eventually, but everyone is carried away. That is one source of war, you know; well, a sort of hysteria possesses people. I remember I felt it myself, but do you know, I have totally forgotten what I felt and even what I did just then. Certainly I wasn't in the least afraid at that time. You see I did not understand. I joined up – yes, I went to Ireland to train. There was, or will be, a popular song called 'It's a long way to Tipperary'. Yes, I suppose it's going about now. I got a telegram from the War Office ordering me to proceed to Tipperary. I thought it was a joke, but I went there, two months after the war started, and found mud, rain, dreary barracks, drill, whiskey – it wasn't a joke after all.

The above description of the impact of the sudden declaration of war on Dr Nicoll is quoted from his unpublished novel *Pelican Hotel*. It is his recollection of it in 1939, described by Gregory Nixon, a character in the novel who has returned to 1913 from the future, having already lived once through the 1914 war.

Dr Nicoll's first impulse was to volunteer. Mrs Elystan Miles, whose husband, a regular officer, was on active service, took over the Golders Green house. He wrote to his stepmother as follows:

Bowden House,
Harrow-on-the-Hill,
Thursday, 13th Aug. '14.

Dearest Mater,

Thank you for your letter. I am sorry you are both so against my volunteering. I saw Connie; poor girl, it is a strain for her. I hope she will feel comfortable at Golders Green. Up at Lumsden it must be difficult to realize the war. I fancy Bowden House will be used for military purposes as it is on the list of reserve hospitals, and we have had a notice. So far I have not heard whether I am needed although I hear they need men who can speak French or German. London looks very empty. Everywhere are transport wagons, territorials, bags of flour, drums and marching. I hear from a patient that 10,000 men arrived at Portsmouth on Friday last, were quartered on the inhabitants for the night and sailed next morning. I have got some of my better patients to enlist. It will do them good.

Best love,
Maurice.

Dr Nicoll was commissioned in the R.A.M.C. He told us with amusement that the first time he went out in his uniform, a Sergeant-Major in Regent Street instructed him how to correct the way in which he was wearing his equipment. He was embarrassed but grateful. He was ordered to proceed to Tipperary, but by December he was in barracks in Limerick and wrote the following letter home for Christmas:

The County Club,
Limerick,
'14.

Dearest Mater,

Many thanks for your letter. This is to wish you all a Merry Xmas. We are quite gay here and shall have a jovial Xmas dinner in Mess. All the men are very well supplied with all the necessaries. It is freezing with snow and the roads are slippery to march on. Work is fairly slack as most of the men are away on leave. We were medically inspected 'for active service' on Monday, so I suppose we shall soon be off.

Thanks very much indeed for the novels. They are most welcome for this time. I am sending you and Mildred a little Limerick lace. Best love, and many thanks to you for all your sympathy and kindness during this last year. It has been much appreciated by this medical officer-man.

Your affectionate son,
Maurice.

Rest after Xmas.

RAMC Mess,
New Barracks,
Limerick.
Sunday.

Dearest Pater,

I did not write a separate letter of Xmas wishes to you. I do so now, wishing you every blessing for the New Year. We had a quiet but cheerful Xmas and things are fairly slack owing to some of the men being away. There is no news as to when we go out – only fantastic rumours. Anyway it cannot be for another month at least as we have got no forwarder with equipment or uniform. I do hope that in spite of the war the coming year will be kind to you. Do not worry about Elystan or me. Whatever happens, one way or another, it will be destined, and I am perfectly tranquil and serene. These blighters must be smashed, although my duty is to patch them up! We are weary of waiting here. Where is Joffre's Xmas present?

All my love. Keep well, and take care of diet, liquid and solid.

Your affectionate son,
Maurice.

His letters home from the New Barracks at Limerick, apart from one which described a visit to the races, were chiefly concerned with lack of equipment and with the fear that the war would be over before they got out to France. He was appalled at the cost to the Government of maintaining these field ambulances during this interim period while they had no equipment, uniform, or supplies. He felt marooned there and lamented the lack of news. 'Never was a place or a life so devoid of news,' he wrote. All the time they were longing for something interesting to happen. He wrote that they had only partial uniform, one wagon instead of thirty, four horses instead of two hundred, no guns, no rifles, no information, no encouragement, no little book, no tips or hints how to conduct their operations. They felt no one seemed to care for them, a fighting force. They received no instructions or orders. He wrote: 'We drift about vaguely, here rumours, here a wave of enthusiasm, which dies away soon. We are all very fit physically and would be delighted to hear we were under orders.' He had heard that Dr Jung was on the frontier mobilized, and that this bored him exceedingly as he was in the middle of writing a book.

Dr Nicoll contrasted his enforced idleness with the terrific activity of his father in the cause of the war. He wrote: 'He is doing splendidly and is on much more active service than we are yet. I was glad to see that he had presided at L. G.'s meeting.'

Since the outbreak of the war, Sir William had worked indefatigably to secure victory for his country. His biographer said of him:

> To him as a Christian patriot, nothing else seriously mattered. Now as never before he realized his calling and election. Surely he had come into the kingdom of journalism for such a time as this! (*Life and Writings of William Robertson Nicoll* by T. H. Darlow: Hodder and Stoughton.)

In the *British Weekly* of 6th August, he had published a clarion leader 'United We Stand'. He considered the war a righteous and necessary war. He considered that the war would be a terrible war, and possibly much prolonged and that it would tax our strength and resources. He warned the people against pacifism. His own personal courage was dauntless. Not the least part of his patriotic service was to fortify his fellow countrymen during the darkest months of the conflict. Moreover, through his friendship with Mr Lloyd George and other politicians, he often had access to uncensored facts and week by week his published war notes signed 'W. R. N.' were scanned eagerly for some inkling of what had happened, or might happen soon.

Dr Nicoll had always expected that his Field Ambulance would be sent to France and he was prepared for the mud of the trenches, but in July he set sail for a very different destination. The following telegram, dated 24th July 1915, was received by Lady Robertson Nicoll:

On active service. All well. No news allowed.

M.

This was soon followed by a letter to his father written on 15th July from an unnamed ship:

Dearest Pater,

We are stopping at Malta for a few hours, so I write this short note. Not allowed to say much. Quiet, calm trip and nothing seen of an exciting nature. More like a pleasure trip. Large comfortable ship, quarters and food excellent. The ship was at the first landing – a big muddle apparently. We passed Gib. bristling with guns in the pink dawn. We all have life-belts. If I can send a telegram, I will, but I fear it will not be allowed or possible. We are not allowed to have anything to do with the wireless on board and hear no news. We can see the mountains of Algeria now. A small library on board. Everyone very merry and careless. Cards and songs and games all day. Passed Italian transport yesterday from South America, packed with reservists, otherwise not a ship of any sort seen. Due at our destination in about five days, I fancy. Very pleasant getting away like this into a non-war atmo-sphere. All peace and sunshine and laziness. Hope you are all well and fit and that a little good news is coming up now for a change. All very fit here.

Love to all,
Maurice.

The only news of his destination received by his parents was the characteristic telegram saying 'an island in Acts'. In August he wrote from Suvla:

We are close up now. Huge quantities of dust and flies and smell. Burning sea in front of me and dust everywhere. I am told that the discomforts are much worse than in South

34

3. Medical Student, Bart's

4. R.A.M.C. 1914, with Constance, his sister

Africa and can quite believe it. I have one book, *Jane Eyre*. I brought it by mistake and am annoyed as I dislike it. Out here Jane Eyre would have learned a lesson to suffer fools gladly, not only gladly but rapturously! My servant says there are no lemons, but a melon is reported a mile away in the hands of a Greek trader moving eastwards. I have sent him after it with one shilling. It is my last shilling. Miss Jane Eyre would have stuck to the shilling and analysed her feelings of thirst away.

Lady Robertson Nicoll recorded in *Under the Bay Tree*:

Maurice returned from Suvla Bay in September invalided with dysentery. Once on the hospital ship, away from all the horrors, he slept so heavily that a kind nurse did not ship him off at Mudros or Lemnos where there were hospitals, but left him undisturbed. So after a week of delay at Malta, owing to submarines, he got safely back. He was very thin, with glittering eyes, and his story of Suvla Bay ghastlier than one could imagine.

In February 1916 Dr Nicoll went to Mesopotamia with the 32nd Field Hospital. Many of his war experiences on active service are described in his book *In Mesopotamia* (Hodder and Stoughton), of which I quote the opening paragraph:

There is nothing to suggest that you are approaching the gateway of the Garden of Eden when you reach the top of the Persian Gulf, unless the sun be that flaming sword which turns every way to keep the way of the Tree of Life. Of cherubim we could see no signs. We lay motionless, awaiting orders by wireless. Of the country before us, we knew next to nothing. We did not grasp that the great river at whose mouth we lay was called 'shat el Arab' and not the 'Tigris' and I do not think that a single one of us possessed a copy of the Arabian Nights. Few of us knew anything of the gun running troubles in the Persian Gulf of recent years and of the exploits of the Royal Indian Marines.

He describes the landing of the field ambulance in very great heat: 'A desolate place beside a creek, looking like a bricklayer's

D

yard.' He describes the toil of unpacking equipment, stores, blankets; how the men chanted a rhythmic refrain in imitation of the native coolies when carrying loads. He quotes a simple, native chant:

> *Singer:* Tomorrow we will eat rice and meat.
> *Chorus:* May Allah grant it!
> *Singer:* We are doing a great deal of work.
> *Chorus:* May Allah reward us!

And then he quotes the more picturesque refrain of the Tommies:

Six men are carrying a crate.

> *Singer* (softly): Is it 'ot?
> *Chorus:* I dont think!
> *Singer:* 'ot as 'ell?
> *Chorus:* I don't think!
> *General chorus,*
> *repeatedly with*
> *passion:* Allah, 'ollar, Allah.
>   Oh – Allah, 'ollar, Allah,
>   Allah, 'ollar, OOO!

At the end of the arduous day, bully-beef was doled out and bottles of drinking water, and the men settled down in the empty sheds beside the creek. They went to bed in a thunderstorm, which Dr Nicoll describes as 'a vivid, zig-zagging, banging affair that circled round most of the night'. He wrote:

> The frogs trumpeted in chorus all night. Packs of dogs or jackals swept about in droves, once at full pelt through our tents like devils of the storm. It was nightmarish, but sleep brought that wonderful balancing force that sometimes clothes itself in dreams and steeps the spirit in all that is lacking. Just before falling asleep, I reflected that Adam and Eve might well have been excused in such a country.

When he reached Mesopotamia, the hot weather was beginning. He said that the wounded and sick came down river in thousands from the campaign for the release of Kut. Men straight out from England, unused to hot climates, were also being sent to hospital in big batches. There was a great lack of ice and no fans, electric or otherwise. There were no nurses, partly because there was no accommodation for them. He describes in his book the hospitals that were set up, fifty beds in a shed, and eventually beds crowded into every available corner of the clearing. New sheds had quickly to be erected by natives and these had to be built on piles driven six feet into the spongy soil. Drinking water had to come from a creek and he describes how it was chlorinated with bleaching powder, which when mixed with whisky was most peculiar.

Practical difficulties which confronted the field ambulance were innumerable. An extraordinary effort was needed in order to obtain soda water because of the lack of bottles. It was necessary to be poled down the creek to the river to a soda water factory, where the bottles were refilled. Dr Nicoll gives great praise to the Y.M.C.A. huts, and as always was most interested in recording what nourishment was available during a period of war. Lime juice and water was the usual drink until the sun went down, 'then,' he wrote:

> It was almost the universal experience to find alcohol necessary in the evening. The mind was exhausted, food was unattractive, conversation was impossible, the passage of time immeasurably slow and a restless irritation pervaded one until a dose of alcohol was taken. Its effect was humanising. But still, it is worth remembering that the Prophet forbade alcohol to the people of the country. But then he permitted other things.

In due course, after much delay, there was an increase in fruit and vegetables.

On 26th April 1916 he wrote to his father from Basra as follows:

Dearest Pater,

I am afraid you are all having a trying time over at home, with political crises, etc. It seems very remote from here. It is steaming hot now, about 96° in the shade and cloudless. The floods are coming down and will probably clear us out of here, so they say. If so, I don't know where we'll go. Everything is of course in a prodigious muddle down and

up river – worse than the P. By the way, Murodin, the
Turkish General here was at Eton with Townshend, which
is odd. He says it can't be done. I wonder if we'll be out here
for more than a year. I shall put in at the end of my year to
get back for a bit. . . . The insects are getting annoying. The
most prodigious winged creatures enter one's tent and buzz
and flap around. I'm a mass of bites and itches, but quite
cheerful. Supply very bad. Frogs croak all night. No transport for river. One sleeps all afternoon but does not get fat.
Jealousy everywhere. I'm looking after all the camp sick of
this area and am busy all morning. The mails get here about
once in 10 days roughly – one is due in today. They are great
days. No tobacco for troops. All papers, books, mags., etc.
are most welcome. I wonder if you're seeing anything of
L. G.? May lose all we've got. If so, give him my regards
and tell him K. is the man for this picnic.

Best love to all,

M.

Two months later his sister, Mrs Elystan Miles, received the
following letter:

Basra, 27th June 1916.

Dearest C.,

Its hot! Nothing metal in the tent can be touched. Water
in a pail is so hot you can't put your hand in it. Through these
thin canvas roofs the sun cuts like a knife through butter.
Butter, by the way, is impossible here – thin, smiling, watery
fluid. And sick – streams of ambulances all day. I see a
hundred cases, I should think, each day – new ones – and
have a ward i.e. a few temporary shelters, tents, sheds, filled
with eighty others, just lying on the ground. Poor devils, its
terrific, heatstroke, heat-exhaustion and malaria mostly. One
staggers round. We go to Amara next week. The new lot of
doctors is gradually taking over, thin exhausted men from
Manchester dazed with the heat. They won't last long. I think
our lot has lasted wonderfully – only six out of thirty away,
the rest slaving and dripping. Of course we should have been
under thick-roofed huts and not thin canvas. A dreadful

rumour has arisen that we doctors have to stay on till His Majesty's pleasure and won't get home after one year. If I last till November I certainly mean to set sail for home. Another hot season here is more than any man can stand. The Indian Medical Service men say there is nothing approaching it in India. The Indian troops are dropping as fast as ours. Well, my dear, they say I am the fittest of the lot. It is because – if it is true – of the Nicoll spirit of knowing how to do a thing with the least possible physical exertion. I perceive it to be Oriental. I give quinine and salts and milk and soda to all my patients and never any fancy mixtures. That and opium. The exhausted men need opium here and they sleep for two days and wake new men. Use the drugs of the country, opium, quinine and salts. You can do anything with these drugs here, add one – emetine, and you have the whole necessary pharmacopoeia. The rest is a matter of cold water, wet sheets, rest and shade, and electric fans and diet. *We have no fans yet after two years occupation.* 'Not foreseen', etc. So the ward gets stifling at night with all the mosquito nets hanging and heat cases get bad again. Big fans – very simple – gas engines, dynamos – wire and fans – would save life daily. 'Not foreseen.' 'No, no, of course not. *You* have your fan and stone house. *You* don't know what heat by day is, because *you* don't go out in it. Oh, You.' (addressed to a certain person here.)

> All love to all.
> Send plenty of stuff to read.
> It follows us up to Amara
> from here.
> Best love,
> M.

'The Nicoll spirit of knowing how to do a thing with the least possible physical exertion' was apparent in Dr Nicoll all his life – and the importance of economy of energy was later to be greatly stressed in his teaching. Moreover, compassion has been described as the last of the virtues to be attained, the culminating virtue, but Dr Nicoll at every stage of his life had this feeling for others, this power of putting himself in their place, which is apparent in these letters. He even had the forethought to take privately extra supplies of morphia to give to those on the beaches who were dying in agony from the shelling. No provision had been made for them otherwise.

Dr Nicoll gives in his book a detailed description of the sufferings of the patients in his hospital. He found heatstroke the malady most painful to witness, with the exception possibly of acute cholera. I quote his description of a typical day:

> To gain some idea of heatstroke, it is necessary to grasp the conditions that produce it. A typical hot day begins with a dawn that comes as a sudden hot yellow behind the motionless palms. A glittering host of dragonflies rises up from the swamps, wheeling and darting after the mosquitoes. In the glowing light, mysterious shapes slink past. They are the camp dogs returning from their sing-song, which has kept you awake half the night. Inside the mosquito net you see various gorged little insects, struggling to get out of the meshings through which they passed so easily when they were slim and hungry. The hot beam of the sun picks out your tent and the mercury goes up steadily. At five you are bathed in perspiration as you lie in bed. It has been in the neighbourhood of 90° throughout the night.
>
> You have probably spent most of it smoking in a chair in the moonlight, listening to horses whinnying, donkeys braying, dogs barking and yelping without a pause, and men groaning and tossing in the steamy sick tents. The business of getting up is one of infinite weariness. There is nothing fresh in the morning feeling. At eight the mercury is probably 100°. At times as you dress, after a tepid bath, it is necessary to sit down and take a rest. Your vesture is simple, a thin shirt open at the collar and a pair of shorts, stockings and shoes. During the day, your feelings do not correspond to the height of the mercury, for after breakfast a certain amount of energy possesses you and the morning's work becomes possible. But after a couple of hours, in the neighbourhood of eleven o'clock, when it may be anything from 110° to 120° in the shade, a kind of enervation sets in. This

partly due to lack of food. For some reason we found it necessary to eat a considerable amount. The theory of a simple diet, a little fruit, meat once a day and in small quantities, did not work out in practice. After midday, the world is a blinding glare and the intake of air seems to burn the lungs. A comparative stillness descends on the scene. On the plain, activities cease. Through the double canvas roofing of a tent, the sun beats down like a giant with a leaden club. The temperature in the wards increases. At the worst moments, you feel distinctly that it would be possible, by giving way to something that escapes definition, to go off your head. A spirit of indifference to everything is necessary. Any kind of worry is simply a mode of suicide. There must be no inner conflict. Cranks soon suffer. Life becomes simplified. An oriental contempt of the West, with all its preoccupations grows insensibly. When a dripping orderly came to rouse you to see some case, you understood perfectly the attitude of mind that produced the idea of kismet. Why move? If the man dies, it is Allah's will. It is Allah's will that he is sick. Let him remain in the hands of Allah. It was during the afternoon and evening that heatstroke occurred in the main, when the humidity of the air began to go up. A great many of the new troops had no idea of the danger of the sun. The Tommy does not estimate a situation very quickly. The attempt to change the main meal of the day to an evening hour did not meet with success and during the afternoon the men would sit bucking away in their tents and refuse to adapt themselves to the idea of a siesta. Moreover, the Tommy is obstinate by nature and does not like to give in. He goes on marching in the sun, even though he feels bad, and the collapse is swift and fatal.

About five o'clock, with the temperature falling and the humidity of the air increasing, a period of intense discomfort sets in. Perspiration was so profuse that clothes became wringing wet like bathing suits, even if you were sitting still. A kind of air hunger ensued. The few birds in the grove sat with their beaks wide open. It was then that the ambulance wagons began to roll in with their burden of heatstroke cases and continued until after sunset. It is a malady which, as I have said, is dramatic and painful to witness.

A heatstroke station was prepared at the water's edge, containing a couple of baths and an ice chest and patients were put into chill water as soon as possible. They were slapped and punched and lay until they began to turn blue and the temperature fell. Then they were put in a blanket. If any collapse showed, they were just left naked on a bed in the open. Fear played a powerful part in the malady. It tended to produce it and to cause relapses and it was good practice to use direct counter-suggestion whenever the patient was conscious as well as brandy and morphia. The worst of it was that many of those patients that recovered over-night died next afternoon as they lay in the suffocating ward. What was possible with wet sheets and small pieces of ice was done, but it was a wretched business and those who were in Basra at that time and saw those spectacles will never forget them. Nor will they forget the silent, impotent rage that filled the mind at the thought of the giant-bodied, small-headed colossus of war, which makes a useless sacrifice of men in ways such as these every day. But it had one useful effect, perhaps. A real Zoroastrian reverence for the sun came, after seeing a case, and a man learned to look on his pith helmet and spine pad as his best friends.

During the later war when we were in Birdlip Dr Nicoll recalled the devastation caused by sunstroke in his Mesopotamian days which could have been alleviated if the discovery of the curative power of salt had then been made. In the 1914 war the doctors were helpless and had to watch many of their patients die, but in the 1939 war the men were given salt which saved many lives.

In his book, Dr Nicoll records the fall of Kut. His comment was that the fall of Kut did not ease the pressure at the hospitals. The sick rate was increasing steadily. A north-west wind, that comes just in time to make it possible for you to believe in Providence, he wrote, was not due until after the middle of June and meanwhile the day temperature was far over 100° and clinical thermometers cracked if they were left lying about on tables.

A New Zealand radio officer, who came in from the desert one day, had an interesting talk with Dr Nicoll about mirage in the desert. What was puzzling was that the same mirage would appear to several people at the same time. The mirage might occur, not only as an oasis of water and palms, where there is no water and palms, but it might appear as an Arab on horseback or an Arab crawling on the ground, or a transport column. Dr Nicoll thought a mirage, in the form which it took, might have some inner connection with a man's psychology.

His medical comments at this period were interesting. He observed that excessive and prolonged heat (the hot season, for instance, lasting seven or eight months) rouses a defensive mechanism of inertia, whose aim is to preserve life. A man would feel all the power go out of his legs and want to lie down and this was the best thing he could do. He said that mental exertion became almost impossible. Reading was not easy, writing a burden and thinking a matter of extreme difficulty. The experience of this effect of the heat made it possible for him to have some understanding of the Eastern character.

In 1916, Dr Nicoll wrote to Lady Robertson Nicoll from Amara. He put at the head of his letter 'Mara – in the Book of Esther – bitter. Amara is bitter so I suppose Amara means a place of bitterness.' In *In Mesopotamia* he describes the voyage through the Narrows as they approached Basra. There is a part of the Tigris that becomes very narrow with sharp turns, sometimes more acute than right angles, so that progress consisted of a series of bumps from side to side. He said they could not help thinking, as they gazed at these bending and twisting Narrows, that it might be possible, with a little cutting, to do away with the worst bits and open up a straight channel. However, Dr Nicoll had the thought also that tampering with great rivers like the Tigris might cause unthought-of troubles, for it upsets the natural balance of the waters.

The nights during that journey up river were made memorable by sandflies, which he said were like a million little red-hot wires. Moreover the mules screamed and fought and gasped for air, so that it was difficult to sleep.

It was on arriving at Amara that Dr Nicoll saw men risk their lives to rescue a mule that had kicked itself loose of its moorings and fell into the stream in the darkness. This he often spoke of in later years. It made a great impression on him. He felt that there was something lacking in their sense of scale. He said 'What is a wife to think of her husband when she is told that he was drowned while gallantly attempting to rescue from the swift current of the Tigris a mule that could swim far better than he could?' 'As no one was drowned perhaps it is unnecessary to ask questions,' he said 'but this is an interesting one to ponder on.'

His letter home describes their quarters. The men were in mud huts on the plains and tents, but the officers had a little pomegranate grove to themselves, with little single tents pitched under trees among the fruit. He described his men 'as fairly thin just like little bits of stick'. He gives a further description of the scene in *In Mesopotamia*:

> Behind the officers' tents, lay an oriental garden supplied with water to it through channels from the river, by means of a machine worked by an Arab who, as far as one could tell, prayed to it. In this garden lived a colony of jackals, those extraordinary spirits of hell whose wailing and hysteria are so amazing. The jackal does not terrify by such obvious methods as the lion. He plays on your eerie, ghostly superstitious side. He brings up into the imagination the malignity and hopelessness of the damned. He seems to people the night with wailing horrors. To a man dying of thirst in the desert, the jackal must just give the final touch of despair that makes death and nothingness seem best. It must be strange to die surrounded by jackals at their colonial litanies.

He had no news of the world at large and had no idea how the war was getting on. Soon after his arrival in Amara, Sir Victor Horsley died, in whom, he said, we lost the finest surgeon in Mesopotamia. He wrote in his letter home:

> He was a fine man, did good work out here and got things better than they were, at least. A fine, high-souled, obstinate, courteous man, a splendid surgeon, both cerebral and general; a man with very high principles, which he carried out to the

last, who hated this place and yet insisted on sticking it out for one hot season. He got a coffin, and eight officers staggered through the dust after him to the cemetery.

Among others who were buried with him, Dr Nicoll recognized two friends from his Cambridge days. The lovely playing of 'The Last Post' over the graves remained in his memory.

In his book, Dr Nicoll made many comments on the drugs that were used. He said that if limited to three drugs and no more for work in that country, he would prefer opium, epsom salts and quinine. The men received five grains of quinine every day. They paraded for it with their water bottles, each man receiving a pink tablet and gulping it down with a draught of water. The Chinese carpenters slept more peacefully than anyone. One could see the little sticky mass of opium, he said, wedged in between the teeth.

He commented on the fact that sometimes for two or three days at a time cases seemed to go wrong and die on the slightest provocation, whereas at other times the most hopeless cases would clear up. This changing of the current, he said, could be observed in every phase of life. The day temperature was now 124° in the shade and it was impossible, he said, to do anything save what was absolutely necessary. He described his day:

> After a somewhat exhausting night, we rose at seven. The best hours of sleep were usually after sunrise, for then the sandflies vanished. After breakfast of tea, eggs and bread the ward work started. This lasted until about midday. Then came lunch, accompanied by many flies, and afterwards a long siesta, during which one wore the minimum of clothing. At four or five, one dressed again, took a bath and took a look at the wards to see any bad cases. Then the evening began, in which life became more possible. Dinner was usually a cheerful meal. After dinner, what to do was a great problem. One just did nothing. During this time everyone became thin. Any sickness, even a slight attack of diarrhoea, brought down weight rapidly. There was the case of a certain sergeant, whose immense girth was much revered by the Arabs. One can understand perhaps how it comes about that fatness is admired in the East. It is so rare. It is so much

easier to be thin. The sergeant went into hospital for a few days. When he came out, he had lost his glory, even as Samson was shorn of his strength in a night. His clothes hung about him in huge folds. What had taken him years to produce was lost in six days, and with it went the respect of the Arabs. There is practically no fat in the country. There was no dripping for puddings. The cattle were all lean.

Dr Nicoll was much amused by a play produced in Arabic at an Arab theatre at Amara, based on a topical incident. The Oriental mind was amazed by the fact that no Arab was allowed to go into camps and hospitals without a pass. This was satirized on the stage. The scene was of the illness and death of a fat man, whose wife lamented beside him, while a fat woman mournfully shook her tambourine between whiles. The part of the physician was played by a local medium, who seemed to be trying to exorcise the devil in the patient, kicking him, hitting him, spitting on him and jumping on him. When the man died, he carried him off on his shoulders to the cemetery, then returned, dumping the corpse on the ground and saying 'It is no good. I cannot bury him. I haven't got a pass.' The finale brought the house down.

At this point, Dr Nicoll said an effort was made to further the interests of medical science and the Amara Clinical Society was started, at which doctors met weekly and discussed cases and diagnoses and papers were read. He said:

> There is, I think, no better proof that in its central core, medicine is an art and not a science, than in the kind of discussion that goes on at medical meetings. It exactly resembles the discussions that go on in political debating societies.

He found the incessant inspections very irritating, for they suspended the work of the hospital while they lasted, making it necessary to hurry through the usual work and take all the books, papers, and games from the patients and wait for the arrival of the inspecting party. The hospital had by now evidently become so comfortable that it was possible for a man to be admitted and to be found with nothing wrong, his excuse for arriving having been that he wanted a sleep in a good bed:

In September he wrote a more cheerful letter to his father from Amara.

> Dearest Pater,
>
> The outlook seems more hopeful. Hot season very long but body adjusts. Yewing to preach who knew you: preaches too long in the sun. Inertia. Arab vests troublesome. We get ice now, which is a kind of lift at certain moments of the day.

He was beginning to hope that it would be possible to leave before the end of the year. He wrote:

> I am absolutely without brains and can't link two words together. One hundred typhoid cases, the featureless brown plain, the yellow river, the sun, the army forms – that's all the life, day by day without any kind of holiday and know-how to get away from it.

However, the weather became cooler towards the end of October and sickness diminished. Dr Nicoll wrote:

> At this season there is a kind of charm about Mesopotamia. Clouds begin to inhabit the skies and the colour effects, especially those of dawn and sunset, are lovely. It is a time intermediate between the season of heat and the season of floods, a brief time but one in which the country is at its best. Mosquitoes and sandflies vanish. A lovely bird, a deep blue and russet, sings in the groves. The blue jay screams and darts through the palm trees. It is possible to understand how in the Eastern poets, the beauty of women is constantly compared with the moon. It is the only thing to compare it to. In a country like Mesopotamia, with its entire lack of scenery, the moon in all her phases is by far the most beautiful thing that one sees. The only objects that the native jewellers etch into their silverwork are Ezra's Tomb, the native boat, the jackal, the palm tree and the camel. And that is about all the material the country yields. It is this simplicity that leaves only two courses open to the inhabitants. They must

either fall back upon their senses and become sensualists or
seek a higher path and become mystics.

He describes his journey down the river at the end of the year,
once more going through the Narrows. He describes a night at
Amara, a night that differed entirely from those endured when
going up.

> There was a concert party on board and a cavalry major,
> who possessed some tomato soup. That night the sky was
> superb with stars. Taurus rose with Aldebaran as red as fire,
> then Castor and Pollux, calm in their symmetry, with the
> Pleiades above like a shattered diamond. Then glittering
> Orion slowly swung above the horizon. In the middle of the
> night there was a crash of musketry and a sudden uproar.
> The major appeared, speaking in Hindustani very rapidly,
> his eyes closed. It appeared that some Arabs had crept on to
> the barge next to the shore and tried to loot some mail bags.
> Quiet was soon restored. At dawn a crescent moon, uphold-
> ing Venus at her fairest, hung in the east, throwing a soft
> white flame over the dark water.

They reached Corna and tied up alongside the Garden of Eden,
where a wedding was being celebrated.

In Mesopotamia is illustrated by the author's own water colour
paintings. He was very thankful and delighted when colours,
blocks and brushes arrived from England, 'but', he said, 'I am no
good at this mud plain. It's the devil to paint. One gets a smudge
as the result of any kind of work here, painting or writing, so I
must not be critical.' He used to tell us thirty years later what a
solace his painting and writing had been to him during those
months in the desert. He did water colour sketches of the Garden
of Eden, of the Tigris, of donkeys and Ezra's Tomb.

On 6th November, shortly before his return, he wrote to his
father as follows, outlining his plans for the future. He had already
sent a cable saying he hoped to be home by the New Year.

> We have decided – I don't know if I told you – to cut
> entirely away from psycho-analysis and not use the name. It

is the only way to clear oneself from a most difficult situation: I mean, our theories, in their ultimate outlook, are spiritual and full of hope: the psycho-analysts are the pessimists (or pessimism) of Schopenhauer and Co. But as regards material, there are so many close resemblances that so far one cannot trace the dividing line. But be assured that we know that there is a dividing line, and I have tried to write a simple non-technical volume – quite polite – on the attitude I take up. It was an offshoot of Zürich, but independent. I don't propose to join any school. But there are many storms ahead and I fear, after the war, in the emotional outburst that is likely, that the darker school will get many supporters. But I believe that in our work lies the germ of something very wonderful and it is strange to think it is traceable to Freud – though, as you know, Freud is one thing, and his American and Jewish followers another – it is almost correct to say his *Jewish* followers, for they are all Jews, and it is a kind of Jewish revival of thought – a sort of archaism – from which all the Christians who were entangled in it as I was, have broken free – but not empty-handed.

When I get home I propose to resign my Commission and enroll myself – that will give me six weeks' holiday at least and it is the only way to get it for certain. With luck I may get two months: it will be a slack time as regards fighting and I must get out of the life for a spell. I am very anxious to overhaul my MS. and have it ready for a favourable moment.

CHAPTER FOUR

Empire Hospital

Dr Nicoll arrived in England early in 1917. His active service was over, and now he entered upon a new phase of war service which demanded the exercise of all his professional skill.

By the end of January he was installed at 10 Palace Gardens, where he was attending officer patients. He was observing war neurotics, taking notes and had the idea of bringing out a small volume on war neuroses. He was aware that the treatment given, electric currents, baths and tonics, was of no avail to cure a diseased mind.

During his years abroad Dr Nicoll had reflected continuously on the plight of those who would return from active service with injuries of the mind which medical skill could not cure. As a result of his studies with Dr Jung he had come to certain conclusions as to a new approach to the treatment of shell shock, an approach hitherto undreamed of by orthodox medicine. He had brought back with him the MSS. of two books.

His work with shell shock patients led him to make some important observations about the symptom of regression which he considered as the result of the retreat of interest from reality and in examining the condition known as shell shock, he demonstrated the effect of the excessive impact of reality on the individual. Victims of shell shock, he said, lay in bed in a state of helplessness of varying degrees. They might even be paralysed, blind, deaf or dumb and at the same time there might be other symptoms . . . and their emotions were uncontrolled. Such a condition, he said, might persist for many months. They had great fears and they had lost interest in life. What had happened in this process was that the force that reveals itself as interest had retreated down to levels that belonged to the first years of their life and this process was called regression. In this conception of regression Dr Nicoll was adhering once more to Dr Jung's views. He observed the spectacle of regression also in advancing age. Whenever a man reaches a point at which everything he says and does leads back to a certain period in the past it is said that he is experiencing regression.

Dr Nicoll frequently talked to us about this subject and applied his knowledge of it to our dreams. Whenever anyone dreamed himself back into early circumstances he attributed this to a state of regression, which was the result of a desire to escape from a situation which had become intolerable.

I quote a clear example of what happens in a case of regression. This is a case described in an article by Dr Nicoll published in the *Lancet* in 1918, 'A conception of regression in psychological medicine':

> The patient had developed symptoms of profound shock regression on the battle field. He had a bad stammer, tremor and vivid battle dreams and was almost incapable of any effort of attention. He gradually improved and the battle dreams disappeared. Three days before his medical board, the stammer got worse and the battle dreams reappeared. The reason for this was not difficult to trace. He had been offered a special post, which he desired, and everything in the immediate future depended on the decision of the medical board. Reality had become uncertain therefore and slight regression had taken place.

Dr Nicoll gave this example as an illustration of the retreat from reality which caused the revival of certain symptoms.

In June 1917, *Dream Psychology* was published by Hodder and Stoughton in a series called Oxford Medical Publications. The reviewers accepted Dr Nicoll as a disciple of Jung, and one critic went so far as to call the book 'a summary of Jung's view'. In 1913 Dr Nicoll had already become clear in his mind that it was necessary to break away from the Freudian system of psychology, from the practice of Freudian dream analysis. No sooner had he made up his mind about this than the war of 1914 broke out. His two and a half years of service in the R.A.M.C. had given him time for further thought which had the effect of confirming for him the direction in which his future work as a Psychologist lay. In the preface to *Dream Psychology* Dr Nicoll stated:

Within the last few years the Zürich School of analytical psychology under Dr Jung has parted company with the Viennese school under Professor Freud, the pioneer of dream analysis. The outlook of the Swiss school differed so fundamentally from that of the Austrian school that disunion was inevitable. In England and America many people are familiar with the Freudian teachings. I shall feel justified in producing this book if it enables its readers to regard the dream, in some degree, from Dr Jung's standpoint, and I desire to place on record here the debt that I owe personally to Dr Jung.

In the book Dr Nicoll outlines the main differences between the methods of dream interpretation practised by Freud and Jung. The basic value of dream interpretation, Dr Nicoll maintained, was that it could give the key to the malady of a neurotic which was never found wholly in consciousness. The patient had to be made aware that the roots of his trouble lay in his own psyche. His dreams would shew him what was wrong with him. The dream is compared by Dr Nicoll with a cartoon.

Just as the cartoon is a symbolic representation of circumstances affecting social or political life, which must be recognizable, if the symbolism is to be intelligible, so the dream gathers certain threads of interest into unexpected juxtaposition.

The symbolic setting was, he said, formed from the incidents of the day, but they were combined in an unexpected manner, and 'what is unexpected corresponds to what is not thought of, or not conscious'. Thus he defines the dream as 'a product of unconscious activity, a presentation of interests in a form unconscious to the individual'. From this definition follows the conclusion that although many people had the same dream, each dream should be interpreted differently, for every individual had his own associations from which arose his use of the symbolism.

He shewed that dreams are comparable with waking phantasies. Many dreams, like phantasies, could be interpreted as compensatory in cases, for instance, where they counteract the distress of physical conditions. Freud had applied his wish-fulfilment theory to such dreams, looking on them as representing the gratification of wishes not to be fulfilled in reality. The compensatory theory of Jung, however, sees in the phantasy and in the dream an attempt to provide that which is lacking in reality and Dr Nicoll stresses that it is protective in meaning, so much so, that in some cases it could protect even from insanity. In the same way, when a waking phantasy goes too far, the dream corrects this. Its purpose apparently is to adjust the balance. The following example given by Dr Nicoll illustrates this:

> A young man began to paint pictures during a period when it was impossible for him to pursue his normal line of work. He achieved a minor degree of success, and gradually conceived the phantasy that art was his true vocation. His normal work followed a different path – art, on the other hand, seemed to him easy by comparison. His phantasy-building system wove pictures of a large studio, pleasant surroundings, easy-going companions, and unscheduled hours. In this state he experienced the following dream: 'I was at an exhibition of pictures; some of my own were hung in a corner. The room was empty – a man entered wearing a fur coat, and I seemed to know that he was a millionaire and a great connoisseur. He began to examine the pictures – he came to a corner where mine were hung and passed on with scarcely a glance at them. . . .'

Dr Nicoll points out that this dream contradicts the dreamer's idea that his pictures were of value. His phantasy had compensated him where his normal line of work failed him and the dream seemed to be correcting the over-compensation of the phantasy-building system. In the undercompensated type, characterized by lack of confidence, the dream would depict a man with more than necessary confidence or joy. For instance, a man called upon to take unaccustomed responsibility would see himself as a failure in his phantasy but he might dream of himself as an actor successfully taking a leading part on the stage.

Dr Nicoll points out that in handling a dream the aim is to discover the motive of the unconscious. When this is revealed the attitude of the conscious mind becomes clearer. In this connection

Dr Nicoll used the word *interest* in a special sense rather than Jung's word *libido* or Bergson's *élan vital*. He defines interest as a force that flows making a man what he is. The pushing out of 'interest' on to life is termed *extroversion* by the Zürich School, and Dr Nicoll writes that the study of the difficulties that hedge about successful extroversion constitutes one of the main tasks or psychological medicine. He thought that the secret of the character of what Jung called the extrovert seemed to lie in the slightness of the barrier that intervenes between feeling and its expression. Dr Nicoll said that the extroverted type was remarkable in its inconsistency and its lack of self-knowledge. In such a type the unconscious in dreams would seek to check it. For instance, a too-active woman would dream that she missed her train because she had too much to pack. The introvert type, on the other hand, could more easily know himself. His task was to discover a means of relating himself to life or he would be in danger of losing touch with reality through living in a fantastic world of his own thoughts. Each type was shewn in dreams how to adjust himself to become more balanced. Dr Nicoll relates hysteria to extroversion and epilepsy to introversion.

In his book he makes a very interesting connection between phantasy and rumour, which he defines, either good or bad, as communal phantasy. He points out that it is possible to regard good rumour as arising under exactly the same circumstances as optimistic phantasy. It arises out of psychic necessity as a compensatory product, when to the community as a whole, or as an isolated part, reality assumes a threatening aspect. He made clear that the Jung conception of the unconscious greatly expanded that of Freud which had seemed to be concerned only with repressed material. Jung found in the deepest level of the unconscious primitive ways of thinking, symbols, belonging to the evolutionary background of Man. This view Dr Nicoll expanded further in a series of lectures given to the Tavistock Clinic for Functional Nervous Diseases. In these lectures he shewed that mythologies of different nations resemble one another because the *collective unconscious* is the common inheritance of man. He stressed, therefore, the necessity of separating in dreams the archetypal constituents from the personal. He said that in the present age of rationalism we have no relationship to the collective unconscious, no mythology, and little religion. He suggested that dream analysis might be necessary in order that man may re-establish a relationship with the collective unconscious.

Dream Psychology went into a second edition in 1919 which Dr Nicoll prefaced with a reply to those critics who had accused him of being unnecessarily hostile to Freud and his school. He admitted his hostility but added that he believed in Freud up to the point that the infantile psychology was contained in the unconscious but maintained that it was not the whole unconscious. He disagreed on the question of symbolism which he considered a primary form of expression, creative and of value to life, and he found in the dream a certain doctrine akin to the central teaching of many religions, a doctrine necessary for the rebirth of self from collective values to individual values. He said that the problem of every neurotic whom he had treated had been one of the development of individual values, whereas the men had fought for collective values. What Freud had done, he said, was to relate the problem of neurosis to the understanding of the instincts and his work on this subject had been unsurpassed.

I quote a letter written on 15th March 1918 in which Dr Nicoll describes a step that had been taken in connection with his work on shell shock:

> *Empire Hospital for Officers,*
> *Vincent Square,*
> *Westminster, S.W.1.*
> *15th March 1918.*

Dear Pater,

Thank you very much for your letter and news. I was sorry not to be up to see you, but have been very busy and it is very nice to rest when one has a short respite. To come up from the hospital is a three hours' business, and somehow there are so many little appointments scattered throughout the day that it is very difficult to get a sufficiently free period. The *Lancet* has taken one of my papers, but there is some extraordinary muddle as regards the paper for the *Nineteenth Century*. It was sent up to the War Office for permission to publish, and the last I heard of it was that it was in the hands of a professor in Liverpool who wrote in a bewildered state to ask what it was. However, I have hopes. An abstract of the reply I made to Dr Rivers' paper before the Royal Society is printed in the Proceedings, which I will bring you some time. There was a review of *Dream Psychology* in the *Lancet* of the week before last. We had a meeting of the shell shock Committee on Tuesday last. The War Office has taken over two or three enormous asylums, and we will have to do what we can with them. Of course it is unfortunate that they should have taken over asylums with the asylum staff, etc., as that was just the thing we wished to avoid. I do not think that there is any prospect for many years of realizing our ideals in this respect, but there is plenty of evidence to show that the movement is a very widespread one. George Riddoch* will be back some time early in April, I hope, and then I will apply for ordinary leave for a fortnight or so. Kenneth Walker is over on a mission concerned with getting human blood, as it has been found that this is the only remedy for the profound shock that follows extensive loss of blood, so you will soon be seeing in the papers appeals for people to come forward and give a pint of blood. The King [King George V] will no doubt lead the way, but I do not suppose he will be able to give a whole pint. It is rather interesting, by the way, that it has been found that there are four fundamental types of human blood, mutually antagonistic to one another, and that it is essential before transfusing a patient with human blood to ascertain what type he belongs to, so that the right blood may be selected.

Your affectionate son,
Maurice.

The article for the *Nineteenth Century* to which Dr Nicoll refers was actually published in the following May. It was entitled 'The Need for Psycho-Pathological Hospitals'. In it Dr Nicoll gives free rein to his indignation at the delay in recognition of the need of these hospitals for the treatment of shell shock and other nervous

* Dr George Riddoch, a Neurologist, who was also a pioneer in Psychological Medicine.

cases. The article might be called an indictment of orthodox medicine. He lays bare the neglect of scientific enquiry into the psychological factor except in such obvious cases as hysteria, neurasthenia and so on. He advocates clinical psychology which, dealing with the individual's own reality, will demand certain qualities on the part of the doctor. He asks for the setting aside of special hospitals for psycho-pathological cases, and deplores the existing habit of treating such cases in the same wards as insane cases. It is evident from his letter of 15th March that asylums had already been taken over which was just what he wanted to avoid.

On 16th July 1918 Dr Nicoll contributed to a Symposium held at a Joint Session of the British Psychological Society, the Aristotelian Society and the Mind Association. To the question – 'Why is the "unconscious" unconscious?' Dr Nicoll's reply was summarized thus:

> Because life is a process of progressive evolutions, and the context of the healthy conscious mind requires to be closely adapted to reality if the individual is to be successful. Therefore, the progressive transmutations of psychic energy are carried out at levels beneath consciousness, just as the progressive transmutations of the embryo are carried out in the womb of the mother, and it is only the comparatively adapted form that is born into waking life.
>
> Thus from this point of view we must regard the unconscious as the inexhaustible source of our psychic life, and not only as a cage containing strange and odious beasts.

In May of this year, Dr Nicoll gave a course of lectures at the University of Birmingham on Psychotherapy at a post graduate course in Crime and Punishment.

In the autumn Dr Nicoll was appointed to the staff of the Empire Hospital for Officers in Vincent Square, where he had already begun his work on shell shock. He wrote to his father as follows:

> Our lot is composed of Dr Maurice Craig, Henry Head, Farquhar-Buzzard, Rivers, MacDougall, Fernside, Professor Elliott Smith, Branwell, MacNamara, Millar, Riddoch and myself and they are, thank the Lord, all as keen as mustard

now this has come to a tussle. But what the thing really means in the spiritual sense is that the orthodox medical reactionaries have been smashed and psychology has been born. The door is wide open for ever, so I feel that all my talks and dinners and harangues and explanations and attacks of the last eight months have not been in vain. For it was I who got Buzzard to move, and he is the pillar, being a square man.

This was what Dr Nicoll had worked for since his return, that there should be a better understanding of the needs of a diseased mind, the needs of a man suffering from shock. At times he wrote as though the end of the war were in sight. He was anxious about his father, who had been ill, having overworked during the early war years, and being reluctant to give up anything of his usual activities.

On 16th September he wrote to his stepmother, who was presumably in Scotland:

Dearest Mater,

I went up to Bay Tree on Saturday and found the Pater very cheerful, and looking better. I thought his cold sounded a little bronchial still. But he was in good spirits, and talked animatedly about his holiday which he seems to have enjoyed very much. I was so glad you arranged the extra week. It was a very clever move, and it has certainly helped him as he admits. I go up again shortly, and Connie goes on Monday, I understand.

I am free of 'Latchmen' and back at the Empire, I am glad to say. 'Mentals' do not interest me. All very busy and tired of waiting for the Dawn, which appears as far off as ever.

Much love,
Maurice.

This solicitous regard for his father's health runs through Dr Nicoll's letters of this period.

While he was on active service in Mesopotamia, various letters from Dr Nicoll had been published in the *British Weekly*. Apart from descriptions of life and conditions in Amara, reminding those at home of what those fated to go through a second or third hot season would have to endure, the letters touched on religion and philosophy. For instance, he wrote saying how it was brought home to all those on active service that they must look for an answer to the question put by so many 'where were the souls of the dead in the after life?' I quote an extract from a letter published in the *British Weekly* on 13th January 1916 in which he expressed views about life after death that he continued to emphasize until the end:

I tell you it forces one to think and I believe that to be one of the many great objects of the war. It has made thousands of soldiers atheists; it has made thousands raging lunatics and it has made more thousands think. And now I wish to ask some great exponent of orthodox Christianity whether the others are utterly damned for being forced by reason and high explosive shells to think as follows – that when we die we do not by any means solve the great mystery. We retain our individuality. We meet our friends who have died before us. We find ourselves still faced with problems, still able to progress and develop by tackling them. We are given a good chance, as we are given a good chance on this earth. But we still have the problems of our own natures to contend with and the great plan is still that of progress by conquest of self. The fact that our bodies lie dead on the battlefield does not mean that our minds and feelings have undergone a complete change. If we were narrow on earth, we retain that narrowness, only we probably have it brought home to us more clearly. If we have left much still to do on earth, then we are sent back again to learn our full lessons and complete our labours. We still make mistakes but there are teachers, as on earth. I dare not go further. I am no doubt sufficiently condemned by Christians at home already. But many of us on the battlefield have found in these simple views a message of comfort and a wonderful lessening of the terror of death.

May I in conclusion thank you for printing the message of Sir Oliver Lodge, the great preacher of continuity, in a recent number.

Another letter was on the subject of old age. Here already is the germ of thinking on this subject that was to develop progressively during Dr Nicoll's life. He wrote:

A man is old just as soon as he shows by his conversation that he looks wholly into the past for his greatest and best. It means that he is looking at *his* greatest and best, which now lies behind him. Such a definition is of greater practical value in the common relationships of life than to say that a man is as old as his arteries, or because their average age is well over fifty. These points do not matter.

But it matters very much if the general mind of the company is fixed wholly on the past. Then one knows they are old, and behaves accordingly.

A man *begins* to grow old as soon as he looks back. In this way he has 'old phases' – which are temporary – during his existence; phases in which he looks longingly back at a lost love, or at a past success which the present denies him. Such phases are of extreme danger, for if prolonged the mind may become a veritable pillar of salt. But some minds become permanently old even before the full maturity of the physical body. One finds examples of these in that large and ever-present class of men whose thoughts dwell continually on their school or college days, as if fascinated by some misty glory of which the present and future are both totally devoid. They are cases of arrested development, and their vision cripples them.

The mind that remains young has to make continual sacrifices. The sacrifices consist in leaving older patterns of thought for patterns that are newer. This is one of the practical aspects of sacrifice, the freeing of oneself from the dependent states, which are satisfactory and comfortable, and the gaining of more independence of people and things; it means being independent of oneself.

Those whose physical bodies are full of years, but who still look forward, are men who have the courage to undergo continually these inner sacrifices. And their achievement is an exceptional thing, rarely appreciated. People say: 'Is it not wonderful that so-and-so keeps so young?' They say it idly, and, if they themselves are old, with some bitterness, because the idea that they are blameworthy stings them. It is a fine thing to see a man far on in years still refusing to admit the tempting thought that he has done his best, still pushing on, and making a continual *synthesis* with modern ideas and modern literature. For such a synthesis is a continual sacrifice, and a man begins to grow old the moment he shrinks from it.

Dr Nicoll, as we have said, had brought back with him the MSS. of two books, *In Mesopotamia* and *Dream Psychology*. *In Mesopotamia* was published by Hodder and Stoughton in April 1917, under the pseudonym of Martin Swayne. Much of the original MS was censored as Dr Nicoll had revealed the scandalous mismanagement of the campaign, giving evidence of the constant shortages in necessary supplies.

Lady Robertson Nicoll, who was a water colour artist, makes the following comment on it:

> This spring Maurice published a book, *In Mesopotamia*, illustrated by himself in water colours. I was particularly pleased about this for he had had no lessons but had shewn a gift for sketching when he was a boy, and when he was starting for the East I had said, 'Do take a paint box' – H. A. Harper said to me in Egypt, 'throw out of your box indigo and brown madder – put in your shadows in transparent greys. Look out for hot reflected light.' Maurice's sketches were most successful in their effects of shimmering heat.

In Mesopotamia was well reviewed and the water colour sketches received much praise. It was recognized that here was a truer picture of the war in the Near East than any given in despatches.

Dr Nicoll had a dioscurian facility for following two lines at once, and his next publication took a very different form. *The Blue Germ* was published in 1918 by Hodder and Stoughton, under his pseudonym of Martin Swayne. Among the numerous reviews of this book, which most critics were at a loss to know how to classify, it is, surprisingly enough, a review in the Parish Magazine of St Andrew's Presbyterian Church, Frognal, which reveals the clearest understanding of its true nature. The reviewer writes:

> The sensationalism of the book is no more than its pretext; its text is the inadequacy of physical life to satisfy or to explain humanity.

Thus Dr Nicoll gave in a new form the message that he had already plainly stated in *Dream Psychology* and which he was to reiterate in all his subsequent writings. He was continually seeking to make men think and to look for meaning beyond that which the senses offer. In this phantasy he describes the invention of a germ which kills all hostile germs in the human body, thereby conferring physical immortality on all those who can escape death by violence. The inventors, a Russian scientist and a Harley Street specialist, present an amusing contrast of the Russian with the English character, and the victims who appear on the scene with their blue nails and eyes, are treated with a humour reminiscent of the author's light-hearted gaiety in *Lord Richard in the Pantry*. Nevertheless the thoughts underlying this very original plot are profound. The results which the inventors had expected from their infecting of the Welsh reservoir supplying Birmingham with water are contrasted with the *unforeseen* results. The emptying of hospitals and the prolongation of life were natural and expected consequences but the epidemic of murder arising from the hatred of the old engendered in the hearts of the young when they awoke to the realization that their seniors would block their way for ever, was something that had not entered into the calculations of the inventors. Fear of physical violence assumed enormous proportions now that it became the only danger that remained. Moreover, a complete cessation of desire threatened to cause the machinery of life to run down and stop. Having lost desire, many thousands of men and animals fell asleep. It is characteristic of Dr Nicoll to remark at this point in his story that dogs remained awake longer than the other animals and longer even in some cases than their masters. He had a great respect for dogs and refers here to a sweetness in their nature that he found rare in men and women. Those men and women who remain awake are people in whom the desire of life plays a minor part, people characterized by a certain sweetness and strength. But they make no attempt to reorganize the world under these new conditions. And now comes the author's concluding surprise: on the seventh day the sleepers begin to wake up, and desire returns. The status quo is resumed.

It is noteworthy that in this year, 1918, before he had met the system of teaching which was to become his work for the last thirty-five years of his life, Dr Nicoll conceived the theme of this novel, illustrating the vulnerability of mankind whose meaning depends on the satisfaction of desires. Likewise in *Dream Psychology* he demonstrated that men who have lost meaning can only be restored to health by being connected with what is spiritual in their being.

It was during this period that Dr Nicoll, Dr James Young and Miss Maud Hoffman shared not only 146 Harley Street, but also a cottage at Chorley Wood in Buckinghamshire, where they foregathered with their friends at the week-ends. This cottage was found to be haunted. Dr Nicoll had sometimes talked about it to us, saying that Dr Jung had stayed there as a guest. More than thirty years later, in the spring of 1950, a letter arrived from Dr Jung to Dr Nicoll asking him whether he còuld recall what happened. I quote an extract from the letter:

> The purpose of this letter is really to ask you whether you still remember the noteworthy adventure we went through in your week-end place down in Bucks, during that summer I spent with you. You remember probably that you wrote me a letter in which you reported about your subsequent experiences with that spook house. Unfortunately that letter has vanished in the course of the years. I should like to ask you therefore whether you wouldn't be kind enough to tell me again about your experiences there after I had left. I remember that you spent about two or three nights down in the garden-room and that you pulled your bed out of it into the garden to have an undisturbed sleep. I have been asked recently about the story and I didn't feel too certain about your report. I should be very much obliged to you, therefore, if you could kindly refresh my memory.

Dr Nicoll's reply gives a good description of the events which took place at the cottage:

4th May 1950.

Dear Dr Jung,

When you were staying at Harley Street you came down to a farmhouse which Maud Hoffman, Jimmy Young and myself had taken in the valley of Aylesbury. In those days we had no motor-cars and I think we rode bicycles from Aylesbury Station. As you may remember, we had to walk through two or three fields to get to this long two-storey house with the awful twisted orchard trees. I think I am right in saying that we got this house very cheap because the agent could not let it owing to the fact that it had a bad atmosphere. I fancy it was here that either you or I saw the ceremony of the Bull surrounded by the cows at the full moon. Now, as regards your actual coming, I know you came in the days of Maud Hoffman, also in the days of my brother-in-law, Major Elystan Miles and my sister, etc. and we had very good talks out in the orchard. I remember how we were so fascinated by your talk among those twisted tortured trees. Also I remember that at least I or you put up statues in plasticine under the orchard trees and you said about the statues to me: 'You must be in love with someone,' and I was furious with you, because I was in love with someone who you told me was typically English. You said my statues indicated adoration. Then, as you will remember, we often had wet days down there and we painted the Garden Room in water colours and you told us all how to paint symbolically (I was always painting adoration!). Then I am not quite sure whether we told you about the legend of the house, but I hope we didn't. Anyway one morning you came down on a nice hot day in your skimpy costume and you sat down next me and said: 'Is there anything wrong with this house?' So I said: 'Well, there are things said about this place. That is why we got it cheap.' And you said, 'There is a woman with half a face in my room and she put it on my pillow and I felt horrible' and I understood you could not sleep afterwards very well. Anyway, the next morning, you said: 'Some old perspiration on the walls is not very pleasant.' I forget how it went afterwards but on one occasion when I simply loathed you for the time being I said: 'You go up to town, Dr Jung. I am going to rest here.' I was left there alone and slept in the upper room, not the one that you had inhabited. I was at the time trying to serve Hecate but I felt the presence round me of evil and I had to get up and walk downstairs in not exactly panic but I knew I had to go. And I went down to the Garden Room where there was always a camp bed and I dragged it out into the orchard and slept quite tranquilly. It was not anything said, but a pressure.

Now you will probably remember how we made enquiries round about of the local folk who of course would never say anything, but the fact remained that the place had been unlet for years and years. Also let me remind you, how you at that time had met a goldmaker. I think we were walking to see an enormous house called Waddesdon Manor belonging to a Rothschild and you were saying to me how you would like very much to own a place like that and then you said: 'How lucky you English are, because you have these aristo-crats and we in Switzerland don't know whether to wear yellow boots with top hats, etc.' You told me then a lot about the possibilities of psycho-material-transformation – i.e. if a man puts his psychic genius into a bit of wood, the wood stands up to him and in fact it is an example of psycho-transformism.

About what happened afterwards I really don't know except that after I married Catherine we used to go down there but we always slept with a double-barrelled gun loaded, and here I will remind you that I did not have a dog then, and I would have liked to know what a dog would have said about the situation.

M. N.

Mr Kenneth Walker, who was a week-end guest there, recalled recently that it was the custom after supper to go into the white-washed garden-room with a paint brush and paint one's own picture on the wall. He remembered the Mithraic Altar that Dr

Jung had painted, in tones of blue, with two figures, evidently the torch-bearers. Dr Nicoll had painted an allegorical journey, and Mr Kenneth Walker a centaur gazing across a valley.

Mrs Elystan Miles also stayed at the cottage with her husband. She recalls that Dr Jung did the cooking, ably frying a steak in olive oil. Of the mural, she remembers, 'Maurice's very tall green Tree of Life with its graceful branches and on the white wall opposite Dr Jung's painting of the Soul taking the Middle Way, a small figure of a man toiling along a narrow dangerous path, a high mountain one side, a precipice the other – full of dramatic colour.' Was this perhaps the allegorical journey that Mr Walker remembered?

5. Marriage, 1920

6. Catherine Nicoll, 1920

CHAPTER FIVE

Marriage — Meeting with Ouspensky and Gurdjieff
Training at the Château du Prieuré

It was in 1917 that Catherine Champion Jones came to stay with her uncle, Dr Leonard Williams, in Harley Street. She had been doing war-work in Aberdeen, having had previous training in massage. On the evening of her arrival her uncle apologized for having a guest. 'We are sorry', he said to her, 'not to be alone on the first night you are here when you must be tired, but we have this brilliant young doctor here.' The guest was Captain Maurice Nicoll, R.A.M.C., in khaki, who was just back from Mesopotamia. He had come in to write an article with her uncle. It was thus that Dr Nicoll met his future wife. They did not meet again for a year, and then he was once more dining at the house of Dr Leonard Williams where he met the two nieces, Catherine and her elder sister. Mrs Nicoll recalled this memorable dinner during which she had observed that Dr Nicoll said some rather extraordinary things and did not talk as the others did. Some time later, when she felt as though on the verge of a nervous breakdown she remembered what he had said and thought of him as the one person who might be able to help her. She conceived the idea of consulting him and set forth across the road and entered 146 Harley Street, where Dr Nicoll was at that time living and had his consulting-room. She told the receptionist, Mrs Rhee, that she wanted to speak to him, but was told that this was not possible without an appointment, as Dr Nicoll was seeing patients every quarter of an hour. Then, Mrs Nicoll said, when recalling the occasion: 'I tossed my head and went away.' The following morning her uncle's butler came up to her room and informed her that Dr Nicoll was waiting to see her in the morning-room. As she entered he said: 'If I had known it was you I would have seen you at once.' He then asked her to go over to his consulting-rooms. In their first conversation they discovered that they both had the same end in life. Mrs Nicoll remembered vividly that morning when, pacing angrily up and down, she told him that she wanted to find the peace which passeth all understanding. 'Why do they write about it if it is not there?' she said. 'I must find it.' These words epitomize her attitude to life which combined impatient questioning of what was lacking and the energy in seeking for it. From that day they began to dine together nearly every evening until the day came when he said to her: 'I remember. I have married you before.'

His sister Mildred writes:

> I remember the first time my brother brought his fiancée to Bay Tree Lodge to meet us. We were naturally very excited and we all fell in love with her the moment we saw her. She was very beautiful and very quiet, an air of great repose and self-command surrounded her. And she was very gentle. She wore, always, lovely clothes, and for this special evening she had chosen a black lace dinner dress threaded here and there with dark crimson velvet ribbon. The next great occasion was a big dinner party given by Dr Leonard Williams at his Harley Street house to celebrate the engagement. At the long, polished table I sat next to Kenneth Walker, who always remained a good friend. Dr Williams' elder niece, Léonor, was acting hostess for her uncle, and I remember thinking what a fine setting this eighteenth-century house was, with its Angelica Kauffmann ceiling in the drawing-room and its dignified rooms, for the two sisters and the white-haired, debonair uncle, who was a distinguished doctor.

They were married in January 1920 at the Marylebone Parish Church, and went to Switzerland for their honeymoon during which they stayed with Dr and Mrs Jung at Küsnacht. Mrs Jung referred to this in a letter written after Dr Nicoll's death. She wrote:

> I remember Dr Nicoll visiting us with his bride on their honeymoon trip. Both Dr Jung and myself were greatly pleased that he had such a charming wife.

After their return they lived first at 146 Harley Street, where Dr

Nicoll carried on his practice, and eventually took a house in Chester Terrace, which was very beautiful. From then onwards they continued to have a common aim and worked together in pursuit of it. Week-ends were sometimes spent at the cottage at Chorley Wood.

Mrs Nicoll's childhood had been very unusual. We delighted to hear her speak of it. She had been born in Mexico, where her father, Mr Robert Champion Jones, was a banker. A few years later he moved with his family to Lima and it was their home in Lima that she used to describe to us. There were three sisters, Léonor, Catherine and Betty, and one brother, Terence. They had a native nanny, and received many fearsome impressions from their surroundings. Beggars with festering sores and lepers made an early impression. Earthquakes were terrifying, but Mrs Nicoll recalled more often the wonderful garden with its tropical plants, brilliantly coloured birds and large butterflies. She had also happy memories of their Chinese cook who created splendid confections of ice-cream and spun sugar in the shape of swans and castles and various set-pieces for special dinner parties. All this made a great impression on the children. In 1899 the two elder girls had to make a long, rough voyage to England, rounding Cape Horn, in order to go to school in Bexhill. They did not like boarding-school life and felt little in common with the other girls, although Mrs Nicoll proved to be an excellent hockey-player. They had had many strange experiences which their companions could not share. Indeed, it is likely that what for them had been of daily occurrence in their Peruvian home would seem exaggerated romancing to the others who had had a conventional English upbringing. They in their turn knew little of the English background. The holidays were spent for the most part with their grandparents. Mr Champion Jones died early in 1910 and Dr Leonard Williams became their guardian.

During the first eighteen months of his marriage Dr Nicoll remained in very close touch with Dr Jung. He and Dr James Young took part in a Summer School at Sennen Cove, Cornwall, where Dr Jung was lecturing. Mrs Jung came over with him. In April 1921 he wrote in his diary the following comparison of Jung with Socrates:

People feel about Jung much what they feel about Socrates
– some think him a violent atheist, others an enlightened
deist, some a sceptic, some a mystic. But we must say, as
Maier says of Socrates (Maier, *Socrates*, 1913, p. 3), 'The
man whose influence was so widespread and so profound
cannot have been like that.'

A principle set up by a master can be applied in different
ways by those who come after, and so gives rise to contradictions. These contradictions arise out of the principle in
application, not in the principle itself.

Socrates was an analyst. He influenced people profoundly
by the peculiar way he spoke to them about themselves.
Biographers dispute why Socrates had such an effect on his
age and the future – they still resolve the problem by all
sorts of contradictory solutions. Socrates remains enigmatical
because of his relationship to the unconscious.

In July 1921 Dr Nicoll recorded in his diary:

Thinking of making a book of Freud's theory versus Jung
in detail.

On 9th August the following entry was made:

Prayer to Hermes.
Teach me – instruct me – shew me the Path, so that I may
know certainly – help my great ignorance, illumine my
darkness? I have asked a question.

Within two months this question was answered and Dr Nicoll
was shewn the way which he was to follow for the rest of his life.

A daughter, Jane, was born to Dr and Mrs Nicoll in October
1921, to whom Dr Jung became godfather and Dame Katherine
Furze godmother. Before Mrs Nicoll had fully recovered her
health an event occurred which was to turn their lives into a
direction from which they never afterwards swerved. Miss Hoffman told Dr Nicoll that she had heard that the Russian philosopher and mathematician, P. D. Ouspensky, had come to
London and would be lecturing to the Quest Society. Dr Nicoll
went to hear him and on his return home rushed in to see his wife,
and, literally shaking the bed on which she was lying, he said:

'You must come and hear Ouspensky. He is the only man who has ever answered my questions.' The nurse was heard to remark: 'I don't know what was the matter with the doctor tonight. He never even asked to see the baby.' But Mrs Nicoll told us that he had appeared transformed, as though irradiated by an inner light. She rose from her bed the following day and went with him to the next lecture, and shared his feelings. Lectures were then continued in a house offered for the purpose in Warwick Gardens, where Ouspensky talked to many of the intellectuals of the day. Often he would dine at Chester Terrace with Dr and Mrs Nicoll, and they would talk on for hours by candlelight, sometimes with Orage, the brilliant editor of *The New Age*, or with Clifford Sharp.

This new link caused Dr Nicoll to break his official connection with Dr Jung who had hoped at one time that he would act as the chief exponent of his psychology in London. Nevertheless his inner relationship to him continued to the end. He incorporated many of Dr Jung's ideas into his own later teaching and was always aware of his debt to him.

Ouspensky, one day in February 1922, some months after his arrival, made an important announcement to his group. George Ivanovitch Gurdjieff was expected in London. This name must be familiar to all readers of this book. It is enough to say now that he was the Russian whose system Ouspensky had been teaching in London for the past four months.

Ouspensky's connection with him is outlined in his book, *In Search of the Miraculous*. On his return from India in 1914 after his search for the truth, Ouspensky had attended Gurdjieff's group in Moscow. He became aware that the teaching that he heard then was the truth that he was seeking. When Gurdjieff moved to St Petersburg, Ouspensky followed and attended his meetings there. Eventually, after the October Revolution, he joined him in the Caucasus where later many members of the early groups in Moscow and St Petersburg also assembled, and a house was taken at Essentuki and organized group work began in March 1918. There came a point when Ouspensky separated from Gurdjieff and completed the writing of his book, *A New Model of the Universe*, but later he worked with him again in Constantinople. When Gurdjieff left for Germany Ouspensky came to London. This was in August 1921. By the time that Ouspensky had collected a group of people, Gurdjieff came to London. This was in February 1922.

Dr Nicoll described to us the first appearance of Gurdjieff in London at a meeting where, with Ouspensky beside him to interpret, the group sat petrified in silence, awed by Gurdjieff's presence. One of the company timidly ventured: 'Mr Gurdjieff, what would it be like to be conscious in Essence?' 'Everything more vivid,' was the brief unforgettable answer. As there were no further questions Gurdjieff left.

The idea of opening an Institute in England was now put forward and many of those who attended Ouspensky's meetings subscribed for this purpose. The Institute was opened but was not continued for more than a short time, and the group eventually collected a sum of money with which the Château du Prieuré in Avon near Fontainebleau was bought, where the Institute was opened in the autumn of 1922. It was called 'The Institute for the Harmonious Development of Man'. It was started with about sixty-six students, some English and American, the rest Russians from Gurdjieff's former Groups. Many of the English had given up their work, their source of income, or sold capital, in order to pay the expense of residence there. There was a rule that people should pay what they could afford, and those who could pay compensated for those who could not, among whom were many Russians whom Gurdjieff sheltered with the utmost generosity. Orage had given up the editorship of *The New Age* which had made his reputation as the foremost English literary critic of the day. Dr James Young, who had already given up his career as a surgeon to practise as a Jungian psychologist, now left his patients in order to go to the Institute.

Among those who sacrificed a career in order to go to the Institute was Dr Nicoll himself who gave up his lucrative Harley Street practice as a consultant, and also borrowed a sum of money from his expectations under his father's will, in order to contribute generously to the expenses of the Institute. This he did with the full consent of his wife. When Mrs Nicoll spoke to us sometimes of their departure from London and the financial sacrifice that it entailed, apart from the risk in taking a delicate baby abroad, deprived of the safety of the English nursery, she never implied that they could ever have acted otherwise and she never regretted it. The courage with which they both surrendered material security in exchange for the possibility of spiritual values was shewn repeatedly in similar situations in the years that followed, but this was the moment of the greatest sacrifice which they never even called a sacrifice. Thus it came about that on 4th November 1922 Dr and Mrs Nicoll with their young baby and a nurse went to Fontainebleau, Mrs Nicoll's sister, Miss Champion Jones, having gone on ahead. There was some difficulty in securing goats to take with them for the milk which had been ordered for Jane at that time. In Paris the only source of supply had been the Zoo. They took with them a great deal of luggage being convinced that they wanted to spend the rest of their lives at the Institute.

The Château du Prieuré was a very gracious building, which had once been a hunting lodge belonging to Madame de Maintenon. There was a tradition that it was built on the site of a Carmelite monastery. It had been the property of Dreyfus, who had given it to his avocat, Maître Labori, in payment for his defence at his trial.

I visited it a year or two ago on a still winter's day. As soon as I entered the courtyard I became aware why Dr Nicoll had been able to make a spontaneous decision some years later to buy Great Amwell House, which must have reminded him of the Prieuré. At the same time I felt that his decision to make a pool in front of our house at Tyeponds arose from his memory of the pool in the courtyard of the Prieuré. I had feared to find the house occupied by people who were not in harmony with its tradition, but I was pleasantly surprised to find that it had become a Convalescent Home, controlled by the French Government, and that there was an atmosphere of peace, and nothing was visible that could detract from the grace of the house. It was possible to see the lovely vista from the terrace, to walk over the lawns with their fountains (no longer playing) and along the alley of lime trees, and to ascend the little knoll with its view of the château on one side and the meadows on the other. I understand that its grounds covered forty acres, all set in the Forest of Fontainebleau.

On the gate a plaque has been put up in memory of Katherine Mansfield who died there.

Miss Hoffman, who was at the Institute at the same time as Dr and Mrs Nicoll, gave some of her impressions of the community life there in an article published in the *New York Times* of 10th February 1924, of which I quote the following extracts:

> You may or may not know about the philosophy which lies at the back of all the activities of this unique community. The American papers have called them the 'Forest Philosophers' and you listen carefully to catch any of the teaching. But the nearest that you get to philosophy for many days is to make the acquaintance of a good-natured, but not well-pointed fox terrier, with a large body and a small head, named 'Philos'. You venture to ask if there are any lectures or classes. Quietly you are told, without further comment, that there are none.
>
> Later you are told that everything that is done in this place of work has a meaning. You work hard – not for the sake of the task itself – but for the purpose of making efforts, and for the purpose of self-observation. You soon begin to suspect that this place may be an outer court of one of those old Mystery Schools about which you have read, over the portals of which were always the words: KNOW THYSELF.
>
> The Gurdjieff system aims at an all-round and harmonious development of Man. It is a place where every one can be an artist, or an artisan, and his own mental, emotional and instinctive energies are the materials with which he works. As most of the energy in modern life flows into mental activity, much physical activity is needed, and many acute emotional conflicts are required to divert this energy into instinctive and emotional channels.
>
> The claim made by the Gurdjieff Institute is that, by the reactionary effect of harmonious movements on the psyche, Man may hope to progress to that balanced development which has been arrested by the cramping of an unnatural and mechanical civilisation. But the work that leads to a balanced development of being is not confined to gymnastics and

dancing. Every kind of manual labour, within doors and out-of-doors, is performed by the students, both men and women doing all kinds of work. Combined with the physical work are difficult mental exercises; and the emotions are kept active by the natural reactions in each person to an environment and conditions that are in many ways the reversal of most of their fixed ideas and habits.

The Key words of the Gurdjieff Institute are WORK and EFFORT. Nothing is made easy in this place. Always the task is a little beyond your strength – you must make an effort; the time is curtailed – hasten – make effort; you have reached the limit of your strength and are exhausted – then is the moment to make effort – and tap the higher energies and the source of Will. Those who are intellectually powerful and emotionally weak cannot be considered successful. Their structures are top-heavy. Exquisite emotions alone, or physical strength alone cannot give knowledge or perfect being. At the Gurdjieff Institute an attempt can be made to fill in deficiencies, correct heredity and habit and to balance knowledge and being. Incidentally and as a by-product of these efforts, you renew your energies and your youth and make yourself more efficient for life.

Miss Hoffman points out that at the Institute irregularity is a principle. On arrival at the gate, therefore, if you have obeyed the instruction over the bell: 'Sonnez fort', the ring may be answered by a gate-keeper or not. The writer explains:

In the meaning attached to this irregularity, which arises at the very entrance to the Gurdjieff Institute, lies a crucial principle of the enterprise. It is a place where habits are changed, fixed ideas are broken up, mechanical routines do not exist, and adaptability to ever-changing forms and modes of life is practised. So 'Sonnez fort' and wait. Some one passing within may open for you. It is really the kitchen-boy's duty. There is a different kitchen-boy each day and it is the most onerous job in the place. Presently he will appear with a large apron tied round him – possibly not a clean apron. He may be anybody, the editor of a London paper, a Harley

Street specialist, a court musician or a Russian lawyer.
England, America, Russia, France, Poland, Georgia, Armenia
and several other nations are represented here.

Someone takes you up to the 'Ritz' corridor, so named
because of its beautiful furnishings, or to the beautiful 'Monks'
corridor above, so named for the cloister-like appearance. In
the 'Ritz' the rooms are luxurious, while in the 'Monks'
corridor they are comfortable and quaint. All pay according
to means. Those who are rich must pay very well indeed
for there are many among the pupils who cannot pay at
all.

Round about midday there is a meal. At noon, if you have
risen at six, at one if you have risen at seven and at eleven-
thirty if you have risen at five. You have probably arrived in
time for this meal. If your room is in the 'Monks' corridor
you take a hasty glance round at the red brick floor, the old
French chintzes on the walls and furniture and the heavenly
forest garden without, before you hurry down to the dining-
room. This is a beautifully proportioned room with red
hangings and fine old paintings. Three windows overlook
the grounds and a door leads to the terrace. If the day is
warm you have your bread and soup on the terrace, or in the
dining-room, or you can take it to your room, or to the
garden, or to the pantry – where or how you like. The food
is nourishing and sufficient, but useless conventions of service
and elaboration of dishes, food and courses are absent. You
receive your food from the hands of the cook in the kitchen,
and after you have eaten it, you wash your plate and cup, and
there is an end of it. In the matter of food there is the opportunity to 'change habit'.

When you enter, Mr Gurdjieff greets you and makes you
welcome with a smile that has both sweetness and spiritual
quality. You get a first impression of a nature of great kindness and sensitiveness. Later you learn that in him is combined
strength and delicacy, simplicity and subtlety, that he is more
awake than anyone you have ever known.

Your first evening is a never-to-be-forgotten experience.
Here from nine o'clock to twelve, to one, perhaps to two

o'clock, the work goes on. When the obligatory exercises begin you receive a shock. You find yourself sitting up, leaning forward and receiving impacts from that moving mass of energy on the stage. The obligatory exercises contain every movement which is later worked up and used in the various special groups and dances. After the first hour of exercises – when the blood is tingling in every accustomed and unaccustomed cell of their bodies – the pupils rest on goat skins and this is the moment chosen for the most difficult kind of mental concentration.

Katherine Mansfield had already been at the Institute for a fortnight when Dr and Mrs Nicoll arrived. In response to her request to be allowed to stay there at this time when she was suffering from tuberculosis in its advanced stages she was told that she could come for a preliminary fortnight. She had heard of the teaching from Orage who was her friend, and was convinced that Gurdjieff was the one person who could help her. It was not only a physical cure that she sought, but spiritual regeneration. During this fortnight in October, when the Institute was not yet officially opened, she wrote frequently to her husband in England, John Middleton Murry, describing all that was being prepared for the work that was to be undertaken. It is interesting that we have her record of all that was going on before the greater number of the English residents arrived. She wrote of her charming room, of the delicious and nourishing food,* of the halcyon days when she was able to walk in the park in the clear sparkling October weather. She made light of the scarcity of hot water, even of cold water, and often referred to the discovery that such deprivations, which would have been hardships in England, fell into place in these new surroundings and were not important. It was the newness of the way of life at the Institute which enraptured her. She very quickly began to understand something of what this way of life was to lead to. She found herself sharing in activities that she would never have dreamed of touching in her ordinary life, and she understood that one of the reasons why so many forms of domestic and outdoor work were organized

* The diet became more sparse when the Institute was officially opened.

was to give the group opportunities of developing new faculties in themselves. I quote extracts from some of her letters:

18th October 1922.

It's a most wonderful old place in an amazingly lovely park. About forty people, chiefly Russians, are here working, at every possible kind of thing – I mean outdoor work, looking after animals, gardening, indoor work, music, dancing – it seems a bit of everything. Here the philosophy of the 'System' takes second place – practice is first – you simply *have* to wake up instead of talking about it, in fact, you *have* to learn to do all the things you say you want to do.

27th October 1922.

I spend all the sunny time in the garden. Visit the carpenters, the trench diggers. (We are digging for a Turkish Bath – not to discover one, but to lay the pipes.) The soil is very nice here, like sand, with small, whitey pink pebbles in it. Then there are the sheep to inspect, and the new pigs that have long golden hair – very mystical pigs. A mass of cosmic rabbits and hens – and goats are on the way, likewise horses and mules to ride and drive.

27th October 1922.

The Institute is not really started yet for another fortnight. – A dancing hall is being built and the house is still being organized. But it has started really – if all this were to end in smoke tomorrow I should have had the very great wonderful adventure of my life – I've learnt more in a week than in years là-bas. As to habits. My wretched sense of order, for instance, which rode me like a witch – it did not take long to cure that. Mr Gurdjieff likes me to go into the kitchen in the late afternoon and 'watch'. I have a chair in a corner. It's a large kitchen with six helpers – Mme Ostrovsky, the head, walks about like a queen exactly – she is extremely beautiful. She wears an old raincoat, Nina, a big girl in a black apron – lovely too – pounds things in mortars. The second cook chops at the table, bangs the saucepans, sings, another runs in and out with plates and pots, a man in the scullery cleans pots – the dog barks and lies on the floor, worrying a hearth-brush. A little girl comes in with a bouquet of leaves for Olga Ivanovna – Mr Gurdjieff strides in, takes up a handful of shredded cabbage and eats it . . . there are at least twenty pots on the stove – and it's so full of life and humour and ease that one wouldn't be anywhere else.

2nd November 1922.

Last night, for instance, in the salon, we learnt to make rugs from long pieces of corn. Very nice ones. Very easy to make, too. I have been in the carpenter's shop all this morning. The small forge is alight; Mr Gurdjieff is planing, a M. Salzmann is making wheels – later on I shall learn carpentry – We are going to learn as many trades as possible, also all kinds of farm work. The cows are being bought today – Gurdjieff is going to build a high couch in the stable where I can sit and inhale their breath! I know later on I shall be put in charge of those cows – Everyone calls them already 'Mrs Murry's cows'.

Katherine Mansfield's Letters to J. Middleton Murry, 1913-1922. Edited by J. Middleton Murry (Constable 1951)*

Such was the Institute as seen through Katherine Mansfield's eyes during those two weeks. Goat's milk was prescribed for her and goats were accordingly bought and placed in the cow-stable, where she was entertained by their gambols. The chaise-longue was duly constructed and installed on Gurdjieff's instructions. It might be expedient here to emphasize that the stable never became her only dwelling-place as some writers have stated in error. She repeatedly refers to her own room in her letters. After the first fortnight, when the Institute was opened, she moved to a smaller room, but her periods of rest in the stable were very much appreciated by her. From her first arrival at the Prieuré she received from Gurdjieff the utmost kindness and consideration. He did everything for her that could be done, and her letters express a radiant joy that continued until her death early in January.

Dr and Mrs Nicoll with Jane and her nurse were eventually

* By permission of the Society of Authors as the literary representative of the Estate of the late Miss Katherine Mansfield.

allotted rooms in Paradou, a house in the grounds where families could stay. Here the children were looked after by the various mothers and nurses who took it in turns to take the elder children for walks. Mrs Nicoll used to say that it was no joke to take out a number of small children of different nationalities for country rambles, the Russians, who were numerous, knowing no English. Jane was taken out by her own nurse, Nanny Nellie, who adapted to the strange way of life there and tended her charge most efficiently with loving care, seeing that she had suitable food and regular hours. Families were able to be together, but other men and women had separate meals and only met together during certain group activities and at the evening sessions.

The first job given to Dr Nicoll was, he told us, that of kitchen-boy which involved the washing up of hundreds of greasy plates with no soap and often no hot water. In spite of what Miss Hoffman said later about the daily change in this office, when Dr Nicoll first arrived he found that he continued washing plates for about three months. Mrs Nicoll was put on to help with the cooking, and her impression was chiefly of the giant iron cauldrons of soup that had to be continually lifted on and off the stove. Miss Champion Jones cleaned the bathrooms daily on the Ritz floor. That she could do this is to be wondered at, as she was very fragile and delicate. The diet at this time was very meagre in spite of the hard physical work that was done by nearly everyone.

They were given a Russian teacher, Olga, from whom to learn the Movements. There were no lectures. They met Gurdjieff at supper on the first evening, and afterwards were able to talk to him occasionally through an interpreter, but he was often in Paris. Many of the English people found that weeks passed before they had a chance of speaking to him although he directed most of the activities. Dr and Mrs Nicoll recalled sometimes in conversation with us the routine of those months – early rising, particularly for Dr Nicoll who had boilers to light, very little solid food, physical work all day long, and then the Movements at nine p.m. with talks by Gurdjieff afterwards, so that very few hours remained for sleep. Dr Nicoll was forbidden to read during his stay at the Institute.

Ouspensky himself visited the Institute in November and remarked on the 'interesting and animated work that was proceeding there'. He wrote:

> A pavilion had been built for dances and exercises, housekeeping had been organized, the house had been finished off, and so on. And the atmosphere on the whole was very right and left a strong impression. . . . They carried on very intensive mental exercises for the development of the memory, of attention, and of the imagination. . . . Then there was a lot of obligatory work for everyone in the house and connected with the housekeeping which required great strenuousness, thanks to the speed of working and various other conditions. (*In Search of the Miraculous* by P. D. Ouspensky: Routledge and Kegan Paul.)

When the group arrived the first task was to construct a Turkish Bath in the form of a grotto on a hillside in the grounds. Like all such undertakings at the Institute, this was devised by Gurdjieff with the utmost ingenuity and completed with a speed that to ordinary standards would seem fantastic. It provided seven kinds of baths, also a rest-room hung with Eastern carpets. This constructive work was in addition to the household duties and the care of the animals which were shared by all. Katherine Mansfield became fond of her cows of which she was for a time given charge. The group soon learned that it was necessary to be able to do everything. For instance, one had to be able to kill a pig without being sentimental about it, and to clean pigsties without objecting to the work. Dr Nicoll used to explain to us the difference between objecting and disliking. He said that they learned to do tasks that they disliked without objecting to them, thus they no longer lost force through the interference of the emotions with what they were doing. In the day-time most of the men looked like brigands in their odd rough clothes, but everyone had to change for dinner into clothes suitable for the Movements for which they later assembled in the Pavilion. Many of the women wore velvet dresses. Dr Nicoll used to describe his efforts and those of the other beginners with humour. He always seemed to be singled out as the scapegoat when anything went wrong. Gurdjieff was constantly calling out: 'Nicole!' and then would make a gesture of despair. Mrs Nicoll often arrived late and was then forced to hold her arms out horizontally for ten minutes, the penalty for lateness. (She was deliberately late, she told us, because it was the only time when it was possible for her to have a bath after being among the pots and pans.) The most supreme efforts in attention were demanded in order to follow the commands given which involved making the most unaccustomed and difficult movements which could not easily be memorized. At the end of the session the group would sit down on their goat skins and there would be exercises in mental arithmetic. Then Gurdjieff would give a talk interpreted by Mr Pinder, an English engineer who had lived a long time in Russia. Dr Nicoll told us that he used to sit beside Mr Pinder who would often have a whispered conversation with him when the Russian proved unfit for English ears. Listening to a talk through an interpreter used to be very tantalizing, Dr Nicoll told us, because whereas Gurdjieff would pour out a torrent of words which lasted for several minutes, Mr Pinder would give a laconic interpretation, just a sentence or two, whereupon Gurdjieff would look at him and shrug his shoulders, smiling sardonically. Thus, in every one of its aspects the system was made as difficult as possible to learn and practise. The talk would go on until the small hours. Those who had to rise early had not many hours to give to sleep but it was taught that during a night's sleep it was only the deep sleep that was really valuable, and after two or three hours of deep sleep one would awake refreshed. The extra effort which they had made physically, emotionally and mentally would make it possible to fall asleep straightaway, whereas normally the first few hours of sleep are valueless. This I proved to be true from my own personal experience when I first went down to Essex where Dr Nicoll had his Institute years later. Would that everyone could know it too and be released from nocturnal worries when sleep is short.

The next group effort was to build a theatre. This had to be completed in a fortnight. Dr Nicoll often spoke of this and later put into practice much that he had learnt from Gurdjieff on the art of building. Katherine Mansfield found herself making costumes, having hitherto in her life avoided sewing as far as possible. These buildings that were erected so rapidly were not intended to

7. P. D. Ouspensky at Alley Cottage

8. Carpenter's shop, Prieuré

last. Dr Nicoll quotes in his *Commentaries* (vol. 1, page 14) Gurdjieff's answer to his question 'Why don't you build more solidly?'
'This is only temporary – in a very short time everything will be
different – everyone will be elsewhere. Nothing can be built
permanently at this moment.' And Gurdjieff added privately to
Dr Nicoll that he thought the Work would have no permanent
home.

Gurdjieff himself was apparently able to do everything and to
excel in everything that he did. Moreover his speed was like
lightning. I discovered later that the same could be said of Dr and
Mrs Nicoll. Speed in working was said to be a sign of inner
harmony, when all functions work rightly without interference.
Gurdjieff would walk around the grounds of the Prieuré commenting on the work that was being done in different places and
say: 'Must be done in half the time.' Sometimes a piano would be
trundled through the park, and it would be set down beside each
group of workers in turn who would then be expected to do one
of the Obligatory Movements, while M. de Hartmann played.
Gurdjieff was aware of everything that was going on and knew
everyone's state. Mrs Nicoll told us once how she had spent a
whole long day scrubbing the floor of the theatre and he met her
in the evening when she was feeling very sorry for herself and
said: 'You had nice day in Paris, yes?' with a gleam in his eyes.
She burst out emphatically: '*No*, I've been scrubbing the floor all
day,' but afterwards she wished she had not given way to her
indignation at having been apparently misjudged, for she realized
that Gurdjieff knew very well how she had been occupied, and
was only trying to test her with his remark. Most of his personal
observations were tests, but again and again those at whom they
were aimed failed to remember that this was his method of
teaching, and repeatedly they would fall into the traps laid for
them. Gurdjieff would say: 'I cannot change your being, but I can
create conditions, thanks to which you can change yourselves.'
He attacked ruthlessly what was called in the System the false
personality wherever he found a manifestation of it. The group
were placed in circumstances where they would feel a loss of face,
in order to force them back to rely on what was real in themselves,
for it was only what was artificial, acquired, that could cause them

suffering when it was attacked. If people were too fixed in their vanity he would discourage them from staying, saying that it would cost him too much blood to work on them. Members of the group were not taken at their own life-valuation. Dr Nicoll, for instance, was no longer a Harley Street Consultant – in the eyes of Gurdjieff not even a doctor. He recalled various occasions on which Gurdjieff would come in asking for a doctor in an emergency, and he would ignore all offers from Dr Nicoll and Dr James Young, accepting instead assistance from an unqualified Russian. This, of course, was deliberate, but each time it was possible to forget that it was a well laid trap and to fall headlong into it. Stupidity also was mercilessly exposed and attacked. Dr Nicoll told us of a man at the Institute who, on finding that the pigs had got into the tomatoes, 'walked very slowly, to avoid identifying and muscle tension, and told Gurdjieff'. His comment was, 'I fear that Gurdjieff roared at him and leapt, so to speak, about a hundred yards to those pigs'. He defined stupidity from one point of view as 'lack of seeing relative importance'.

Winter came early. Katherine Mansfield in her letters refers to the fact that she was now living in her fur coat and had bought some fur boots, and yet suffered less this winter than any other because it was possible to take external conditions differently. The heating of the Château was quite inadequate. There were stoves in the passages here and there but often they did not burn very well. Some of the rooms had fire-places and the residents could get wood from the grounds. But there was no question of ever being warm and comfortable even in bed, for the beds were hard and the coverings sparse. Christmas was approaching and although the Russian Feast was not to be celebrated until later Gurdjieff gave permission to the English to make all the necessary preparations for a traditional Christmas Dinner. The Russians were invited to this and eventually sixty-odd sat down to the Feast, Mrs Nicoll at Gurdjieff's right hand. Dr Nicoll recalled the contrast which this festival, with its abundance of wine and food, presented to the ordinary routine fare of semi-starvation. The whole atmosphere was transformed. Gurdjieff allowed a pig, a sheep, two turkeys, and a goose to be killed. Those who had not killed before in their lives were given the task of killing, and others who could not endure the sight of blood were to watch, as in order to be trained in the balancing of one's functions it was expedient to have all experiences. The plum pudding contained a silver coin entitling the lucky receiver to a prize – a new-born calf. There was a big Christmas Tree to decorate. All the English took part in their Christmas event. Gurdjieff certainly knew all that there was to know about the art of celebrating festivals. Something memorable was thus created in the life of the group which had henceforward a permanent place in all recollections of it.

The theatre, called afterwards 'La Maison d'Etudes', was scheduled to be completed and opened by 13th January, Gurdjieff's birthday. During the last week or so extra effort had to be made and the men were ordered to go out at two a.m. after the evening session instead of going to bed and to work for two or three hours by the light of electric lamps. The women had made costumes – Gurdjieff had skilfully cut the material. Visitors to this building later speak of it as a 'hangar' or even, rather oddly, as an 'aerodrome'. This was because the basis of its structure was the framework of an old hangar which was erected on an extensive surface which had been carefully levelled, and prepared with much labour. The walls were decorated with lath-work, inside and out (a method which Dr Nicoll afterwards used in his own building in Essex) and plastered with a kind of mud and straw. When the building had been dried, the walls were painted and then hung with Persian carpets of which Gurdjieff always seemed to have an abundant supply. Visitors often remarked on the value and beauty of these carpets. But then Gurdjieff really knew about Persian carpets.

Meanwhile, on New Year's Eve, Katherine Mansfield, having become aware that her time was short, wrote to give her husband Gurdjieff's invitation to spend a few days at the Prieuré and to be present at the opening of the theatre. Middleton Murry started on his journey at once on receiving her letter. He arrived and found her pale but radiant. She took him to see the theatre to which the finishing touches were being added, and introduced him to her friends – M. de Hartmann, M. Salzmann, Dr Young, Olga Ivanovna, and others. He already knew Orage whom he found much changed, gentler and softer. Katherine took him to her cowshed where a special gallery had been erected for her with a balustrade. There were two divans here spread with Persian carpets. M. Salzmann had painted designs on the walls and ceiling. The outside had been painted with the Signs of the Zodiac. Middleton Murry remarked on the simplicity and the serious demeanour of those whom he met. The same evening his wife died from a haemorrhage after climbing the staircase to her room in the Prieuré. Mrs Nicoll was with her at the end. She and Dr Nicoll had become her friends after being in close touch with her since their arrival two months previously.

On 12th January, the day before the Birthday Feast, Gurdjieff with the Russians, and Middleton Murry with the English, were present at her simple funeral in the communal cemetery.

Gurdjieff now asked Dr Nicoll to work with him in the carpenter's shed in the mornings. Gurdjieff was a superb carpenter. His father had trained him as a small boy during the period when he had fallen back on carpentry as a means of livelihood after he had lost his wealth. Dr Nicoll also when we knew him had considerable skill with any tool. This apparently he had always had, for his family told us of his early dexterity in setting up electrical experiments. He looked back with much pleasure to the hours spent with Gurdjieff who had taught him to handle wood, as well as men! Gurdjieff had a certain knowledge of English in spite of his insistence on teaching through an interpreter. His broken English conveyed many truths to him. In the middle of the morning Gurdjieff would say: 'We old men, Nicole, we have coffee,' and would call for Big Nina, to bring coffee to the carpenter's shed. (Dr Nicoll at that time was nearly thirty-nine!) One of the trials connected with this period was that Dr Nicoll would frequently find that pieces of wood which had been sawn to the correct length and prepared for some constructive work had disappeared, and it would eventually be discovered that one of the Russians had taken them for firewood. It was no use expostulating. The Russian would simulate innocence and would say he did not understand English. There was no redress.

Gurdjieff bought a car which seemed to give him great pleasure. He taught himself to drive it by experiment, with much grinding of gears and squeaking of brakes. To drive with him was terrifying.

Dr Nicoll told us of one adventure. He and one or two others received a message one evening that Gurdjieff wished to sleep at a high altitude that night, and proposed to drive to Switzerland. So off they went at break-neck speed. I think it was on that occasion that they got out of the car and ate roast goat by the wayside, and Dr Nicoll was reproved for letting his attention be diverted from the feast by the sight of a beautiful view. They arrived at their destination and had only been in their rooms about three hours when by order of Gurdjieff they were all awakened and told to be ready to return. Gurdjieff had had the good night's sleep that he sought at a certain altitude. They returned at the same incredible speed as on the outgoing journey and by some miracle reached the Prieuré in safety.

During April Dr Nicoll had received disquieting news of his father's health which had been failing for several months. At the beginning of May he was called to his bedside and arrived in time to be with him at the end and to be recognized by him. He was always very thankful for this. He knew that his precipitate action in throwing up his promising career, towards the furtherance of which Sir William had contributed with the utmost generosity, must have been a great shock to him, and the culmination of many disappointments. He had been aware that he had wounded his father deeply and yet had seen no way of making him understand that he had made the only possible decision.

Sir William Robertson Nicoll died on 4th May 1923. His biographer records that among his last words were these: 'I believe everything that I have written about immortality.' (*Life and Writings of William Robertson Nicoll* by T. H. Darlow: Hodder and Stoughton.) He had continued his work on his sickbed almost to the last in spite of very great weakness, and thirty years later Dr Nicoll shewed the same indefatigable devotion to his work during his last illness, and continued to write until a fortnight before his death. Mrs Nicoll came over for Sir William's funeral but returned to the Prieuré soon afterwards as she had left Jane there with her nurse. Dr Nicoll stayed in London for three months as there was much for him to do in connection with the settlement of his father's affairs.

During the summer of 1923 demonstrations of the Movements

were given on Saturday evenings for the public. The residents and visitors in Fontainebleau and Avon attended these presentations in great numbers. I quote Miss Hoffman's description from her article in the *New York Times* referred to above:

> The demonstrations are given in a large aerodrome [*sic*] erected by the pupils, which comfortably accommodates more than sixty pupils and several hundred visitors. The stage is large enough for forty people to take part in the exercises at the same time, and a large space, covered with Persian carpets, remains free in the centre.
>
> The pupils sit around this square space on goatskins and cushions in the Oriental fashion. The interior of this study-house (Maison d'Etudes) has been decorated with colour, drawing, stencilling and designs. The whole of the extensive canvas ceiling – and every buttress, beam and space – is covered. The colours are rich and vivid, as are the windows. All the work of painting and designing has been done by the pupils themselves.
>
> The demonstrations are unique in their presentation. They consist of movements which include the sacred gymnastics of the esoteric schools, the religious ceremonies of the antique Orient and the ritual movements of monks and dervishes – besides the folk-dances of many a remote community.
>
> The movements are not only bewildering in their complexity, and amazing in the precision of their execution, but rich in diversity, harmonious in rhythm, and exceedingly beautiful in the gracefulness of the postures, which are quite unknown to Europe. To the accompaniment of mystical and inspiring music, handed down from remote antiquity, the sacred dances are executed with deeply religious dignity, which is profoundly impressive.

These demonstrations were evidently rehearsals for the public performances which were to be given in New York by specially trained pupils who accompanied Gurdjieff to America the following winter, when he had closed the Institute.

Dr Nicoll returned to the Institute in August 1923. He wrote in his private diary that Gurdjieff said to him:

When you return to Institute two men – one happy to meet friends, old associates, etc. The other does not begin to be felt until you arrive. Suddenly you begin to fear. He thinks of all the difficulties to be faced. He thinks seriously. (So it happened with me.)

Soon after his return Dr James Young left. He had been at the Prieuré since October 1922. His reasons for leaving have now been published, so it is unnecessary to refer to them here. He had worked with Dr Nicoll in close association at 146 Harley Street for many years. I quote the entry in Dr Nicoll's diary:

> Jimmy has left. G. gave lecture on importance of remembering that we came here with a definite object – that we found life unsatisfactory and wished for another form of life. This place gave opportunity of finding another way of life but living here we soon forgot why we came and identified with everything.

Dr Nicoll recorded about himself that by returning to London and coming back to the Institute he gained in resolution. He made an aim 'never to forget that G. is circular – not to take one point in that circle and criticize it'. Through remembering this aim he was able to endure the discipline until it came to an end three months later when the Institute was closed. He looked on the difficulties as the price asked for self-knowledge. However, at one point he was led to remark that he wondered 'whether the difficulties Gurdjieff knows he creates are equal in value for work with those he does not know he creates'. The Institute was described by Gurdjieff as 'a hatching place for eggs. It supplies the heat. Chicken inside must try to break shell then help and individual teaching is possible. Until then only collective method.' This image was used throughout the years when Dr Nicoll taught us.

I quote a conversation which took place at that time between him and B.M., one of Ouspensky's group.

> I first met Dr Nicoll in the summer of 1923 at The Priory. For several days I had noticed him during the recreation hour after lunch. Most of the people sat about in the sun, or strolled and chatted, but he kept apart steadily pacing up and

down very intent, very solitary. I myself was feeling rather bewildered by the experience of life at the Priory. At last I plucked up my courage and went up to him. 'Dr Nicoll', I said, 'can I speak to you? Could you help me to understand what we are doing here?' He stared at me, almost glared at me.

'How can I help you?' he said. 'Don't you know I need to help myself? We have to help ourselves.'

About to walk on he stopped. Seeing he had rebuffed me he smiled, very sweetly and kindly. 'You see, don't you? I can do nothing for you.' Then he walked off, and again paced up and down.

I felt deep respect and admiration for him. For I saw that it was the truth that he had come here to find, the truth as inwardly experienced, and I knew that already some great struggle was going on in his soul. About a year later I heard him say before a group of about thirty people, and in a voice trembling with emotion: 'You must understand that this that we are doing cuts at the very roots of one's being.'

Much of the training was designed to free people gradually from their associations. Gurdjieff himself was able to think sometimes without association. He would point to a flower bed and then to himself and say: 'As if one – here and there. Direct. All different.' This meant that to him everything looked different and distinct – not all one. He was continually trying to make people see that they recognized by association and did not see differences, that to them everything became the same through association. When Jane was ill, Dr Nicoll was told that she was ill associatively and that her parents must not be afraid for her. He stressed the fact that the body must and could be trained to believe and then it could be strong. The man who is afraid, he said, was always ill, but if the body believed we could resist infection by strength of bodily belief. At the Institute many associations were broken. I quote Dr Nicoll's description of a typical evening shewing the method used, and his comment on it:

> Tonight G. gave typical muddle scene – counting – no one knew what to do – orders – running about, etc. till one-

thirty. Felt demon get up – would not endure this nonsense. This is his method of making difficulties. He acts all the anger, aggrievedness, etc. If you make effort and do not identify and not let self-pride get up you end up with gain of energy. Also another method that he has is to tire people beyond the first accumulator. Then when at two or three a.m. he stops no one seems to want to go to bed and general feel of everybody is changed.

To be without associations, e.g. It is late – everything pulls one internally to the idea of tiredness, late, ought to be in bed etc. If possible to stop this, not tired. To stop it new life is necessary – quite new ways of life and thought and of what is important – and ultimately these lead to God and the Kingdom of Heaven – i.e. aim would direct matters. This is energy releasing thought because if I no longer care in the ordinary way of caring I do not lose energy in caring and because I step outside my circle of limiting ideas I find myself nearer my living being.

Dr Nicoll recorded in his diary certain exercises which were done in the evening for the purpose of developing attention. There was the repetition of difficult words against which he rebelled at first, thinking the exercise silly. Then there was an exercise in which each row had to count to a different place in the music and then act. There was practice in having a brief look at a diagram and then having to reproduce it. There were many other exercises during the last months at the Institute, examples of which were published by Orage. Experience had made Dr Nicoll see the necessity for not being affected by other people, or interfering with their actions, even if he thought them wrong. Whatever the defects in other people, it was necessary to see them objectively. Other people were freed by this separation. He had found that Jane was liberated when her parents overcame apprehension and carefulness for her safety. It was necessary to be continually aware that all those who were at the Institute were in the Work and had experienced its perplexities and 'had got a small part of themselves "gymnastic" enough to go on, a part which could at moments think and act in a different way from any other part of the machine.' He put it thus: 'A little leaven leaveneth the whole lump.' Note *leaven* – a lightening living effect. 'All of the world lumps or tightens and binds – only what is stronger than the world loosens and frees.'

He spoke of the method used, physical work and dancing, as something that is a framework which if used exceptionally could give unusual results. He found it needful to remember always that nothing that happened there mattered but only its effect on him. He observed that the pendulum swung the whole day back and forth and that it was necessary to remember oneself when it was forward and simply to wait when it swung backward. He recorded an occasion when after a bout of violent imperious feelings against Gurdjieff the latter had said his neck needed massage and gave him a shoulder-shaking exercise which gave physical relief and quietness.

In the autumn Gurdjieff decided to close the Institute. A suggestion was made that Dr Nicoll should go to America with Orage to teach the System. He felt doubtful and wished to withdraw from this, preferring the idea of teaching later in Scotland. Eventually Orage went alone, to be followed later by Gurdjieff when he took his dancers to give demonstrations of the Movements. In October Dr and Mrs Nicoll returned to London.

Dr Nicoll gave a curious impression of Gurdjieff at the end of his diary, remarking on his weightless eyes, his blushes, his hesitation, his strange power. He summed up his work as basically the breaking up of mechanicalness, and the making of new associations for the purpose of shifting the basis of oneself, with an insistence on individuality, which was impossible without *sincerity*. He never saw him again, but all that he had learnt from him was built in to his character and he acknowledged him as the source of his change of being. He and Mrs Nicoll relived their experiences, physical and psychological, at the Institute for us when they were teaching us on the same lines. In this chapter I have endeavoured to represent their experiences as they recalled them. We were only able to understand them when Dr Nicoll reproduced the Institute with his own group later. Therefore I will postpone further comment until a later chapter.

CHAPTER SIX

Relationship with Ouspensky

Mr Kenneth Walker, in *Venture with Ideas*, refers to a meeting with Dr Nicoll soon after the latter's return from Fontainebleau in the autumn of 1923. His book for children, *The Log of the Ark*, had just been published, and Dr Nicoll invited him to join a group of people who had begun to build a spiritual Ark, a refuge against a pending flood of violence prophesied by Gurdjieff. Having heard that his friend had thrown up his excellent practice in Harley Street for a year previously to go to the Prieuré, Mr Walker was convinced that he was very much in earnest, and thus it was that he went along with him to a meeting taken by Ouspensky in Warwick Gardens. Dr and Mrs Nicoll had begun once again to attend these meetings on their return from France when they found the group working in the same way as before. Ouspensky was continuing to give his exposition of the System. For those who had worked with Gurdjieff at the Institute, however, there was now a difference. Formerly they had received the ideas intellectually, but now the ideas had become alive for them, as they had during the past eleven months come to know what it meant to apply them practically to themselves.

It was necessary now for Dr and Mrs Nicoll to make plans for the winter as they had no home and were both exhausted after the strain of the sustained physical effort demanded by the rule of the Institute. It was arranged that they should take over The Old Manse for the winter, and they soon went to Scotland and settled into the house with Jane and the devoted Nannie Nellie. All that they wanted to do was to rest physically and emotionally. Here it was possible to lead a quiet life, eating and sleeping and reading, and to relax. Snow came early to Scotland that year and they were confined for some weeks to the house and village. Jane's perambulator was put on runners, and her adaptable Nannie continued the nursery routine that she had somehow always managed to maintain under the varied conditions of a changing environment. Dr Nicoll gave himself up to the relaxation of browsing among the miscellaneous books in his grandfather's remarkably extensive library. This was for him a real form of rest. After a while his creative faculty reawakened and he began once more to write short stories for the *Strand Magazine*. When spring came Dr and Mrs Nicoll planned a return to London. Bay Tree Lodge now became available for them, as Lady Robertson Nicoll was preparing to retire to The Old Manse. The family came south and installed themselves in Frognal. Dr Nicoll began to gather his practice together again, but his work was hindered by an attack of scarlet fever which was not diagnosed as such until too late, so that he had a relapse through driving when he should not have done and an operation became necessary. He was ill at Bay Tree Lodge for about three months. He told us that at that time he lay in bed, having lost interest in life, and what cured him eventually was not any particular treatment, but some good news which arrived to the effect that a legacy left to him long ago by his mother had come in (presumably through the settlement of his father's estate), which meant that his financial position suddenly improved. He got up on the day the news came. He used to cite this personal experience as an example of the truth that good news is a powerful curative. Dr and Mrs Nicoll then bought two cars and arranged to share the house, which was much too big for them, with Mr and Mrs Healey. Dr Nicoll was now able to continue the work of his practice which steadily developed, and he saw patients at his consulting-room at 146 Harley Street.

It was now possible for Dr and Mrs Nicoll to attend Ouspensky's meetings again at Warwick Gardens which they did for the next seven years, while Dr Nicoll gained increasing insight into the psychological state of his patients through his own self-knowledge gained from the System. A very deep personal relationship developed between himself and Ouspensky. Other members of the group have told me that Dr Nicoll was apparently the only one of the group with whom Ouspensky could really relax, and, more than anyone else, Dr Nicoll could make him laugh. Ouspensky told him later that this relationship developed because Dr Nicoll was the only one of his group who would really speak to him emotionally of what he had said at a meeting. He and Mrs Nicoll would attend these meetings on three nights a week, and he used to start the meetings for Ouspensky before he came in, asking for questions. Extracts from these early meetings have been printed in *The Fourth Way* (*The Fourth Way* by P. D. Ouspensky: Routledge and Kegan Paul 1957) in which selected questions and Ouspensky's answers are recorded. The actual reports of the discussions, however, shew that often most of the questions were dismissed summarily by Ouspensky as theoretical, not real, until perhaps a question based on psychological experience would evoke an unforgettable answer from the depths of the Master's being – in fact, it might be the preliminary to an hour's talk. If there were no questions at the beginning of a meeting, Ouspensky would leave, and the group would be obliged to disperse. Dr Nicoll thought it was a Russian characteristic that made it possible for Ouspensky to put up his deaf ear and say 'What?' to all questions that he did not want to answer. He himself found he could not do that.

One of the tasks of the group was to help with the revision and preparation for publication of *A New Model of the Universe*, a volume containing the writings of Ouspensky completed by 1916, before he had met Gurdjieff. The chapters were read out to the group who had to make suggestions. The book was published in 1931 by Kegan Paul. Dr Nicoll referred in his diary to Ouspensky's method of working on the New Testament in the preparation of his chapter on 'Christianity and the New Testament'.

> O. has the New Testament in German, French, Russian and English, and when he is speaking of a verse he looks at the translation in each of them and in the Greek version. He has a number of dictionaries in his room. He is fond of pencils sharpened to very fine points and always has several on his table. His mantelpiece is covered with old photographs, prints and packets of toning paper. He sits on a small uncomfortable chair. The walls are covered with a miscellaneous collection of pictures belonging to the landlord, all of which I have stared at many times without being able to remember any of them.

This method of working on the New Testament was later used also by Dr Nicoll himself. When studying the Gospels he would have beside him the Authorized Version, the Revised Version,

Monsignor Knox's translation from the Vulgate, Moffatt's, and later to his collection were added the Standard Revised Version and the Gospels from the Aramaic. He would compare the translations. He was delighted with Monsignor Knox's rendering of Galatians VI, verse 2, where the translation read: 'Bear ye the burden of one another then you will be fulfilling the law of Christ.' He said that this was the first time that the real meaning of the original had been made clear, and wrote to congratulate him. Dr Nicoll connected this teaching of St Paul with the teaching of the System that it is necessary to bear each other's unpleasant manifestations without irritation – these are 'the burden'.

Eventually in 1926, Dr and Mrs Nicoll moved to a flat in Netherhall Gardens where Mrs Nicoll's younger sister, Betty Champion Jones, joined them. In 1927 they rented for six years an old cottage at Sidlesham called Alley Cottage. It was surrounded on three sides by stretches of marshland and the sea used to come up twice a day to the garden-wall. When the spring arrived Mrs Nicoll would go down with Jane and the Danish nurse, who had replaced Nannie Nellie, and Pushti, the dog, and settle in. Then Dr Nicoll would go down in the Buick every Thursday driving through the night to spend long week-ends there. Every other week-end Ouspensky would join him. It was here that he was able to relax in the quiet surroundings and their relationship grew in silence or in long talks, or simply in companionship on drives, or in the Crab and Lobster. The cooking was done on oil-stoves, and there would be great preparations for these week-ends. The wine would be ordered, the candles placed ready for lighting, fresh lobsters bought, and a large quantity of bortsch was prepared.

I recently went down to the Cottage. The tide was out, and the pale April sunshine made the marshes shimmer in rainbow colours. The scene was deserted save for sea-birds and small crabs. No ships were on the horizon. Dr Nicoll has expressed the loneliness and stillness and the peace of the scene in his paintings. The garden behind the sea-wall had been the place of his happiest memories. The air was invigorating with a tang of seaweed in the wind. The Crab and Lobster is as it was. Mrs Richards, who still lives at the house next door, recalls how Dr Nicoll used to like to take out the wooden plug which had been fitted into the wall to keep out the sea-water at high tide. It amused him to let the sea-water come into the house through the front door and go out at the back. Mrs Richards remembers how she used to find, when she went into the Cottage in the early morning to get breakfast, that Dr Nicoll had slept in the car, as he had driven down in the small hours and had not wanted to disturb the household.

Dr Nicoll records in his diary how he took Ouspensky down to Alley Cottage on his first visit:

> We took him down to the sea. He walked a little in his overcoat, carrying a great number of glasses and cameras. He looked at a smack for a long time. He said his eyes improved as he grew older and pointed out that the binoculars he used did not have to be corrected for his vision as before. I shewed him a house near the beach said to be occupied by an Englishman turned Mahometan. It was covered with ornaments, gold work, statues of women, etc. After staring a while, he said: 'This is paranoia!' and turned away.

Dr Nicoll describes his impressions of the first evening:

> O. ate lobster, fresh caught, and cucumber, and good Southdown mutton at supper. 'This is really food,' he said. He looked intently round the cottage room. 'One can almost feel the world turning here,' he said.

Ouspensky found that he slept better at the cottage than he had for a long time and remarked that he had been able to sleep with his windows open without feeling the cold whereas in London he would have been chilled as it was early spring. He thought that this was because the air was so good. He liked Pushti. He would pinch him and make him yelp and then fondle him. He found his portrait in Sykes' *Persia* and after that he used to tell people that Pushti was a Persian dog. He had a cat at home, Vashka, of whom he was very fond, a big, brindled beast with brilliant eyes, which was about eight years old (the equivalent, he said, of seventy for a man). It no longer caught mice but ate liver and lobster. Dr

Nicoll described how, on that first evening, they burned the remains of the old boat *Sally* on the fire and the tar and copper-nails made a fine effect in coloured flame.

I will quote extracts from the diary that Dr Nicoll kept at that time, recording incidents and conversations during the week-ends when Ouspensky stayed at Alley Cottage:

O. said that Alley Cottage always struck him as an extra-ordinary place and that he knew no place just like it. He was standing in the garden by the sea-wall looking over the marshes. The tide had just gone out and a low sun lit up the sand bay and crowds of gulls. In the afternoon he had sat for a long time reading a novel, without stirring. I asked him how he read – if he thought of the story, etc. He said he usually was thinking of something else. He was sometimes silent for almost the whole day, even at meals, and heavily preoccupied. I played him a Russian song on the guitar but he did not seem to recognize it. He looked at a portrait in oils which I had done of him from a photograph, smiled, took it in his hands and then put it down without saying anything. . . .

Sitting in the Crab and Lobster Inn at night among the farm hands, he said he liked the sound of a tavern and that he thought his liking for it was in his very bones. They were talking in broad Sussex and somebody was playing a con-certina and the place was dimly lit with a swinging oil lamp. He said I should paint a sign for the Inn – which had none – illustrating a crab and lobster toasting one another. I ob-served that all the conversation going on round us was boasting in one form or another. 'All over the world', he said, 'everyone is boasting.'

O. was much amused watching Jane playing 'Old Man' with W., H. and S. and laughed heartily. This was after the game had gone on some time quite close to him without his apparently being aware of it.

He wished to take photographs at Bosham. The tide was in so he could not get the views he wanted but he made friends with a swan. We took him into the church to see the tomb of Canute's daughter, of which he took no notice but observed the framed reproduction of signatures of royal visitors hanging on a pillar and peering at it quizzically said: 'I do not see the signature of Canute's daughter.'

Standing beside W.'s car before going up to London about ten at night he fell to speaking of going distances with horses and reckoned that driving with four horses he could get to London at about two or three next day (seventy miles). He entered into such calculations with animation. He said it was necessary to drive horses at constantly varying rates to get the best out of them over long distances – also that in Russia they drove at night without lamps usually.

One day he came by car to the cottage with Madame Ouspensky. He was quiet and rather absent. We lunched at a hotel on the way down, where I recommended steak and kidney pie as a sample of English food, but it turned out poor stuff. He played with the dog Pushti. He said it was ill because I gave it meat. 'In Russia', he said, 'the borzois are only fed on very coarse porridge. Pushti will never be well unless you stop feeding him on meat, especially from the table, and give him only porridge and some bones without meat now and then.' I said I knew that was true but it was difficult to do with an amiable dog that lived in the house. He smiled and said: 'You will not be able to do it. I said only what was best for it. To do it is another matter.' He asked after the mouse. I said it had a family now. 'How is that?' he asked in astonishment. 'It lived by itself in its cage.' I told him I had let it run on the floor one evening and it had gone down a mouse-hole and had not come back for four days. A little later it had begun to tear at its wooden ladder and half demolished it. 'Ah,' he said, 'it wanted to make a nest,' He laughed at this. I said we had simply taken it as a peculiarity at the time and had not realized the future event as the explanation. He said his cat was now not only growing broad but was becoming longer. 'It becomes a cat. It eats only fish. It likes asparagus and olives very much. It does not eat meat but plays with it – throws it in the air.' His hands are not covered with scratches from this fierce beast as formerly.

He was always very patient with this cat though he complained it often scratched him in the morning in bed and interrupted his waking dreams.

We went with Madame O. to the Black Mill the first night. O. said: 'Even in such a lonely place they must all make negative emotions. In fact, more so.' He referred, I think, to a conversation we had once had there one evening with the owner of the mill, who lives in a fine house by the water's edge. This man had spoken in a heavy dreary way about family jealousies and quarrels over the mill. Next day we went to Warsash to the 'Crab and Lobster' and had lunch on the lawn. The air was magnificent and the sunshine brilliant. Only three other people were there, though it was Saturday and the place one of the finest open restaurants in the country. We ate a great many crabs and lobsters, drank chablis and watched the big liners passing up and down Southampton Water. One big ship on her way to Southampton dropped anchor opposite this restaurant. We speculated why and I said because the tide was going out fast. We began to imagine the disappointment of her passengers – the boat just missing the tide, etc. But it only shewed how rarely one finds the right explanation for anything as we found later that she was a Dutch boat and did not want to go further, so as to save harbour dues.

There were many small sailing vessels and seaplanes and all very lively and fresh. O. was pleased and Madame O. seemed to enjoy it. We went on to tea at Bosham. We returned by the marsh road past Dell Quay and so home to Sidlesham. I said to him that one could experience two quite different sorts of feeling alive – one when you went out of London into the country in air and sun; and one when suddenly after the mind had been stopped for days it awoke and thought flowed. I said that the first feeling did not produce the second. The second could happen anywhere and was the best. He looked at me some time and then said: 'But people have their minds shut all the time. They only know the first feeling.'

That evening he was himself. By this I mean that he looked

well; he seemed bigger, his eye was bright, he smiled a little at times and spoke in a lucid rich way about anything that came up. He said there was a mountain in the Caucasus called Ouspensky Mountain. One of his ancestors was a general who in fighting the mountain tribe had conquered this stronghold with a few men by giving each of his men several guns which they fired in rapid succession. One of these tribes had a habit of playing a game called Cuckoo. Four of them, clad in thick cloaks, with guns, went into a dark room and sat one in each corner. After a time one would call 'cuckoo' and the others would fire in his direction. If he called 'cuckoo' again they fired again. 'The Circassians', he said (he pronounced it Kirkassians), 'are not a bloodthirsty lot like the ———. They are gentle and always sing a lot and are gay and hospitable. At the same time one must offend nobody of these hill peoples. Even if you go to the smallest village the chief, who calls himself a prince, will entertain you lavishly – kill a sheep for you and so on.' How can you pay them back? In this way. You say that you admire something they have – a salt cellar or something quite cheap. Then according to their customs they must say: "Please take it." So then you say that you will take it only on condition that they accept from you a revolver. I carried several cheap revolvers for this purpose.' He said some of them could drink eleven bottles of red, thick wine, of which he could only manage two. In every valley they wore their distinctive dress. He described various dresses and costumes, but I have forgotten them. His description at the time was very clear. I said 'You come from a very big country with many sides to it. Our country must seem a toy.' 'Yes,' he said, 'no one realizes how big Russia is. There are twenty Switzerlands in the Caucasus (Caucasses). And then, Russian Turkestan, where you must ride for weeks to come to a place.' He said that Russia had its England, Scotland, and Ireland. 'The Poles were our Irish,' he said, 'and the little Russians our Scotchmen. There are many stories of little Russians like your Scotch stories.'

O. said about drinking that it was like borrowing – as

something borrowed from tomorrow. Usually he eats something when he drinks – cheese, sardines, or olives, uncooked
bacon, ham, etc. He does not take whisky, which he says is
too much flavoured. English gin he compares with good
vodka. He said he had never been able to overcome his
dislike for milk. Knowing this, G. once told him that he
must drink milk – but he could not. He said: 'I found it
absolutely impossible to overcome this dislike. I have overcome many, many dislikes but never this one.'

Speaking of his childhood, he said he never could properly
deceive himself with toys. He said that when he was a boy
he realized many things which people do not realize till late
in life, if ever. 'I saw many illusions,' he said, 'quite clearly
and naturally.'

In speaking of food and habits of eating, he said that we
certainly ate too much meat, and that in parts of Russia they
only have meat twice a year, and are yet big and strong. He
said in hot weather even a little meat makes you feel the heat
at once, and also makes you thirsty. He told B., who is too
fat, to eat only black bread and cucumbers and drink gin if
he wishes to. He said people should not reduce the bulk of
food they take if they alter their diet, as it gives the instinctive
machinery too little work. Tabloid food was a stupid idea
and concentrated foods were bad – an example of bad science.
I once squeezed the juice of half a dozen oranges into a glass.
He said: 'Why separate it in that way? It is wrong. It may
make a strain somewhere – perhaps in the kidneys. Why not
eat six oranges, simply?' He said hotel meals were difficult
for him: 'I cannot eat the ordinary meals of breakfast, lunch
and dinner for long without feeling ill. It is possible to do
with one meal a day very well.' In spite of what he says
about the bulk of food I am sure he often goes for long
periods without eating. . . .

We drove down to Sidlesham before dawn. We stopped
on the way and ate bread and raw bacon and drank wine
which tasted good in the chill air. We went by Goodwood
and stopped there in the early dawn. O. used his glasses of
which he was carrying a great number and looked all round

at the view. We went down to the Witterings and looked at the sea. We tried to make out a tall object on the horizon with all the glasses. We could make nothing of it. It seemed to be a tower in the sea. We came back to town in the afternoon. I reminded O. of the drive to Chamonix with the roasted goat, and G. and the precipice. He laughed and said: 'The Suicide Club'. . . .

In the early spring we went to Bournemouth by car. We started in the afternoon, meaning to stop the night at Romsey, I having an idea there was a pleasant old hotel there. He observed on the great number of inns called 'White Hart' on the way. It rained and got dark early. We found ourselves in what I thought was Romsey, but it seemed bigger and I said it had grown since I was last there. It turned out to be Southampton. We stayed at a small hotel in the old town and discovered very good hock in half bottles. . . . Very courteous waitresses. He always appreciates courteous servants. As G. does also. He detests people who are rude or cross to waiters.

Next day we arrived rather late at Bournemouth for lunch, in a severe and correct hotel, where my wife had got rooms for us, the town being full with people recovering from influenza. The dining-room hung with atrocious oil paintings and containing many small tables mostly with a flagon of Australian wine on them. I had explained a long while before to him that Australian wine is drunk all along the South Coast of England, chiefly by English Aunts. He looked at the flagons in silence, and then acknowledged my observation to be correct. 'The doctors encourage this,' I said. 'Doctors have much to account for on the last day,' he replied. He never fails to hit at doctors.

We found Bournemouth heavy. Everything was closed on Sunday. He experienced to the full the atmosphere of English respectableness. We escaped to Swanage and lunched at the 'Grosvenor' which we found pleasant and easy and almost continental in feeling. The view of the wide bay, lit with sea lights, and the cliffs and brilliant sunshine were almost Mediterranean. It was early spring but mild.

In the hotel at Bournemouth we had the greatest difficulty in talking late at night, as all lights were put out at eleven. It seemed as if every bedroom listened to us. . . .

We got into difficulties with a policeman at the cross-road in the town. I backed the car. The policeman objected. 'Now whatever we do he will object,' he said, which proved true enough.

He said that England had a bad climate and that winter was something that one had to recover from in England, and that people did not grasp this. England was the worst country in the world, he thought for the respect they paid to regular times for things – regular meals, regular habits, customs and routine, and that to miss lunch was a kind of catastrophe for an Englishman that he could not forget easily. He said many people had insomnia simply because they tried to sleep at the wrong time and that it did not necessarily mean that one could fall asleep at a fixed time just because it was customary. Some people, for instance, required to sleep in two periods every 24 hours. He said people with ingrained reverence for regular habits often did themselves great harm, without noticing it, being upheld by the idea they were behaving in the correct way.

He said London was not a large city, but was a number of towns all joined together. It was unlike Moscow which was one large city.

He said Germany before the war was to Russia what America is to England.

He said that he had wondered whether he should come to England to teach or to other countries – Spain, for example – when he was with G. in Constantinople. Lady X had written him from England. He eventually decided to come to England. He had done this from himself. G. later had signified his approval by coming to England to see results of his work. The Institute in France had been made possible through his work in England in one sense. He said that people who came into contact with him came not necessarily from anything serious. It might be accidental. But what kept them in contact with him after a certain stage was not accidental. At the same time what brought them in contact with him was not that which eventually made them continue with him.

In 1926 a further connection had been made which was of the utmost importance for Dr Nicoll. Mr Fulford Bush became one of his patients on his return to this country from China. At their first meeting a link was formed which endured as long as they lived. Mr Bush became first Dr Nicoll's most responsive patient, then his most loyal supporter and most devoted disciple during the twenty-two years in which Dr Nicoll taught Gurdjieff's system to his own group. I quote his own written impression of his first meeting with Dr Nicoll:

> I first met Doctor Nicoll in the beginning of 1926 on my return from China where I had been practising law in Peking and Tientsin. He had, after leaving Fontainebleau, resumed his practice in Harley Street as the leading neurologist in London and my call was made upon him in his professional capacity, as I had been advised to consult him by Mr Kenneth Walker, F.R.C.S., to whom I had put up a question of a psychological rather than a physiological nature.
>
> 'Maurice Nicoll is your man', said Walker with his characteristic directness – and so it proved.
>
> My first impression in that to me momentous call was of the man's presence, that indefinable quality one so rarely encounters and which is so unmistakable. I do not think I am easily impressed. I have met many remarkable men – in China, Japan, Germany and England, particularly in China where I saw something of the China-Japan War, the Boxer trouble, and the Russo-Japanese War. They all had presence, a certain inner poise, a dignity born of self-command achieved by recognition of a purposed way to some definite objective, the power of detachment enabling them to view your problem objectively. But the man I met in Harley Street had and has this quality in a more remarkable degree. Of middle height, a classically shaped head, clear-cut features, light blue eyes that see right through you with understanding kindliness, making any attempt at evasion or deception futile, hands capable and artistic, a voice of which the diapason

holds infinite range of expression; that is an attempt to give some idea of the man – Maurice Nicoll – of whom the passing twenty-two years have served to intensify the impression formed at that first interview, in the course of which I put forward the difficulty that had obsessed me for some months.

The answer was simple and direct. It involved the application of psychological force which I – in common with the average man – thought I already possessed. At that time there were few limits to my imagined capabilities; like most men I imagined I could do what I made up my mind to do – without any conception of what making up one's mind entails.

Mr Bush used to say that he had considered his enforced departure from China for reasons of health as a minor calamity, involving as it did the giving up of his legal practice in Peking, but he afterwards came to regard this event as a blessing.

He now recorded his conversations with Dr Nicoll week by week. His diary reveals the gradual subtle change in the writer which took place as the psychological and spiritual wisdom penetrated the chinks in his armour. Mr Bush was a proud and violent man of fixed principles who had all the faults and virtues of an Englishman brought up and long resident in China in the days when British prestige was at its height there. Nevertheless towards Dr Nicoll he shewed from their first meeting a humility which remained unchanged, so great was the respect and admiration which he always had for him. His loyal affection and keen sense of discipline made him a most valuable assistant to Dr Nicoll when his group came into being.

The first thing that Dr Nicoll made him aware of was the expediency of not insisting that everyone should see things from his own view-point and of not wounding anyone by word or deed. Then he stressed the importance of relaxing and suggested that relaxed muscles prevented the creation of antagonism in others and pointed out that such relaxation enabled a man to pass through dangers unmolested, as Christ passed unnoticed through a crowd. He used Mr Bush's knowledge of ju-jitsu to provide an analogy to shew that psychologically also it is possible to conquer by yielding so that one's opponent is overbalanced by the force of his own momentum. Through his understanding of these three things Mr Bush came to approach life differently.

After some months Mr Bush consulted Dr Nicoll about the advisability of giving up his legal work and opening a studio for physical culture of a remedial nature, which was the kind of work that appealed to him particularly. Dr Nicoll approved of this, as it was apparent that his profession had always engendered a contradiction in him, whereas this new work was what was essentially harmonious to him. The Studio was therefore opened and it was clear that Dr Nicoll's advice about his patients was a great asset to his work. At an early stage he advised him to break routine in their training before the novelty should have worn off – that is, to change the routine constantly. Then he pointed out to him the value of exercises that increase nerve-strength rather than muscular strength in that it was usually the nerves that tired first. Dr Nicoll advised him about the psychological causes of many illnesses. In 1926 there were not so many publications dealing with psychosomatic causes as there are today. For instance he suggested that despondency was the cause of rheumatism, emotional interference the cause of asthma, and narrow thinking the cause of many nervous complaints. The most striking advice however that Mr Bush received from Dr Nicoll at this juncture was that an increased use of the mind for new thinking would be beneficial to health in that this made it possible for energy to be generated from a source that had in many people not been fully tapped.

Mr Bush was directed by Dr Nicoll to a new line of thought that gave him great mental stimulation. This was the result of a renewed study of the New Testament and of Plato. His reading led him to put many questions to Dr Nicoll from which it is apparent that the latter was already thinking on the lines of his later interpretations. For instance, he stressed the importance of distinguishing between what Christ said to the disciples and what He said to the multitude. This was the beginning of selecting the esoteric teaching that was within the exoteric presentation of Christianity.

Dr Nicoll was already studying the parabolic teaching of

Christ, wherein there is an inner meaning underlying the surface meaning. He was speaking of the Sermon on the Mount and of all that was demanded of a man if he were to reach a certain state called in the Gospels the Kingdom of Heaven. It is very interesting to observe in the record of these talks how gradually Dr Nicoll placed the esoteric meaning before Mr Bush so that it eventually superseded the orthodox standpoint of exoteric Christianity. For instance, there is an entry as follows:

> Strong dissent from my statement that the lesson running throughout the New Testament is one of Love and Service to mankind in general. Contended that mechanical man is not capable of service – only Conscious Man is capable of that. We call that Service which is only a form of Self-service – what circumstances, artificial self-pictures, demand that we shall do. To love is very difficult – to learn to love those who are our colleagues, working with us towards knowledge and self-consciousness, takes years of apprentice-ship. One's natural leanings are all towards criticism of others, satisfaction at finding them wanting, and so on.

In 1929 Mr Bush took a large house in Redcliffe Gardens which contained a big studio suitable for his remedial work which demanded much heavy apparatus (for weight-lifting and so on). The surplus rooms in the house were let off to tenants. His practice had expanded so that he now had a resident secretary. This studio afterwards was used for meetings.

On Wednesday, 9th September 1931, ten years after his first meeting with Ouspensky, Dr Nicoll was, to his surprise, author-ized by him to teach the system. This necessitated complete in-dependence of the main group taught by Ouspensky. One or two people came with him from Ouspensky, but for the most part he collected his own people – people with whom he had talked during the past year or so. Mr Bush also brought some people. It was now that Mr Bush became invaluable. He under-took all the organizing work, became Treasurer of the group, and by freeing Dr Nicoll from responsibility for all business details made it possible for him to devote all his energy (apart from the demands made on him by his consultant work in Harley Street) to the teaching of the System.

Dr Nicoll related to us the short conversation in which Ouspensky gave him this authority – 'Nicoll,' he said, 'you had better go away. . . .' Then, after a long pause, he added, 'Go away – and teach the System.'

CHAPTER SEVEN

Group Work in London and Essex

On Wednesday, 9th September 1931, Dr Nicoll took the first meeting of his own group at Mr Bush's studio in Redcliffe Gardens. At this meeting he spoke of the Fourth Way, the Way known to only a few people, although those who follow it go through life in the company of the rest of the world. They do not retire from the world: they simply live in the world but are not of the world. The teaching was carefully guarded in case it should fall into the wrong hands and become distorted, and this was how its original truth had been preserved intact, although it had taken many different outward manifestations, such as Gothic architecture, Alchemy, and the Art of Chivalry. Dr Nicoll explained to the Group that the ideas which they heard at the meetings were not to be spoken of. They were receiving instructions, the same instructions that had been handed down through the ages to those who were prepared to accept them as truth, instructions as to how to live as though walking on the waters of life, as Christ did – and indeed, one name given informally to the System was Esoteric Christianity. This was the teaching that Dr Nicoll had received from Ouspensky during the previous ten years.

At the third meeting those who were present were asked to say whether they wanted to continue – they all wished to do so. They were then instructed not to speak of the ideas to anyone except those who, they considered, would be responsive to them. It was remarkable, as they surveyed their friends and acquaintances, how few seemed suitable. The ideas were acceptable only to those who no longer believed that life had meaning in itself. For his groups Dr Nicoll wanted people who had become strong in life, who had a sense of responsibility, as parents, householders and citizens, and who had come to see that there was a meaning behind what life could give. Gradually new members were added to the original group. Mr Bush brought his two sisters, his secretary, Miss Dorothy Corcoran, and several of his patients. People began to hear of the group in various odd ways. I quote the description of the manner in which one member came to be introduced:

How and why I first met Dr Nicoll has something of magic about it. A good many years ago I experienced a state that I can only describe as – of despair. I could see no meaning in life, and could find no way of struggling out of the morass I was sinking into. I burst into tears for ridiculous and unexplainable reasons and became an embarrassment to myself and everyone else.

One day, out of the blue, a name flashed into my mind – 'Dr Maurice Nicoll'. Where did it come from? Who was he? It did not come to me once but more or less stayed with me until at last I was obliged to face it and use my reasoning powers. The result, after some search through the previous four to six years, was the localization of the name in connection with a friend who had mentioned the help she had from him over some trouble, the nature of which I could not recall. Nor had I seen my friend since.

I tried to put the name from me at first, but it was no good. It had come to stay – and the need to find the owner now became an urgent necessity. I was living in the country at that time. At the first opportunity I went to London and at once on arriving went to a phone-box in the station to find his address. There were two Dr Maurice Nicolls, both with letters after their names, but different ones! I felt my determination and courage ebbing, but after staring at the two addresses for goodness knows how long, I took the plunge. I rang up the one in Harley Street, and asked the secretary for an appointment for following day. It was the right one.

(I will not relate here my impression on first meeting the materialization of the name that had been with me continuously for it was the incredible and mysterious side of my first contact with Dr Nicoll that I set out to write about.)

After I had visited him three or four times he said: 'You no longer look the poor ghost you did the first time I saw you. Would you like to come and hear me answering questions and talking at a meeting tonight?' He gave me the address, and time, and told me to sit in the front row, and not to ask any questions during the meeting. Although this happened more than twenty years ago, I can still vividly recall the extraordinary state of anticipation and excitement that I felt as I sat in the bus on my way to my first meeting, as though I were conscious of the importance of the event, which in itself sounded nothing in particular yet actually was going to change the whole of my life.

I arrived at a tall grey house in Redcliffe Gardens. The front door was ajar. I went into the hall and found the door on my left was also open and I could hear a murmur of voices. Without hesitation I went in, and found myself in a room that looked like a gymnasium – there were about four rows of straight-backed chairs, facing a small table and chair and blackboard. The back row was fully occupied, and a sprinkling of others also. A tall man stood up and came forward. 'Are you Mrs X?' he asked. 'Sit anywhere you like.' Remembering my instructions I took my place in the front row and I felt no embarrassment even though I thought I detected a smile on somebody's face – and there were only two others in the front on either extreme end.

Dr Nicoll came in, when we were all assembled, quietly, with lowered eyes, as though the room were empty, and his mind was occupied with other things. He sat down facing us, and for a few minutes remained silent, eyes still lowered. The tension in the room became taut and increased momentarily until he released the pressure by looking up and glancing round the room, taking in each person with casual attention. He paused for a moment, when his eyes arrived on me, the newcomer, sending me a message of friendly recognition. This little introduction over, I realized that we had entered a new phase – the phase of waiting for someone to ask a question to start the meeting. Again the tension rose, and for what seemed like ten minutes, though was probably only ten seconds, we sat in strained silence, until eventually someone with extraordinary calm and collectedness asked a question – and I couldn't help wondering why he hadn't put us all out of our misery, and asked it sooner. To my relief, although it was no responsibility of mine, having (quite unnecessarily) been told not to ask a question, the meeting was built up on this first question. Others were able to speak more easily on the same subject though from different aspects, and each question was answered at once, curtly, if it was asked formatorily – and at length if the question sprang from a genuine desire to know the answer. Long silences occurred again and again, each as electric as the last, and when eventually after about an hour Dr Nicoll stood up and said: 'We'll stop now,' and went out – quietly, as he had come in – without a word or glance to anyone – we, who were left behind, began immediately to fidget or chatter, as though filled to the brim with energy, we must use some sort of safety-valve.

Meetings continued and as the group became enlarged it was divided and people met on different nights in the week, sometimes in Redcliffe Gardens, sometimes in Harley Street and occasionally in the elegant flat in Kensington occupied by the Misses Bush where the surroundings were in great contrast to the gymnasium background in Mr Bush's house. Eventually Dr Nicoll insisted that it was necessary to find a room for meetings which was more like the room in Warwick Gardens, and for some years the groups met in a bare lecture room at a Dancing School in Finchley Road.

It was to a meeting in this room in Finchley Road that I was brought by Mr and Mrs Casswell one Wednesday evening in the spring of 1935. I had no idea to what I was being introduced. I had recently moved to Hampstead after having divorced my husband and had been invited to dine with the Casswells who, newly married, had settled in a flat close by. During the evening they remarked casually that they were attending some psychological lectures which might interest me and suggested that I might accompany them to one the following week. I agreed to do this but I did not expect anything more than some intellectual diversion. I knew nothing of psychology. My experience of my first meeting was not quite like that which I have quoted above. I had not already met Dr Nicoll. I had not even heard his name, and I was not at all nervous as I was quite accustomed to going to lectures and had no preconceived ideas about this one, nor did I know that this new contact was going to mark the division of my life into two distinct parts, as clearly as if I were crossing the Rubicon.

It is interesting to know that Mr Casswell himself had gone to his first meeting with great reluctance, having been persuaded to accompany one of his contemporaries at Oxford with whom he had been having some talks. His introducer was certainly justified in his choice for the reluctant new member soon became attracted to the System and had he not stayed I have sometimes wondered whether the course of my own life would have been different.

My memory of my first meeting is selective. I do not recall an atmosphere of tension, perhaps because I was so innocently free from it myself. I appreciated the quiet way in which Dr Nicoll answered questions. I became aware of the fine quality of his mind during this quiet, almost informal, conversation, and of a spiritual certainty that seemed to be the source of all that he said. Yet my moment of recognition had not yet come. I continued to attend the meetings and appreciated them but found no continuity in them as each time the subject of the previous week was apparently ignored and a new subject spoken of which I could not connect with what I had already heard. One evening a passage from an unpublished chapter by Ouspensky was read to us and when I asked to borrow it, it was explained to me that the teaching was oral, and nothing could be read. This rather disconcerted me, as I was accustomed to having the printed word before me and liked to be able to read widely on any subject and to make my own connections. However, the Casswells came to my help at this juncture by lending me *A New Model of the Universe* which had been published in 1931 by Kegan Paul. The passages that were being read to us from manuscript were from the book that was later published under the title of *Fragments of an Unknown Teaching or In Search of the Miraculous*, but here was a published work of Ouspensky and it was in reading this that I had my first moment of recognizing truth. (I still had not recognized Dr Nicoll.)

It was when I came to the chapter called 'Christianity and the New Testament' that I had an emotional experience, unforgettable, of recognizing something I knew to be true but had forgotten. This was my first moment of becoming aware that all knowledge is but remembering, as Plato taught. It seemed that in one instant of expanded time I saw the adventure that lay before me of discovering the inner meaning of the New Testament, and knew that if this system taught by Ouspensky were Esoteric Christianity then it was this study that I wanted to follow. The intensity of the revelation faded, but its effect was permanent, and the interest of studying esotericism in the Gospels in particular has never failed. I read the whole of the *New Model of the Universe* and also Ouspensky's earlier book, *Tertium Organum*. Although these writings had preceded their author's meeting with Gurdjieff, yet here was already a new way of thinking presented, which gave me a background to the ideas which were discussed at Dr Nicoll's meetings. The idea of scale, of many dimensions, of the unmanifest as the cause of the manifest, of the continuation of teachings which linked the great Religions – all was here.

Sometimes I had the privilege of sitting beside Mrs Nicoll at the meetings and admired her beauty, her deep rich voice, and above all, her stillness, which made me aware of my own fidgeting, my inability to be still. Soon she asked me to tea at her flat where I found much joy in a real conversation with her. I realized years later how in such initial talks with new members of the group she must have consciously made herself passive to listen to what they would reveal of themselves.

My first real talk with Dr Nicoll was of a very different nature. One day I received instructions to make an appointment with him through his receptionist at 146 Harley Street. I went to his consulting-room one morning and although he was not sitting at his desk, but in a chair by the fire, while we talked, nevertheless the surroundings were somewhat awe-inspiring, and so were the stern words with which he immediately shook me out of self-pity. However, when he had found out what my interests were he began to tell me about his own literary work and we discussed books and films and writings.

These visits to Harley Street were repeated at intervals and some time later Dr Nicoll suggested that I should collect material for an anthology of passages referring to death. He had always wanted to make such an anthology, he said, but was always otherwise occupied. This work was a great solace to me for years and that was, I believe now, what it was intended to be. The task made me turn first to my favourite reading among the Ancients. I re-read in translation, Plato, Xenophon, Plutarch, Herodotus, Epictetus, Cicero, Horace, and Marcus Aurelius, until it began to dawn on me that many of the psychological truths which we were studying at Dr Nicoll's meetings had been expressed long ago in Greece and Rome.

I remember that one day I was moved to take Plato's *Republic* from the shelf where it had stayed unopened for some years. All day I read it – in the evening I went to the meeting in the Finchley Road and Dr Nicoll made an announcement to the group: 'I think you should all read the *Republic* of Plato.' This was the first experience that I had of finding that once one was working in a group it was possible to find oneself tuned in beforehand, and already thinking on the lines to be discussed.

Dr Nicoll had for some years made it a practice to spend any hours in the daytime that were free from appointments in the Reading Room of the British Museum where he was working on material for the book that was afterwards published under the title *Living Time*. Here his American secretary would spend her days reading for him and copying out relevant passages in her neat, clear handwriting. Miss Frances Ney had arrived from Buffalo U.S.A. in 1927, at the right moment to give him the assistance he needed in the collection of his material. She had come a long way, having no idea of the outcome of her journey. She had come over to England to see Dr Nicoll because she had read his *Dream Psychology*, and certain works of Jung, and wanted to talk to him. I quote her letter recollecting her first interview with him:

> I had read Jung, Eckhart, Dr Nicoll's *Dream Psychology*, etc. and simply wanted more. I reached London April 1927 – an interesting period. Dr Nicoll's first request was to find this quotation, if possible: 'There are two streams of knowledge, one rising and falling, one . . .' he could not finish with the exact words. He added – that at various times there was special teaching – one might find traces of it. I think he also spoke of the Gothic period – wandering scholars, etc. I am not sure how it came about – but I found this: 'The Canon.'

Anon. (publ. 1896?). It had some material from Fludd and a
picture. This brought Dr Nicoll to the Reading Room to
see Fludd. There are several volumes in one of the special
rooms. I copied some of the Latin text, also traced a picture
or a diagram. . . . of the two streams of knowledge, there
was no trace. . . . About this time he dictated a few pages
about being *invisible*. I think that this book *Living Time* was
taking shape. He came to the Reading Room one or two
mornings each week – sometimes with a definite request for
material – sometimes simply for the translation of a word.
He knew his Greek – and Plato. Sometimes I simply recopied
his pages, he corrected, then they were typed – not necessarily
as chapters, or in sequence, but more as if certain aspects had
to be seen – typed – then revised. This did not last long – the
extra notes perhaps simply were parts of this picture, making
the subject clearer, or to keep a right continuity. The last two
or three years he simply dictated new or revised chapters.
(This was at his home.) His book as a whole – and its parts –
grew and developed – but I think while the *whole theme* was
quite clear to him he was thinking of the reader. . . . My next
task was to make a list of material about Scottish Mysticism.

Dr Nicoll did not complete his monograph on Fludd for which
a certain amount of material was collected, but for several years
he re-read widely in Greek Philosophy, the neo-Platonists, the
Hermetica, and the Christian Mystics, and formulated his thoughts
on scale and Eternity, on the reality behind appearance. Ouspensky's ideas, absorbed by him, were expressed in the light of his
own philosophical and psychological knowledge. *Living Time* is
a study of the inner man – a study of reality from various points
of view, of scale, dimensions, time, Eternity, recurrence, and
concludes with a hint of the possibilities of integration in Living
Time.

In 1931 Dr and Mrs Nicoll and Jane had begun to spend week-
ends with Miss C. M. Lydall who had been at the Institute and
was godmother to Jane. They all shared Lakes Farm, Miss Lydall's
house at Rayne, near Braintree in Essex. The original owner had
sold the farmhouse and now lived in a modern house while he

continued farming the land. It was approached by a very muddy
drive, but when the sea of mud had been safely crossed one came
upon a most attractive house, with gables, surrounded by a
medley of flowers and old fruit trees. There was a certain amount
of livestock – cocks and hens, rabbits and guinea-pigs and three
pet sheep, of which Jane was very fond, which contentedly
cropped the grass in the field, answering to their names when
called. Members of the group would come down by invitation
to spend Saturday or Sunday there. I quote a description given by
Miss Selene Moxon of her first visit with her friend Miss Sunday
Wilshin, during the summer of 1932, both extremely nervous as
they were very new members of the group.

> The house itself was old and had a delightful atmosphere.
> Along the back wall a verandah had been built where all meals
> were served during the summer. A long trestle table covered
> with a gaily coloured cloth and equally gay china looked so
> delightful that it was a pleasure to sit down and eat the food
> that Mrs Nicoll provided. In those days Mrs Nicoll did most
> of the cooking herself and she was an excellent cook. One or
> two people would help her with the vegetables and salads,
> and everyone took a hand in the washing up afterwards. Dr
> and Mrs Nicoll were always tremendously active, Dr Nicoll
> making things in his workshop or writing in his own room.
> Mrs Nicoll worked harder both indoors and out of doors
> than anyone I've ever met. She seemed to have a tireless
> energy. I never saw her hurried or flustered over anything.
> The garden at the Farm was almost entirely her doing; she
> grew lovely flowers all the seasons. Dr Nicoll built a little
> greenhouse for her and in it she grew cucumbers and many
> plants. It was a mass of Morning Glory one year, I remember.
> Never having seen it before, I was dazzled by the wonderful
> blue.

Miss Moxon's first visit to the Farm was memorable in more
ways than one. She had with her an order to view a cottage at
Little Saling. Having recently made up her mind to leave London,
she had made enquiries about properties in Essex before she knew
that Dr and Mrs Nicoll were at Lakes Farm. She was surprised to

discover that Little Saling was only a few miles away, and the following morning she made an offer for the cottage, Wymers, into which she and Miss Wilshin moved two months afterwards. From that time onwards Dr Nicoll used often to dine at Wymers when he stayed down at the Farm during the week to write. He was able to relax there and would talk sometimes until dawn, while every now and then some biscuits attractively spread with cream cheese or patum peperum would be placed beside him which he would eat absent-mindedly but with evident appreciation.

Dr and Mrs Nicoll liked to celebrate Christmas in the country, but in the year 1932 Mrs Nicoll was called away to nurse her mother who was very ill. Miss Moxon and Miss Wilshin were asked to hold the Group Christmas Dinner at Wymers. Miss Moxon was a superb cook, but she was somewhat shaken at the prospect of being responsible for dinner for eighteen.

On the morning of Christmas Eve Dr Nicoll's car was heard advancing up the lane. It was a vintage car that rattled and clanked; the windscreen wiper, a pair of forceps, and part of the wiring had been gathered together in a lemonade bottle. His dog Pushti as usual perched up at the back somewhere. Pushti and he were inseparable. Pushti was a remarkably intelligent animal of no known breed, big and handsome however with a beautiful coat. When asked what *kind* of dog he was Dr Nicoll said he was a 'Persian Greyhound' (which silenced anyone silly enough to ask). The car having arrived at our gate, Dr Nicoll emerged carrying in his arms a large turkey with its long legs dangling. All went off well and the party continued into Boxing Day and Night. After that year it was laid down that a Boxing Night party at Wymers should follow the Christmas party at the Farm.

In 1933 the Ouspensky group had acquired a house in the country which Mr Kenneth Walker describes in *Venture with Ideas*. Here Madame Ouspensky who had been so long with Gurdjieff at the Prieuré was in charge of the practical work and it certainly appears from his description and from all that Dr Nicoll told us that she used some of Gurdjieff's devastating methods of producing the necessary friction for work on the development of being. In 1936 a larger house was bought with land for farming, and group work was carried on on a very extensive scale and a number of the group became resident there. Dr Nicoll did not attempt to form a residential group until the outbreak of the war. We were however always aware that we were working in a parallel way to this senior group.

In February 1934 Miss Lydall died, leaving Lakes Farm to Jane. Soon afterwards Dr and Mrs Nicoll conceived the idea of building on the land a house which would be suitable for group activities with large rooms on the ground floor and bedrooms upstairs for the increasing number of people who were coming down to work at the week-ends. The site chosen was the field called Tyeponds. Plans were drawn up by George Kadleigh, who was then very young, but has since become distinguished in the world of architecture. On 12th March 1938, Mr Bush recorded in his diary:

> With reference to Work parties at Lakes Farm – to be started to give people some idea of the atmosphere of work as it exists in common effort. Proposed to build Ex. Room – Kitchen – Sleeping-room etc. Building of lath and plaster to be built by group members – constructive, practical work for men and women.

On 18th May 1935 the first working-party took place. I quote Mr Casswell's description of this which he recorded in his diary, and of the initial work which took place a few days previously:

> I have a very distinct recollection of a day which we spent at Rayne just before this. I do not remember that anyone else was there but I helped Dr Nicoll to prepare for the beginning of work by constructing a plank bridge across the ditch between Lakes Farm garden and the Tyeponds field. There was a strange satisfaction in the work intensified by anticipation of things to come.
>
> The first work was the building of the workshop. This did not take very long, and as soon as it was finished we had a celebration feast in it.

It now became customary for all those who came down to help with the building to stay over Saturday night. Some of them slept at Lakes Farm, some at the 'Swan', one or two in small outbuildings in the garden, and others stayed with members of the group who had week-end cottages nearby. Meals were all at the Farm indoors or out of doors. After a meal, it would probably be Dr Nicoll who was first at the sink for washing up. Mr Casswell recalls the progress of the building:

> By September 1935 the outline of the house was complete. The near end was solid and covered with laths but the far end was still a skeleton of beams. I and my wife spent our holiday staying with the Parfits at their cottage, going over every day to work on the house, mostly lathing. One night there was a fierce gale and when we arrived in the morning the open end of the house was leaning over at an angle of about 75°. There was nothing we could do about it, but the next week-end with the help of block and tackle it was pulled straight.

I came down to the Farm for the first time during the early summer of that year. I remember driving down one Sunday for the day with the Casswells. The work for the women at that time was chiefly lathing. I had not done it before but once one got the knack of it, it was pleasant. We worked almost in silence in our different rooms. Luncheon was out of doors and the conversation has not stayed in my memory. What I recall most clearly is the new feeling of sharing in the building of a house. Energy was conducted through the single-minded way in which the group worked together, inspired and directed by Dr Nicoll. Mrs Nicoll was radiant when we arrived at the luncheon table. We all felt joy in being there.

The house was gradually completed. It was called Tyeponds – the name of the field on which it stood. Dr Nicoll had learnt much from his building experience at the Institute. The hardest work had been the initial digging of the foundations. Once the house was constructed plastering was the order of the day. The men used to mix the plaster. I remember that the buckets of it were heavy to carry up ladders, but I learnt to plaster and again it was a question of discovering the knack – a certain movement of the wrist was required. When I plastered ceilings I always seemed to find my hair covered with it even although I bound up my head with a scarf. The most skilled carpenters were given the work of making and fitting the windows. When we reached the stage of painting the house the work became most pleasurable.

Mr Parfit recalled recently certain preparations that Dr Nicoll had made before the building work began. Week-end after week-end he had given himself tasks to be completed in a set time – for instance, he would knock up a chair in half an hour. He was all the time experimenting to see what he could expect from the group. Everything that he gave us to do he had already done himself.

A water-diviner had been called in to find a suitable place to sink a well, but as the only spot that he suggested after dowsing was too far from the house, the matter was left in abeyance. Mr David Squire recalls a conversation with Dr Nicoll who asked him where he thought the well should be and he pointed to a spot just outside the kitchen at the back of the house. Dr Nicoll said that that should be the place and there the well was dug, a pipe having to be sunk in the centre because of trouble with sand. The water supply turned out to be adequate. This was typical of the way in which decisions were made.

A local thatcher was called in to thatch the roof of the house as this was specialized work which was not within our scope. When Christmas came four of the bedrooms were habitable and there was a giant Christmas tree in the Big Room.

It was during this period of building that Dr Nicoll was in his element. All that he had learnt from Gurdjieff about building at the Prieuré was now put into practice – the methods, the speed, the working for quick result rather than for durability, his skill in carpentry. His presence inspired us as Gurdjieff's presence had been the inspiration at Fontainebleau. The group found themselves discovering new faculties, that had previously been unsuspected – nothing was impossible. Meanwhile, under the direction of Mrs Nicoll we learned to cook for great numbers. The process of gaining experience was gradual. First, one would be one of two assistants to the chief cook in the kitchen. Then the day would come when one found oneself responsible for dinner for thirty. I remember that I myself began by assisting with the preparation of breakfast. This was not difficult but needed a certain amount of calculation, as the various oil-stoves had speeds of their own for boiling kettles, and it was important moreover not to let any of the thirty or so eggs boil hard.

Looms were installed in one of the sheds and stair-carpets were woven for the staircases at either end of Tyeponds. Curtains were made. One of the results of assisting in the building of a house is that you always recognize your own work. Any mistakes face you permanently. At first you have some compunction when confronted with them, but eventually you can accept your early mistakes with a kind of tenderness.

Certain aphorisms from the Study House of the Château du Prieuré were written up in beautiful lettering. The most memorable was:

Remember that you are here to contend only with yourself
– thank everyone who gives you the opportunity.

This was the Key to our group work – a reversal of thinking was necessary in order to accept that all difficulties encountered were in oneself and that we owed a debt to all who, through our reaction to them, were the means of shewing us something about ourselves. Normally one thinks that other people make difficulties. It took a long time to become aware that all irritation, exasperation, anger, were the result of one's own mechanical habits of reacting to certain manifestations in other people.

These week-ends of hard work during the building had a very special quality about them. One would arrive in the early afternoon on Saturday (one or two people having come down on Friday to help Mrs Nicoll, who did all the catering and shopping in Braintree herself on Saturday morning). At dusk we would perhaps gather in the kitchen where there was always a blazing fire, everywhere else being very cold, and a bottle of sherry might be opened. Then we would assemble in the large dining-hall for dinner. The tables were arranged sometimes in a square, sometimes a T-square. There was always wine, generally claret, and a feeling of leisure after the efforts of the afternoon. This was the time when Dr Nicoll liked to talk to us. There was no organized meeting at the week-end at this period. Dr Nicoll himself took meetings in London on four nights in the week with late talks afterwards. At Lakes Farm and Tyeponds he liked to talk and to teach informally. We knew what it was to have real conversation. This might go on for hours, well into the night. The mental exercises used at the Institute might perhaps be given, but for the most part he would speak of the ideas of the System, of memories of his training at the Institute, of Gurdjieff himself, of Ouspensky, of the work that he wanted to do here at the Farm. He had in mind to make an Institute here where things could be organized so that extra effort could be made, as at the Prieuré. It was here that he was able to attack vanity and anything false in people. This was always done in public, generally during meals. There was no escape. Then the conversation might turn on his own reading. He would talk of the mystery of Time, or Recurrence, and dwell often on passages from Plato. Special passages would be read aloud. Later in the evening we would go to the kitchen and clear away and he would take his guitar and play Spanish songs which one or other of the group would sing, Miss Sunday Wilshin, or Michael Streatfeild. The talk would continue interspersed with guitar music.

Mr Bush asked whether it was possible to use the knowledge and the powers which we gained from our training in the System for material effect or was it the fact that any such attempt would defeat its own object. Dr Nicoll replied that certainly such acquired power could be used for material gain but that the acquisition of such power would probably mean the absence of any desire so to use it. 'One does not use a £1000 bank note to light cigarettes,' he concluded. 'If we want to impress others we must be concerned with their affairs, unmindful of what effect we may be creating. To pose is to defeat the object of the pose. When a man makes an impression upon one it is usually because he is not trying to create an impression but is concentrating upon doing something for one or understanding something of one.'

On Sunday we would be up very early and all those who were not doing domestic work would work on the house or the garden. A rockery was being built by Mrs Sandheim and Miss Reekie. Mrs Sandheim was renowned for her gifts to Dr and Mrs Nicoll. The first gift that arrived was a troupe of peacocks. These were shut up in the dark carpenter's shed for the night as there were beams there on which they could perch and we did not know where to house them safely. Mr Gloster arriving later in the evening and not knowing of their presence went into the shed to get something and was startled to see eyes glaring down at him through the darkness. The peacocks did not stay long with us as they were always straying on to the railway line nearby, and we were too often called to the telephone by an irate voice saying, 'Come and collect your peacocks.'

It was decided to dig a pool for goldfish in front of the new house. This was hard work as the ground was clay. It was then lined with concrete. This was the pool which resembled the one at the Prieuré. Once the house was finished and the pool and the garden well under way, we had time to paint, and art classes and guitar lessons were organized.

Meanwhile in London in 1936 Dr Nicoll began to recollect the music of the Movements, which he planned to revive for use in his group. On 12th May, he called on Miss Marjorie Stalker, a pianist in the group, and spent two hours in humming the tunes which she tried to harmonize on the piano. She could not write music, but she came down to the Farm and played the tunes bar by bar to Miss Wadham who wrote them on a score. Dr Nicoll had recollected the Obligatories, the March and the Counting Exercise.

In the autumn it was arranged for Mrs Howarth, accompanied by Mrs Nott, to teach us a few of the Movements in a basement of the Finchley Road house where we had the meetings. This was not the most convenient room for the purpose. I myself always seemed to be behind a pillar. Now that the music, so beautifully played by Rosemary Nott, became familiar, all the musicians in the Group, Mr Squire (senior), Miss Marjorie Gordon, Mrs Parsons and Miss Stalker, were able to reconstruct it, as they foregathered after the sessions.

By the time that Tyeponds was completed we found that it was not large enough to accommodate the increasing numbers who were now assembling at the week-ends. The senior members of the Group considered the situation and it was decided that a further house should be erected by a builder who would be asked to work at the utmost possible speed. Funds were raised among the Committee. The new house was built at right angles to Tyeponds – not joined. The space between was reserved for a studio which we later built ourselves; it was not urgently needed and it provided further work for those who had not shared in the construction of Tyeponds. The new house contained one very large room extending over the whole of the ground floor which gave us space enough for the Movements to be performed and for displays of acting and for dancing at parties, and for a meeting of the whole group. Upstairs there were a dozen or so small bedrooms and one central music room with a bay window looking down on to the garden enclosed now on two sides, the pool being outside the main door. Each room contained its own radiator. The house was built very rapidly. It was interesting for us to watch professional builders at work, but they did not work for the most part during the week-ends when we were there. The house was very attractive, in particular the floor surfaces surpassed the rough boards in Tyeponds, but we had more affection for the original building which preserved marks of the being of all who had worked on it. I know that my eye was attracted constantly to an inept bit of plastering in the bathroom that seemed to be a part of me. A grand piano, the property of one of the group, was now installed at one end of the large room, and it became our custom to go over there on Saturdays late in the evening when we had talked for a while at dinner. Mrs Currie taught the Movements.

Mr Bush had a Parsee friend, Mr Pagose, who was instructor in ju-jitsu to the Police. Dr Nicoll arranged for him to come down with Mr Bush on several Sundays to teach us ju-jitsu. We were lined up in rows facing one another – I remember that we were out of doors. What we appreciated most were the demonstrations given by this thin, lithe instructor who with a minimum of effort seemed able to throw Mr Bush who at that time must have weighed twenty stone. The art of ju-jitsu, Dr Nicoll said, when we talked about the demonstrations afterwards, bears upon this – 'to conquer by yielding', which means that recognition of one's opponent's intentions enables one, instead of resisting, to lend force to and thereby unbalance him and make ridiculous his effort. Dr Nicoll said that this was an illustration of what should happen in us psychologically. 'It is not by resisting but by recognition that one conquers. Freedom from certain desires in oneself is obtained not by fighting against them so much as by observing them, by expressing in words the peculiar antics they induced – thereby loosening their grip of one.'

Meanwhile the four meetings in London during the week continued. I went to one of them only, but small sub-groups now used to meet fortnightly without Dr Nicoll under the direction of the senior members of the group where it was possible to discuss more freely.

Occasionally a number of us were invited to Warwick Gardens to a meeting taken by Ouspensky. The setting for such meetings was as Mr Kenneth Walker describes it in *Venture with Ideas*. We were in great awe of Ouspensky but he always answered us very kindly and smiled benignly once or twice. In the earlier days of the group I heard that Ouspensky sometimes came to take Dr Nicoll's meeting for him, and it was Dr Nicoll then who was more nervous than his pupils as he was presumably hoping that Ouspensky would think that they were not completely foolish, and was doubtful of the impression that they would make.

Sometimes after the meetings at Finchley Road, Dr and Mrs Nicoll would take a party to the Café Royal where we would talk until late. It was interesting to see the change in him when he relaxed into being a genial host.

A day came when Dr Nicoll asked me if I would like to type and handle some short stories for him. I was delighted to do this. Some of them were already typed and corrected. I re-typed these and started on those that were still in his handwriting. And now it was that I experienced a curious feeling of familiarity as I typed from this most original handwriting. I suppose it was then that my destiny as Dr Nicoll's future secretary was confirmed. Members of the group told me afterwards that no one so far had deciphered his writing. His American secretary who was now working with him at his flat wrote only from dictation. His literary agents had no success in placing any of these stories which were startling in their originality. Soon Dr Nicoll began to give me other MSS. to type for him. He would ring up early in the morning and say 'Casa Prada, seven', and that would mean that

I would dine with him before the eight-thirty meeting. He would talk very freely to me of all the things that he wanted to write.

In June 1938 Professor Sigmund Freud was forced to leave Vienna. He came to London with six of his analysts who were all well received by the Freudian psychologists. I was rung up one day and asked if I would undertake to teach English to some of the analysts and assist them with the translation of their articles. I saw them all and arranged to have three of them as pupils. Through conversation with them I began to acquire some knowledge of the Freudian methods which I found extremely interesting, especially as I had by now sufficient knowledge of Ouspensky's System to contrast them. I was amazed to find that Freudian psycho-analysis seemed to leave the patient at the end with no inner contact, and for the first time became aware of the vast gulf between this psychology and the system that I was studying. The analysts themselves were charming people, completely sincere, devoted to Freud himself, and convinced of their vocation. Several were doctors. I began to enjoy the companionship of the woman among them, Mrs Hoffer, who was widely read. I had revisited Germany the previous year, and had spent some time in Weimar, renewing my early love of Goethe, whom I had come to recognize as a deep student of esotericism, and Dr Nicoll had urged me to read his 'Letters to Zelter' which we discussed sometimes.

The Munich Crisis of 1938 cast its shadow, and Dr Nicoll was at that time dwelling on the possibility of war with Germany and making plans for such an eventuality. His American secretary returned to the U.S.A. In the early summer of 1939 he rang me up one morning and said 'Go to the British Museum and give me a picture of December 1913 from the newspapers and periodicals.' I found that all newspapers were now housed at Colindale. There I made notes from the press of the period – of the events and fashions of the day. These notes were to form the background of the novel that he had in mind to write, which was afterwards called *Pelican Hotel*, but not completed. He had been thinking over the possibility of preventing war, and devised as the framework of this novel a return from the future (1939) to the past (1913) with memory of the future.

We had long discussions about the inadequacy of memory after seeing how little we remembered of the events of the period which he wished to make the background of his novel. However, fortunately there was the evidence of the newspapers for the main events. Dr Nicoll made great efforts to recall small personal details about himself at the time, and gradually built up a picture of himself to represent the character called Gregory Nixon who was to play the part of a messenger from the future to the past, from 1939 to 1913, who vainly attempts to stop the coming war. The opening sentence describes Dr Nicoll as he was on a June morning in 1939:

> I was walking across Regent's Park on a misty beautiful morning in early June in the year 1939. The sweet smell of new-mown grass hung in the air. The lawn-cutters were at work. The clock on the Pavilion pointed to ten o'clock. The sound of chiming bells came from the concrete tower beyond the trees by Baker Street Station. I fell into a reverie.

Gregory Nixon's awakening into his past on a snowy December day in the year 1913 is described as a series of shocks, for the discoveries of his situation are made in the light of the mature mind of a man of fifty-five with his memory as it was in 1939. These minor shocks culminated in the thought: 'Was it conceivable that I had come back in time for a certain purpose – *to stop the war?*'

Nixon's efforts to stop the war of 1914 were to be the subject of the novel. Dr Nicoll's mind was dwelling on the new war that had seemed to him to be imminent since the Munich Crisis of 1938. This exercise of ingenuity in working out how far it was possible to change events was a means of releasing him from such thoughts. He was well prepared for the war when it came. The following description of Gregory Nixon's thoughts was, I think an echo of his own:

> The people eating in the restaurant were just ordinary decent people who, like people in a railway carriage, travel comfortably along, unaware of the catastrophe ahead, people who perhaps sometimes discussed its possibility, but did not,

like me, know its reality. For no matter what we may say, the life of the future is never a true experience, an absolute fact . . . so, although we know we must all die, the reality of it is not grasped. The humdrum mind is incapable of it. But sitting there, the reality of the future was greater to me than that of the present.

In this manner Dr Nicoll was writing on the eve of the Second World War.

CHAPTER EIGHT

Outbreak of War 1939 — Move to Birdlip 1940

In August Dr Nicoll went on holiday to Veule les Roses in Normandy with his family, Mrs Humphrey Butler, Mme Kadloubovsky, who was Ouspensky's secretary, and John Mounsey, an artist, who was later to become his son-in-law. This was the kind of holiday that he loved. I remember driving into Braintree with him to buy paints the day before he left. Anticipation of the pleasures that France always offered to him, the restaurant life, the language, café-scenes as subjects to paint, seemed to have made the shadow of war recede for a moment.

Ten days after his departure ominous rumblings of war were heard. We all received brief messages from Dr Nicoll directing us to go down to the Farm. I had gone down on Saturday for the week-end as usual. The weather was perfect. Colonel Maffett and his wife and children were there and he had already organized the digging of a trench. He was just the man for it, a Gunner, in his element in such an emergency, and thanks to his skilled direction it was completed. Various people joined us and we waited for the return of the Nicolls, who just managed to get their car across the Channel in time on the last ship. They told us that Mrs Butler had received a telegram from her husband, Colonel Humphrey Butler, the previous evening at dinner, urging the immediate return of the party to England.

What Dr Nicoll had anticipated for a long time had happened at last. He had always intended the Farm to be a place of refuge. He now sent out messages to all in the Group that anyone might come to the Farm to take refuge from the expected bombing of London. We all thought that London would be bombed immediately. Friends came down in crowds and we found room for them all. Some brought their babies, others their dogs. Some came laden, feeling that they had left their homes for ever; others brought no possessions.

We organized night watches and paced the garden in twos for two hours at a time each. I have a vivid memory of pacing up and down with Mrs Taylor looking at the stars as we talked in low voices, almost wishing that something would happen while we were on watch.

War was declared on Sunday 3rd September. Early that morning there had been an air-raid warning at about seven o'clock. Jane and a young schoolboy, Peter Riley, were on watch, as we had allotted the early morning watch to them while the grown-ups had undertaken the night watches. They gave the alarm most promptly. They were very efficient, ringing bells, banging on the doors, calling everyone. We all rushed down to the trench, several people carrying their dogs, one or two of which caused rather a disturbance. It was very strange in the crowded trench. We all felt we were in danger and expected the bombers to arrive at any moment. After a while we heard aeroplanes overhead, which of course we thought were the German bombers speeding towards London, and all our feelings then went into anxiety about our friends and relatives in London. Many of the women had left their husbands in London. At last the All Clear went and we came out into the early morning sunshine and had a wonderful breakfast in the open air of coffee and hot bacon sandwiches, which two people prepared very rapidly. I remember the fresh-ness of that morning. Afterwards, of course, we found that it had been a false alarm! We had heard our own aeroplanes.

At eleven o'clock we heard the voice of Mr Chamberlain over the radio saying 'A state of war exists between England and Ger-many.' It is interesting to recall that the Ouspensky Group at Virginia Water were having a similar experience on that eventful Sunday morning. The air-raid warning went for them later in the day (I think it was soon after eleven o'clock) and the children hurried down to the basement room prepared as an air-raid shelter. Mr Kenneth Walker was reminded of the day fifteen years previously, when Dr Nicoll had told him of Gurdjieff's prophecy that there was a war ahead in which much that humanity had built up would fall in ruins, and had spoken of the Group as forming an Ark in the event of another Flood. At Lyne Court, as at Rayne, arrangements had been made for those who lived in London to come down to the country, and stores had been accumulated for this purpose.

Dr Nicoll now asked me whether I would stay at Tyeponds

permanently and work for him as his secretary. I had never anticipated this beforehand, but that moment had an eternal quality, and I knew that this was what I really wanted. I recall only one other sentence of our conversation: 'You'll have to learn to forge my signature, you know.' I worked with him from the outbreak of the war in 1939 until his death at the same time of year in 1953, a period of fourteen years.

A strange period followed – three weeks of golden September, the loveliest weather of the year, and evacuees came pouring in. We were allotted a great number, in spite of the fact that all our bedrooms were already filled with our own group and their children. The large and pleasant music-room housed seven school-children: the carpentry shed housed thirteen expectant mothers and mothers with children. The washing hung in never-ending lines. Dr Nicoll received all his guests into the warmth of his heart, and spent all his available money on buying necessities for them, perambulators, stoves – everything that was needed – and he spent a great deal on having a second trench dug for them, as there was no further room in the one we already had. This was for him a time of fulfilment as he felt that Tyeponds had come into its own.

We now organized a complicated time-table of duties. There was so much to do, so much cooking and so much care of the children and so on, that the duties had to be divided up amongst us. I was rather relieved not to be put in charge of the school-children. This fell to Miss Wadham who seemed to take naturally to dosing them and looking after their clothes and so on, while Miss Lance seemed to delight in bathing them. I felt that I was fortunate to be occupied with secretarial work, which left little time for domestic duties. However, such things as washing-up were done for two or three days at a time by all of us on a rota. The numbers were extraordinary. I think at this point our numbers had reached fifty and the washing up seemed to be endless!

We were soon able to arrange for the children to attend the village school and they went off down the lane each morning, returning home about half past four, hoping for fish and chips, and being continually disappointed. The expectant mothers and mothers with young children soon became very restless and discontented and in a few weeks' time arrangements were made for them to move on to Frinton. They felt lost, finding themselves marooned in the country several miles from the nearest shop. Moreover they did have certain discomforts, for the carpenter's shed where they were housed had no floor – you stood on the bare ground – and they had only oil-stoves for cooking. They were really crowded together on camp beds in a limited space. Dr Nicoll himself was relieved when the expectant mothers had gone because he had no wish to be called upon in a medical capacity! One mother remained, Mrs Stidston, with her child, and she afterwards spent the whole winter with us. Dr Nicoll bought her a fine perambulator. The children also became discontented and asked to be taken away and by November we were left with only three, who stayed for the winter.

We now concentrated on group work at the week-ends, as we had done before the war broke out. As many people as possible would come down on Friday night or Saturday morning and we would have meetings and talks over dinner and the Movements, followed by further talks and music continuing late into the night. Now that our numbers had become smaller during the week Dr Nicoll was able to continue his writing which the outbreak of war had interrupted. He wrote many experimental chapters of a book, to which he continually wrote new beginnings, on the subject of regeneration. He was seeking a way of writing for the public which should convey to those who could understand some of his thoughts about the teaching of Christ. He wrote the first chapter on the Lord's Prayer which was afterwards published posthumously in *The Mark*. I remember reading this chapter aloud to the Group – it was a new and wonderful experience for us to have this first Gospel interpretation. Dr Nicoll was also able to return to his novel *Pelican Hotel*, on which he had been at work before his holiday.

As London appeared to be free from raids, certain people who had been returning from their City offices to Essex to sleep every night now went back to their homes. Dr Nicoll himself went up to town occasionally to take meetings. It was very interesting to compare the group work that now became necessary after the outbreak of the war with the previous work at the Farm. Before the war certain difficulties had been created for people to work on, but once the evacuees had come down, it was no longer necessary to create difficulties. Circumstances increased our difficulties day by day. There was the question of overcrowding, muddle, complaints to see to, extra work.

During the week there were now only four of us in residence at Tyeponds: Miss Wadham, Miss Demery, Miss Lance and myself. Mr and Mrs Currie were at their cottage across the fields and Miss Powell in her house nearby, Dr and Mrs Nicoll and Jane, and John Mounsey at Lakes Farm. Miss Wadham undertook the care of all the oil-lamps and stoves, of which there were a terrific number, occupying her the whole morning in trimming wicks and cleaning, refilling lamps and stoves, which she did very patiently. Those of us who were younger took it in turns to rise early. We would descend to the kitchen and light the oil-stoves and boil kettles, which took rather a long time. Then we would light the boiler and the kitchen fire. By that time the kettles would have boiled and we would journey around the buildings with morning tea. On our return to the kitchen, the next job was to prepare breakfast. At this point it was possible to begin to enjoy oneself, provided that the fire was flickering gaily, as the kitchen then began to look very cheerful and it was quite a pleasure to make coffee and cook bacon and eggs and make toast. Whoever had prepared the breakfast was then free from domestic work for the rest of the day: someone else would prepare luncheon, and so on. In the end it worked out that we each prepared one meal a day, and the rest of the time was devoted to our own special jobs. Mrs Currie came over from her cottage each day and shared the cooking. Her husband was now working in London again.

My own room was in the west wing. I had painted all the furniture and the bed buttercup yellow. I had a view of wide flat fields and the sunset, which was a pleasure to watch after tea on those wintry days. Miss Moxon who was a Cordon Bleu cook, began to come over from Little Saling once a week in the afternoon to give us cooking demonstrations. These we enjoyed very much. We were amazed at her spotlessness. After cooking for an hour, she never seemed to have a hair out of place. We would have long talks after dinner and sometimes Dr Nicoll would play his guitar. We all played various musical instruments. I remember that I began to play a recorder and also tried the concertina, but did not get very far with either. Miss Wilshin held classes in miming and drama. One of our week-end activities was to learn the Morse Code. I remember the day when at last I knew it perfectly and was hoping to acquit myself well, but found that the lessons were to be discontinued. This was always what happened when we learnt anything new, as an exercise; it ended when we were beginning to enjoy being proficient.

Mrs Nicoll suggested that we spend one afternoon a week in religious discussion with her, and this proved to be a source of pleasure to us all as we studied passages in the New Testament and attempted to link the ideas with those of the System.

Mrs Sandheim had brought down some pullets in the late summer. They began to look very woebegone. She herself was now with us only at the week-ends and during the week they were fed by anyone who remembered. She suggested that I should take charge of them, and I reluctantly agreed to feed those unattractive birds regularly. Then an extraordinary thing happened. I began to be fond of them. And they began to flourish – they filled out and lost their woebegone look. Soon Dr Nicoll began to take an interest in them, and he suggested that they should be moved to pleasanter quarters nearer the house, so the move was scheduled as a job for the men. This made the chickens more easily accessible as the winter was coming on. Shortly afterwards I found that a herd of bullocks had broken into the hen run from a nearby field and I had to chase them round and round the hen-house before I could get them out of the enclosure. They left behind them a battered hen-house, and the chickens suffered from nervous prostration. When at last they recovered, they began to lay.

I remember that there were many weeks of snow, when the fields looked very beautiful all around us and the bare trees sparkled. I remember getting up in the dark to light oil-stoves and so on. This was the external life, but always there was a double life. There was my work with Dr Nicoll who continued his writing. He was interested in the subject of transformation and wrote about it from many different angles. He continued his study of the New Testament. We continued the novel *Pelican Hotel* which was a source of great amusement to both of us and he produced a new chapter nearly every week. I had to insert the French conversation. All the time he felt a sense of foreboding as to what was to come. He knew that the real war was ahead of us. I remember being perfectly content to live in the present. I was simply happy to be living in that community. In the spring Nancy Lance married John Edwards and Marjorie Demery married Bill Hodder. John Mounsey who had stayed with us for many months, and had become part of the household, now became engaged to Jane and we prepared for their wedding, which was to be on 26th May at Rayne Parish Church. The weather became glorious and all our friends, all the group, assembled for the wedding, which took place on a Sunday. I remember all the preparations that morning. After the wedding, a photograph of us all was taken in the garden of Lakes Farm. This was the last occasion for a very long time on which we were all to be assembled together. In the evening, Jane and John went off in a car for their honeymoon. We then gathered together to discuss some news that had been brought to us by Colonel Butler that morning. He had had warning that Lakes Farm and Tyeponds were to be taken over by the Military at twenty-four hours' notice because the area in which we were living was now to become a military zone, being on the expected invasion route. This was a great shock. It meant that we had to move the whole household immediately, and to take as many of our possessions as possible. However, we had to find somewhere to go, and after trunk calls had been put through it was eventually arranged that Dr Nicoll should rent a furnished house in the Cotswolds, which a member of the group had found for us in response to our telephone call.

The extraordinary difference between the morning and the evening of that day is unforgettable. In the morning we were preparing for Jane's wedding. In the evening we were facing a new life, having been turned out of our home, and we felt very deeply for Dr and Mrs Nicoll, who had put so much effort into this place. However, they worked with their usual rapidity. We all had our instructions about the packing next day. We got up early in the morning and packed what was necessary, bundling our things into great sheets and blankets. We had been able to get one van, so we took as much as there was room for. Mrs Nicoll felt that it was essential to take as many sheets and blankets as possible, for wherever we were we would want to be able to put up members of the group. We took also silver, cutlery, kitchen utensils, and a certain number of our provisions, for we had great stores which had been laid in as we had such numbers to feed. By evening the van was packed and we all went off to London to stay in different places with friends to be ready for the journey the next day.

The following day, Tuesday 28th May 1940, I went by train to Gloucestershire with Miss Wadham and Mrs Currie. The journey was a strange interim of a few hours, dividing one phase of life from the phase that had preceded it. We had left many of our possessions at the Farm and little knew that we should never see them again. Perhaps it was as well that we did not know that the Farm would never again be the Headquarters of the Work or our home. I was only to revisit it once in the future, on a grey day when we drove over from Ugley where we had moved five years later, to pick apples when the place was empty and derelict. On this glorious summer's day we arrived at Stroud Station and drove in a hired car to Birdlip where we spent the night at the 'Royal George', comfortably enough, a place that was going to be very important to us in the next few years. Dr and Mrs Nicoll had driven to Birdlip from their flat, taking Mrs Hodder with them. There was not an inch of room to spare in the car – Mrs Nicoll was completely hidden by an ironing board, wireless, etc., and Mrs Hodder had to wind her legs around a large drum which they thought would be useful for storing oil. We heard that Dr Nicoll had been very quiet, but took great interest in the journey, and enjoyed a good lunch in a large hotel at High Wycombe, where they had the dining-room to themselves. They arrived at The Knapp in brilliant sunshine, and Mrs Nicoll was much impressed with the vivid red peonies in the garden – she said we must try to remember this first impression as later it would be clouded through associations. When we walked down the hill to The Knapp the following morning we found that they had unpacked and were already installed. The house which had been taken furnished had been built in the late Victorian period, with gables, set back from the road at the place where Birdlip Hill at its steepest point turns slightly to the left. The terrace in front of the house had a wonderful view of the Vale of Gloucester, and the garden extended along the hillside and also sloped upwards behind the house, rising to a plateau set in woods. But at first we had no eyes for the garden. That first morning we roamed through the house, looking at the rooms that had been allotted to us. Dr Nicoll had chosen the dining-room for himself because it had a conservatory attached to it which gave him a private entrance. (It was a private means of exit rather than entrance that he liked to have when he wished to escape from the conversation.) He always liked to be on the ground floor. It was extraordinary how the Edwardian dining-room with its mahogany furniture, which gave so absolutely an impression of being a dining-room and nothing else, was transformed in a moment into a study, where the furniture was soon almost invisible under a litter of books and papers.

Mrs Nicoll had chosen a pleasant room above the dining-room facing the valley. I was given a small room at the other end of the house on the first floor overlooking the vegetable garden. Its simplicity reminded me somewhat of my room in Essex and I was pleased with it. Our sympathy however was with Miss Wadham who as the eldest of the party was given the large drawing-room which had a very pleasant bay window looking out on to the garden but was so full of furniture that it was difficult to thread one's way through to reach the window. Each time anyone walked firmly across the room, to our dismay one or other of the brass cranes from Burma collapsed with a great jangle. For the first few days we used to put the fallen birds together and stand them up again but time soon became too short for this, so we removed them to a quiet place where they could be undisturbed. We felt quite lost for a time in this strange house full of furniture and ornaments from foreign parts after the simplicity of our thatched home with its spacious almost bare rooms which had a certain austere beauty. We gradually unpacked our possessions and adjusted ourselves to our new environment. We made the oblong-shaped hall into our sitting-room as we were expecting quite a large party and had to reserve most of the rooms for people to sleep in. It was an odd room to sit in. We always called it the tram as the shape of the room obliged us to sit in two rows facing one another – not the best arrangement for informal conversation.

My most vivid memory of those first days in Gloucestershire is of the scent of hawthorn in the lanes, and of the golden beauty of the buttercup fields stretching out below the woods. It was the most enchanting weather that formed a background to our sadness, just as the outbreak of the war in the previous September remained always in the memory set in the glowing sunshine that we had longed for all the previous summer. In the garden we were able to pick sweet peas and there was promise of strawberries and a wealth of young vegetables to come. We wore cotton frocks the next day, when Dr Nicoll drove us in to Cheltenham to discover shops, banks, and libraries. It was strange to be walking along the elegant parade, where there were no signs of war, to see women strolling by in a leisurely way in pretty summer frocks, and to have ices in a café, after living in the depths of the country for so long.

We soon had a visitor. Mrs Maffett drove up on our first afternoon having discovered where we had gone. She had been to see her daughter Ann at Cheltenham College. We were pleased to see a familiar face so soon after our arrival. Our second visitor was Mrs Hicks-Beach who came up from her house down the hill to warn us that there were adders in the garden. This news was a shock and for a time we walked warily in the long grass, but soon forgot about this warning until the summer of 1942 when Miss Corcoran actually was bitten by an adder.

I had packed a number of Dr Nicoll's books, all that were indispensable, every version of the Bible, all the volumes of Swedenborg, the Hermetica, Plato, and all notebooks and manuscripts. But it was clear that writing was impossible at present. All his thoughts were for his scattered people. He began at once to explore the village to look for a house that could be a refuge for mothers in the group who had young children. Meanwhile the news of the German invasion of France and her capitulation came through, and he felt this deeply. He had always a great love of France and mourned the loss of her spirit. The Dunkirk evacuation took place and soon survivors began to arrive in the village. Dr Nicoll talked to some R.A. men who had swum out to a destroyer and got back to England. The national shock absorbed into itself some of the personal shock which he had suffered in having to leave the Farm at a moment's notice. He admired the simple, uncritical way in which these men talked of their experiences, blaming no one, praising the courage of the Scottish Regiments, and the French Infantry, saying that it was a question not of men but of aeroplanes, for the German Air Force was terrific. Dr Nicoll lived through all their set-backs and sufferings, knowing from his own experience at Gallipoli what it was like to be on a beach under fire. He spent many hours at the 'Royal George' in conversation with these men, and it was after such talks that he conceived the idea of writing a diary commenting on the War, which he continued until 1943. He used to write this diary every few days, generally at night.

By this time various friends had joined us at The Knapp. Mrs Butler came with her two dogs, the poodle and Shan, the blue Chow with Chinese-looking eyes, and she brought with her two faithful servants, Barrow, her butler-chauffeur, and Edith, her housemaid, who were a great asset to our household and soon endeared themselves to us all. Jane and John returned from their honeymoon. The bombing in London was now becoming serious, and Miss Corcoran came down. As The Knapp was now full, Dr Nicoll rented the King's Head, a roomy stone house which had once been an inn, opposite the 'Royal George', in order to house those of the group who had young children or who had lost their homes. Mothers with their children soon arrived. Eventually all those who could get away from London at the week-ends undertook the long journey in order to have a night or two of peaceful sleep. The real reason however why people came was to see Dr Nicoll, and it was not long before most of the group had managed somehow to come down to what was now our new Headquarters. I quote a letter written by Dr Nicoll to Mrs Syfret, whose husband was at sea:

I hope you are reasonably all right. I can only say that

down here you have a place of retreat if necessary, and if
circumstances are severe you will know that we all have to
live a very communal existence, but this part is on the whole
probably safer than other spots although we have air-raid
warnings and are near an aerodrome. I only write to you to
keep in touch with you and make you aware that we have
prepared a place for our people.

God bless you. Give my love to your husband when you
see him and remember that nothing in life is very important.
What is important is the way one takes it.

Jane is with us and her husband who is shortly to be
called up.

Yours.

M. N.

In such a manner he would write to those who were at a distance
from us, assuring them of his thought for their welfare and of the
continuity of their contact with him.

One day in late July there was gunfire during lunch, whereupon we rushed out to the terrace and were diverted to see the
smoke-rings high up in the sky. From the terrace we had a good
view of the Nazi raider pursuing his way round Gloucester, the
shells always just missing his tail, until he finally disappeared in
the direction of Bristol. Our barrage balloons took nine minutes
to get into their places in the sky. One of them, apparently hit by
anti-aircraft fire, fell ignominiously, looking most pathetic with
the stuffing pricked out of him. We thought at first that it was our
own pet reservoir balloon, but no – it was his fellow from the
hill beyond. We were interested to be able to trace the planes by
the vapour trails that they left in the sky. We soon identified
another, and as it passed over the house we hid in the air-raid
shelter. A baby owl, perched on the telegraph wire in the hayfield
next to us, was a silent and unperturbed witness of the proceedings.
When it flew away we gathered that the show was over and went
indoors. We heard afterwards that a plane had been brought down
nearby having dropped four bombs a mile away.

John Mounsey joined up and Jane would at intervals go to
visit him wherever he was stationed. Tanks would now some-

times pass in procession down Birdlip Hill. Beer ran short. Smokers began to adopt the fashion of rolling their cigarettes. Our daily correspondence at this time began to contain interesting anecdotes of our friends' experiences during air-raids. Miss Keane wrote of her descent to a cellar accompanied by her dentist after the warning had sounded as she sat down in the dental chair. The cellar was well equipped with magazines, as one might expect, and she had the unusual experience of seeing the dentists and doctors who had their consulting-rooms in the house, each filing in with his victim, one patient causing her medical adviser some discomfort through her irrepressible tendency to talk about her symptoms.

Another correspondent wrote that, hearing the sirens announcing the first air-raid of her experience, she had collected everything necessary for a night in a shelter and marshalled her family downstairs, slamming the front door after her as they went out, only to find that she had forgotten both the key of the front door and the key of the shelter. Unable to go back or forward they all perforce spent the period of the air-raid sitting on the steps in the open, reading their books, until the All Clear sounded, whereupon they broke a window in order to return.

Our daily life gradually settled down into a kind of temporary routine. Miss Wadham was given a room on the first floor instead of the drawing-room where she had not been very much at ease. All jingling brass had been put away in an empty locked room to which a neighbour had the key, and which she solemnly opened for us to store away what we felt was superfluous and then locked up again. So we made the pleasant sunny room, which was now quite spacious, our main sitting-room and later used even to have breakfast at its round table. For the time being it seemed that we had become a family rather than a group. Breakfast became a family meal, Dr and Mrs Nicoll both being present, and we opened our letters and exchanged news of all the scattered members of the group. From the bay window we had a view of the valley which had been transformed by the addition of the network of barrage balloons, which became a very familiar sight during the years to follow as we watched them going up and down. In the spring of 1957 I was driving down Birdlip Hill, past The

Knapp, now unoccupied and neglected, which I had not seen for twelve years, and became aware that there was something missing in the lovely Vale of Gloucester. It was, of course, the barrage balloons, whose very existence I had forgotten. Dr Nicoll had done a very delightful painting of them.

In the autumn of 1940, Dr and Mrs Nicoll, Jane, Mrs Butler, Miss Wadham, Mrs Currie, Miss Corcoran, Mrs Hodder and myself were the Knapp-dwellers, and Barrow and Edith looked after us with the greatest devotion, the former being cheered up whenever Colonel Butler arrived for the week-end which gave him the opportunity of polishing his boots and his belt for hours on end. Miss Corcoran took over the cooking, and we, the other women, deputized for her on occasion. Dr Nicoll insisted on washing up after breakfast. He had his own method. He would use neither soap nor detergent, maintaining that traces of it always remained on the silver and cups, causing indigestion. Greasy plates were re-washed after he had left the scullery.

We soon joined the local W.V.S. and used to go up the hill to afternoon meetings in Birdlip Village. Twice a week Miss Corcoran drove Dr Nicoll's car into Cheltenham to buy dog's meat of which a great quantity was needed. I often went with her so that I could visit the various libraries in the town in order to bring home detective stories for Dr Nicoll, of which he liked to read about half a dozen a week. I therefore had to bring about six at a time because of course they were not all readable. He very much enjoyed a good detective story and would tell us about the plots. He liked Sherlock Holmes above all and read all the Sherlock Holmes stories many times. When we acted charades he would like to play the part of Holmes in his cloak and deer-stalker cap. He could not read novels at this stage in his life, but liked books of travel and biography, and we shared all his reading, as he often entertained us by discussing points of interest at meals. Mrs Butler drove Mrs Nicoll in her car to do the household shopping. She turned out to be the best shopper of all, and we owed much to her later on when things became scarce because she had a flair for finding what we needed. She also brought an air of frivolity into everything that she did, even the household shopping, so that unexpected, exciting things were found among the necessities.

Miss Wadham soon began to occupy herself, as she had done at the Farm, in preparing canvasses and completing her stocks of painting materials so that when people were able to join us at the week-ends they were able to continue their artistic activities. She always had the necessary tool or brush and when anything needed to be mended she produced the seccotine and made a neat job of it. I soon found myself involved with the care of the ration books and made many visits to the Food Office. The roses in the garden were a great joy to us and Dr Nicoll never tired of painting them. Painting was his solace at this time. He was unable to continue his novel *Pelican Hotel*, which never was finished, in spite of all requests. The current had been cut by the shock of having to leave the Farm and his work there. His speculations about the possibility of preventing war had been cut short by the shock of reality.

Sometimes we received news of the Farm from Miss Powell who had stayed on in her house nearby. She had heard rumours from the village of much damage done to the furniture and of the ruin caused in the garden by the lorries that drove over flower beds and rockery. A detachment of the R.A.S.C. was quartered there. A correspondence with the War Office began which was to drag on for years about the amount of rent and compensation for damage which was to be paid. Mrs Currie was asked to take charge of the King's Head, which she did with considerable efficiency until the end of the war.

People in the group who had had to remain in London or in another danger area because of their work had said good-bye in much desolation on that Sunday evening after Jane's wedding, thinking that Dr and Mrs Nicoll were going away out of reach and they were being deserted. Yet in his practical wisdom Dr Nicoll knew that once the Farm was no longer available as our Headquarters it was expedient to find a place that was remote enough to be undisturbed by requisitioning or bombing. And his intuition was unerring, as always. Within an incredibly short time I had notified all the scattered members of the group that Dr Nicoll was continuing his teaching of the System at Birdlip and that all who could get there at the week-ends would be housed. At once people began to find their way to us. The London people came and rejoiced in one or two nights of quiet sleep at the King's Head after many nights in shelters or on duty in air raids. They returned refreshed by the meetings and talks that we all had – sometimes also by the gaiety of acting and of music when Dr Nicoll would play his guitar and we would sing. It was necessary to have these gay evenings after the meetings so that energy could be released. One week-end Dr Nicoll's old friend, the surgeon, Mr Kenneth Walker, came down. He proved to be admirable at charades, and organized the most wonderful operation act that I have ever seen done by amateurs, cutting up the patient, Mrs Butler, with a carving knife, with a large circle of anaesthetists and theatre sisters in attendance.

The meetings went on as they had done at the Farm. Mr Bush had remained at his post in London as an air-raid warden. He now wrote to ask Dr Nicoll's permission to hold meetings for all who could manage to come to his house. So, after a long interval, Redcliffe Gardens once again became the London Headquarters of the Group, and those who worked in London were thankful for this central meeting-place, where they used to assemble to begin with on Saturday afternoons. One result of these London meetings was that Mr Bush began to send to Dr Nicoll questions that had arisen during the discussions. A detailed reply would be sent to London for the next meeting.

Early in 1941 we had the idea of making a letter from Dr Nicoll to Mr Bush in reply to a question the subject of the week-end meeting to be discussed by the group at Birdlip before it was sent out so that it might be reinforced by the thoughts from us that it had attracted. Thus the Birdlip and London meetings became parallel. This arrangement worked very well, and I began to type a number of copies of each paper to send out to some of the scattered people who were stationed in remote places and unable to visit us, so that, gradually, the group became linked up. Dr Nicoll would now write a paper every week, generally on Friday evening. This he did for the rest of his life. The weekly papers were published many years later, but at the time they were written the System of Gurdjieff had to remain esoteric and the papers were of necessity kept within the group. Dr Nicoll soon began to call them Commentaries on the basic ideas of the teaching. They were indeed practical observations, comments on

9. After Fontainebleau, with Jane

10. The Old Manse, Lumsden

11. Bay Tree Lodge

our daily life, in relation to the System within the discipline of which we lived.

Two long letters to Mr Bush on the subject of Man's awakening from sleep were followed by a paper called 'The Fourth Way', in which Dr Nicoll answered once and for all those people who were still expressing regret at leaving the Farm.

He wrote:

This Fourth Way is not romantic, and it is no use having romantic feelings about the Farm in Essex. This Fourth Way is quite ruthless and as soon as something is finished – that is, gives no longer any real value, it is abandoned. By this I do not mean that we cannot go back to the Farm, but that this is a great chance for everyone to adjust himself to the external form and physical situation of the Work at the moment. This applies equally to those who cannot come here and to those who can.

I would be very glad if you would all try to understand what I mean because it is important to draw attention to this point owing to the fact that so often everyone begins to 'settle down' after a time into some form of the Fourth Way work which he thinks is going to go on and on just like that. Unfortunately, such mental and emotional habits can be formed.

I once said to G.: 'Why don't you build more solidly?' (we were building a theatre). He said: 'This is only temporary. In a very short time everything will be different. Everyone will be elsewhere. Nothing can be built permanently at this moment.' So it is necessary for everybody to understand in a way what this means. Many times G. had no work 'externally' – that is, no place, no habitation. Everything seemed to have been dissolved away and from the external or sensory point of view to have vanished, yet, as you know, the Work went on and was finally transmitted to this country, and yet this had nothing to do with the external form of the Work, with the actual house or situation and so on, and in view of what G. told me privately, I fancy that we can have no permanent home for the Work and that we shall have to adjust ourselves to every kind of situation in the future. But all of you who have heard the teaching over a sufficient time should be able now to be quite tranquil about change in the external form or the external demands of the Work and to relate yourselves instantly to them from the Work point of view. The trouble is that things become mechanical and it is necessary for a shock to be given so that things are no longer quite mechanical. But the Work continues in the same way and speaks with the same voice and gives the same force to those who acknowledge and practise it.

I must add that the centre of gravity of this talk to you lies in the meaning of what is called the Fourth Way. We are not Fakirs holding out our arms year after year; we are not Monks living in monasteries; we are not Yogis going to remote schools or sitting and meditating in caves in the Himalayas. We belong to what is called the Fourth Way which is right down in life. So we have to work in the midst of life, surrounded by all the misfortunes of life, and eventually life becomes our teacher.

CHAPTER NINE
Extracts from War Diary

The following extracts from Dr Nicoll's Diary contain some of his thoughts about the war, comments on his reading and impressions of our daily life in Birdlip.

June 8th 1940

I talked to R.A. men evacuated from Dunquerque. They came in a Destroyer, swam out to it. Said French were afraid of bombing planes. Hid in holes and said British Tommies lay on their backs firing with rifles at them and brought several of them down. All complain: 'No British planes'. (Churchill explained in the House that the R.A.F. were fighting at other points and high up in the air, attacking the German fighters accompanying bombers.) They said they could have held the Germans if Belgium had not 'gone all bloody'. They said the Scottish troops, Camerons, Seaforths, Black Watch, Gordons, took no prisoners – i.e. they killed them all. 'They were terrible.' They held on to every point, every house, every village. They said they blew up their own guns with a grenade in the breech. All say German Air Force is terrific. This is what our Munich folk never grasped, although the country did. They are a strong-looking lot, drink little and seem to share a common strong brotherhood of feeling. All talked very sensibly and gravely. They said it wasn't a question of men yet but of aeroplanes. They criticized no one. They had little to eat and nothing hardly to drink. Could not drink Belgian water. Scraped holes in sand. All said Navy marvellous. German 5th Column misdirected the B.E.F. at all points, down roads leading to Germans. They were ordered to ask for Identity Cards of people asked to direct them. All say the French infantry wonderful fighters when they get going. Have good respect for their allies. Said Belgians were also fighting up to the moment of betrayal. 'Then we had the Germans outflanking us all the time. Had to retire.' They said that at one place the Germans used gas. They also said, as far as I understood the speaker, who spoke in a dialect, that the French had no gas masks.

July 8th

Today the local constable came in a car with a sergeant in mufti. We had all gone to view the Roman Villa opposite in the valley. The constable said: 'I came here, knocked at the *open* door and looked through the window and saw a lot of pennies on a table.' (This is because I always empty my pockets of copper and stack it on the table, which for the moment seems to have some marmalade on it, so everything is sticky.) I did not know whether the constable was serious or not. He was muttering a gruff 'We don't know who you are, Sir.' After a time, helped by Mrs B., everything was shifted. A wink appeared. (Spoke vaguely of Gallipoli.) He had come because I wanted a single long barrel pistol .22 that I had arranged for. 'How do I know,' he said, 'if you're not using it to shoot me.' Proof impossible. He winked again. I said: 'It's a very interesting pistol – hard to buy today and costs only £6. Yet it is a real shooting-target pistol.' He said: 'You have a fairly long garden here', and consulted his notes. The mufti sergeant winked. The constable said: 'I should have to come to see you again.' I said: 'Why not meet me up the hill at The Royal George?' The constable (who lives in the village) was admirable. 'The Royal George?' he said. 'Yes.' I replied, 'I hear it is up the hill somewhere.' (I had met him there last night.) 'And I am told they sell some odd drink called Bass.' He said at once: 'I have never heard of Bass,' and then, after consulting his notes, added, 'My private number is Witcombe 8.'

July 24th

All fighting is Anti-Christian. The whole of Christ's teaching is about a higher form of *truth*. It has nothing to do with the world or war or politics: and finally, *there are no Christians*, as Dr Mandeville pointed out some time ago. A Christian is not a church-going man or a moral pious man, but an utterly new kind of man 'Born of the spirit'. And no one knows what that is or has ever seen anyone so reborn, or could probably endure such a man; just as so many could not endure Christ and were offended or outraged, or furious with Him; or, like the disciples, very much afraid of Him. Then, later, people invented this long-haired sick Christ, carrying lamps or lambs about *à la* Holman Hunt and the insanity of Nietzsche conceived the Gospels as teaching nothing but a slave-morality and sentimental slopperies. Whereas they contain the most terrible and most harsh and most aristocratic teaching ever given to man, and expressly say that few can be saved, and that we are chaff.

September 29th

I am reading Edward Thompson's *Burmese Silver*, a book, once one catches the atmosphere of the writer, very richly connected and well-done. Possibly an allegory. There is nothing I enjoy more than to get into a book that has some stuff and thought in it, and go slowly along, noticing every detail and allusion, as one walks in a wood at leisure *alone*. I suppose 'modern thought', with its strange lack of understanding anything, would call this 'escapist' or some such jargon-word. The whole art and meaning of life is to 'escape' its crudity and meaninglessness and horrors and transform it as best one can. I would like to hear one of our young modern immature psychologists, who rush, bespectacled, along a path which leads nowhere, but is called 'reality', apparently, ask Dr Johnson at table whether he did not agree that all literature is nothing but 'dope'. But I fancy the doctor would have gone on eating as noisily as possible. One good thing Edward Thompson puts in the mouth of a Scotch engineer on the Burmese river, who doubts the God of mercy of the New Testament and inclines to the God of punishment of the Old: 'Mackenzie continued: "Not but what there *is* something in the warld that'll help you – and, if you find it, it wull grip you fast, so that naething can hurt you further. But you find it with trouble and suffering and infeenite sorrow. And when you have found it it isna God A'mighty at all, but someone that's *in* the business, just as you are. His *mind* is guid, in the main, and he'll save you wi' himself, if you dinna expect tae much from him. For there's ither than purely *guid* mind in the universe, and he canna help himself all that he wad." '

October 22nd

The landlord at the pub is in good form tonight. His talk is something like this: 'Yes, they got the raider yesterday over at so and so. Four of them in it. The villagers saw them all struggling to get out. Well, four less Germans is what I say. I don't like killing, but there it is. The balloons were up all day here because there was a row. Second time the balloon barrage wasn't up when damage was done. God bless them, they say they have to bring 'em down to scrape the fleas off them. Now this is my last single whisky glass. Got nine dozen of them. They all went. No, not smashed. They looked so nice that people thought they would like to see them on their sideboards. I have to use these now and a single whisky looks like a damp nut in them. Yes, sir, lager is stronger than Bass and I well know it. No, sir, there's no hair-dresser in the village. There was one only he's in the Artillery. He was a professional. Yes, sir, he could talk all the time he cut your hair, which takes a lot of training. I had my hair cut by a man across the road. When I came back to the bar they said they were sorry the pub had changed hands.'

October 31st

As a physician, I sometimes watch people coming here from London. In the last war, in the last year of it, I had connection with what were called then 'shell shock' hospitals. It occurs to me to write down my reflections at this moment, as one forgets after-wards, and one forgets nearly everything, in fact. Some people have come down white and shaken. They take two or three days to recover and do not say much. At least, they look better but I cannot say if something more lasting has not happened to them. Some, who come regularly, at week-ends, when they can, look thinner, more finely-drawn perhaps, with brighter and larger eyes, as if they had been starving. I hear from all sides that Londoners suffer from indigestion and have little appetite. But it is the nervous strain that is prior to the dyspepsia, of course. The impossibility of *reasoning* with fear has struck some. Some who have been bombed say they cannot help feeling terror when they hear a plane overhead at night here. I hear of some who, leaving London, want to go back, feeling the country is dull, and wanting to see what is happening. They are, I believe, people who would be very surprised if they were bombed – as if some connection were lacking in their minds. One letter I had from someone bombed, expressed this amazement, as if it were incredible to be personally bombed. I fancy some get an unhealthy excitement out of it all, and like to see all the horrors and destruction, so far as they are able. But most feel an endless fear and anxiety, which at times, in the long nights, becomes almost insupportable and unless dawn came they would totally collapse. All say that in daylight everything is easier to stand. The sight helps the ears. I have heard of no dreams comparable with 'battle dreams' yet – a sure sign in the last war of nervous breakdown. But I confess I have little to say on this subject, as yet. I notice in myself always a tiredness, and a lack of inclination to make mental effort. There are, of course, this time not only the air-raids but the depression all of us feel about the war and our dread of any clear action. The news is intolerable – mean, in the form it is given. We are all prepared to hear that any action we take to help Greece proves a failure and that our forces will once more (if we have any) strategically withdraw. What is the army doing? We must have more than 3,000,000 men in arms surely? Yet we heard our forces in Egypt are numerically inferior to the Italians – who seem to be doing as they please – and our Navy does not seem to have acted in the Mediterranean.

November 3rd

Last night we had a merry party. It is like those gusts of wind that suddenly drive the leaves up in a whirl. This whirl came and touched us all. A lovely, mad night, with music, singing and everything good and we all went to bed late without knowing whether there had been planes overhead or not. When one *arranges* a party – well, sometimes it goes a little bit. But these gusts of mirth seem to descend from heaven, and a man is a fool who cannot respond to them. On the guitar the old songs of Thomas Moore sound well. We played an old Irish song and an old lady began to weep. They are wonderful these melodies and seem already to belong to a better age. But I still feel that the guitar is a solitary instrument and is even upset by a mandoline and cannot take part in any mass-band. *It is for the single voice* – for a love-song – and must, in its original meaning, be struck lightly, to give the voice just its right support and background. It is far better as an accompaniment to a voice than a piano, to a slender delicate and sweet voice – just a few chords, so soft, so charming – and that is all that is required on the guitar. I do not like the 'great masters' of the guitar who try to make it what it is not, as Segovia.

November 4th

I have been reading the Count de Beugnot's Memoirs. (This is the only way to learn to grasp history – Memoirs.) He lived through the time of the Bourbons, then the revolution, then Napoleon, and then the restoration of the Bourbons. Last night I read what he says of Napoleon after he had invaded Russia so uselessly. Up to that point everything Napoleon did was marvellously successful. . . . All Europe was in his power. Beugnot met Napoleon. 'He was utterly changed.' Why had he done this – why go into Russia? Beugnot says because of the inability to invade England and the presence of the Duke of Wellington in Spain, which was a sore spot in him. Because of this continual irritation he turned his eyes eastwards and began to dream of a final smashing blow. But such dreams which apply to our present situation in this war seem to me to be vague – that is, England is still not dealt with. To overcome the irritation of England's holding out by invading Russia seems at first sight strange. Yet it is not strange. Neither Russia nor England is a part of Europe and yet each is closely knit with Europe. To conquer 'Europe' one must conquer Russia and Great Britain. And that is the present situation – once more repeating itself. Hitler cannot conquer England as Napoleon could not. So he looks *east* – not yet to Russia, but to the Danube and the Black Sea.

I notice that I always watch how people live. But I have always done this. I watched even my father when I was a boy. Sometimes one finds something good for the moment. But we do live poorly, weakly and dully and some really live badly, especially those who have some right form of living, I fancy. Yet I do not know. One looks for freshness and livingness and especially from a person who has learned that *life must be taken* in some way or other. I began to talk to someone in a certain way that I rather dislike – a stranger – and he said after a time: 'Well, sir, I think such questions are very monotonous and lead nowhere.' This gave me great half-pleasure.

It seems to me that, whatever theories we hold we have to learn a great deal from *society*. I mean, it is quite impossible for life to have any sort of proper form unless there is some sort of society. I enjoy Beugnot's Memoirs because they are written from a good intelligent point of view – that is, from the point of view of a socially trained man who knows what to eliminate and what is important. *I do not see how any social life is possible without society* – and by that I mean a group of people who are a little more expert in manners and address than the rest. A year ago I was arguing in Harley Street about this to a well-known scientist, a distinctive man, who believes he is a communist. His wife is a cultivated woman and has, in fact, a better idea of how to speak and behave than her husband, though the latter is also of good position. The scientist argued that all social distinctions are ridiculous and that all men are equal. I am always secretly delighted by the word 'equal'. In what way? It means, ordinarily, I believe, *equal in riches* – in money. But it is surely obvious that some men are more intelligent than others and that although as regards *quantities* people may demand equality, as regards qualities people are different even from their birth. Dr Johnson always said that well-bred society women were vastly superior to any others and it is surely obvious. But modern science, once it becomes infected with communism – though the body itself shews any scientist that it is not built up on equality – seems incapable of treating of the obscure. Just before the French Revolution, which ended in Dictatorship under Napoleon (as all such revolutions do, as today we have Hitler and Stalin) the text-books of science were full of revolutionary ideas. I can scarcely think it possible that this was so. But I have bought several cheap text-books of science recently and find they are full of non-scientific ideas – i.e. communistic ideas – and even books on physiology, which is surely a science of *hierarchy*, that is, of higher and lower, speak of communism. And this goes, I fancy, with the general diminution of sex-feeling and the rise of homosexuality. But I may be wrong. But heterosexuality – it is based on the power of seeing *differences* or wishing for what is different from oneself. If only science, which is so utterly lost since matter has turned into energy and the three-dimensional world of our senses has turned into a four-dimensional, could give a message that, in ordinary language, is spiritual, man might again feel it worth while to live.

November 7th

The balloons are all up shining in the high skies and the wood-pigeons assembling for migration exercises are beneath – about two hundred passed over with a rushing noise, flying very fast and making the small squad of jackdaws under them talk a lot. The jackdaws are always practising different flight-exercises but nothing like so seriously and swiftly as these pigeons, which suddenly descend on a small area of trees, covering the branches. Watching a magpie land on the tip-top of a tree, I saw how it used its long tail to balance.

November 8th

It is the ape in science that needs purifying. Indeed, science has brought back the Titans, who are again tearing up everything sacred and holy. But in the legend all is restored eternally.

We had some friends, from London, today. They say that in small dug-outs it is impossible to sleep, if one cannot make all the movements of legs and arms natural to sleep and that it becomes unbearable unless one can do so. They say all the private dug-outs made below the earth-level are flooded and impossible to use. They spoke of Sam Copley who, amongst other properties, had a *bird-seed* factory, which was set on fire. He got to it, after being telephoned for, with great difficulty in the night, his car ending up in a shell-hole in the road. The first thing he saw was the A.F.S. men (Aux. Fire Service) carting away all the typewriters, etc. He had them arrested on the spot. I hear he had twenty thousand pounds worth of seed – and half saved. Someone said it was difficult to imagine there were so many pet birds. Still, even here there are two love-birds in the pub and a canary up the road in the village. A clear night of stars and a half-moon, but nothing as yet – it being nearly midnight now. We tried in vain to complete the last line of a verse in a French poem:

> Les sanglots longs
> Des violons
> Blessent mon coeur

I memorized the poem as a boy, but Mrs B. told me no, it was a well-known song. Taking our average knowledge as average people, we realize how little exact ordinary knowledge we have. I remember clearly why I memorized it – so badly. It was the idea of the long sobbing of the violins – les sanglots longs – that struck me as a true description, probably at a time when I wished for pain and useless suffering, such as we ask for when young and believing in life, when we feel the uniqueness of ourselves and our real immortality. Am enjoying in my mind a 'Penguin' called *Within Four Walls* by two officers who escaped after many attempts from a German prison camp in the 1914 war. In that war parcels and letters were exchanged between England and Germany. Things are worse now – war is worse, evil is worse: and science rides the heavens with meaningless gestures.

November 16th

Pilot-Officer K. missing since the 11th.

November 17th

A delicious morning with a shining blue sky. A long scarlet cloud is advancing slowly from the opposite side of the valley just at the level of the house. High above hang the barrage balloons, looking today as if painted in chinese white. The cathedral is gleaming in the distance, outvying the gas-tank near it, for once. Cows gaze just over the hedges – and suddenly there is a roaring from the valley and up shoots a Hurricane vertically into the calm sky. Last night was wet and nothing happened save that at about two o'clock in the morning, while I was reading, the electric light flickered and dimmed for at least three minutes and then went out. A barrage balloon had got free; and when it does, its trailing cable moves over the countryside catching in everything it can, including of course the grid-wires. But those three minutes of flicker must have meant an exciting struggle 'twixt balloon and grid. The gale a few days back broke some wiring and we had no light or cooking heat: then the main fuse blew two days after and now the outside wires are down again. But we are lucky to have any light. In London there is a universal run on oil-stoves.

I hear one of the big nursing-homes in Beaumont Street is destroyed. Also that Sloane Square Station has 'vanished'. Mr C. says to get from Piccadilly to S. Kensington by tube took him an hour – this was at five p.m. – the platform being jammed with sheltering people. Mr G. here is a fireman three nights a week and was at the Holland House disaster. He said the place could have been saved, only there was no water. There were proper places where hose-pipes could be fitted, only the main pipe supplying all their hydrants had been mended with a length of one or two inch tubing, for some inexpressible reason, and there was no pressure. He says water damages things terribly, fire usually starting on the roof, from the incendiary bombs, and so the whole house is soaked with water, even if it is saved. Mrs F., a French woman, said last night at dinner that Churchill's recent speech in French was just like a schoolboy recitation, to French ears, and very charming to them. Everything continues to remain dark to me. I cannot see how any *victory* can come about. Germany has only to despatch half a dozen divisions to Greece, and she will have the Aegean in a week. I don't see how any conquest of Europe is possible. Mrs B. off to see her Prince – and probably heard something of the big raid on London two nights ago (Friday).

November 20th

Nothing appears to have been dropped last night. The bombers passed overhead to the Midlands. I walked down to the Reservoir and looked at the village nearby, but there is no sign of damage and no cracked windows though they have had a good many bombs dropped just across the water. An old little church, with a sundial, a clock, a flag-pole and a big weather-cock; and a tiny school beside it from which came the sound of children's voices. Men working on the farm, and a big windy sunny sky. 'Noisy night, sir,' said one. Today Madame K. writes: 'I keep on thinking of the *Jervis Bay*. I cannot help thinking that a thing like that is one of the greatest things men are capable of, ordinary men, without any religion perhaps or knowledge. And a death like that is no ordinary death, so those men who went down with her must have taken something with them that death was powerless to kill, because it does not belong to the physical body and goes against all the interests and desires of the physical body.' The *Jervis Bay*, an armed merchant ship, was apparently in sole charge of a large convoy of over thirty ships from America, and when a German pocket battleship appeared she steamed in to action, telling the others to scatter under smoke screens. A posthumous V.C. was given to the Commander.

November 21st

A wet windy night and I hope it is so all over Europe, for then what a relief everyone will feel, airmen and civilians of all nations – and what nonsense to imagine otherwise. A long walk this morning down the hill round by the aerodrome and up the southern hill and along its crest. A strange name on a cart 'A Bugbird' and on a gate 'Anchordyne'. The air-factory buildings are very well camouflaged, so much so, that standing about half a mile away in full sunlight, looking down them idly, I noticed I lost sight of them easily. A barrage balloon at close quarters, tethered; it seems very light and with its rounded sacks of sand that looked like sacks of gold, resembling a moose with flopping ears. Passed an observation post on the top of a little hill – men looking at all training aeroplanes overhead through glasses and a couple of long-snouted machine-guns pointing up to the skies. Everywhere digging was going on – shelters, pits, emplacements. On the wireless we hear the King has opened Parliament today, without pageantry of course, and a little of the speech was broadcast. I hope we are not going to fall into those over-worn tirades about 'justice', etc. and all the vilifications that are used when the word is uttered. Mutual praise would be far better. War is part hatred but most wounded vanity. Mutual appreciation would soon dissolve hatred and hurt vanity. Our political leaders talk of the German as the Hun and the Boche but the ordinary Tommy calls him Jerry.

November 22nd

At this moment, about ten p.m., all is quiet. The stars glitter, the slight wind from the valley, passing between the cables of the barrage balloons, makes a faint shrilling. The owls are calling. I am going to poke the fire and read. In a green vase before me there are some pink roses slowly unfolding in the warmth of the room. The clock is ticking. I hear a car beginning to climb the hill far below in the dark.

November 24th

Tonight a clear starlit night and away south towards Bristol a white flaring in the sky caused by searchlights. Shells bursting and red dots in the sky. No sound. An air-raid on Bristol and Avonmouth. God help them all. We stood on the terrace watching and everyone felt an ache in their hearts. Flash – flash – flash – and each flash the lives of mortals. How long will man remain so asleep to others, so dead in feeling! Today, Sunday, was fine. High skies, sailing clouds, sunshine and lovely air. The jackdaws very interested in performing some strange new exercise in the higher winds above the rim of trees. They talked a lot, and pleasantly – unlike the crows. A hawk hovered and stood marvellously, but was not attacked by the daws, as is usual – usually the daws driving him down by dive-bombing him into the hedges. Several magpies tried to volplane in the moving wind but their very long tails make trouble for them.

The Home Guards mustered importantly and modestly today in the 'George' at noon after drill. A lot of talk about delayed action bombs and those that had fallen near by. P., the actor, back here from a brief tour, who says that Stratford is full of evacuees and they played to poor houses, taking only £200 in the week. At Cambridge they made money. The play is *Thunder Rock*. He has to go on to Bristol this week. It is now close to midnight. The glare towards Bristol has ceased. Perhaps the raid is over – perhaps it will start again. All England at night is open to these bombers and there can be no remedy, in spite of all the papers say. I will be glad to find I am wrong. How can they be stopped? Only by mutual realization of this useless destructive horror. But 'mutual realization' seems very far from human consciousness as things are. Warlike inflammatory speeches go on and on – in the name of justice, etc. and everyone is determined to fight to the 'last ditch'.

November 25th

There was some talk of Spoonerisms. I gave the classical one –
when the Rev. Spooner told his congregation: 'Everyone here
carries a half-warmed fish in his bosom' (a half-formed wish).
Someone gave a new one: 'You have hissed all my mystery
lectures.' I confess to a delight in them. Anything that tosses life
up is good. I was sorry to see my jackdaws mixing with a lot of
vulgar crows in a field of winter wheat. I asked the farmer why
he didn't train a dog to guard the field. He said he had never
heard of the idea, but had wondered if cats could be used. The
little son of P. the artist came to tea, a year and a half old, and
played a long game with six teaspoons on the parquet floor. He
has remarkably good movements. Going out, he saw the barrage
balloons high above him and flung out his arms, smiling up to
them. I have just noticed: spoonerisms – spoons – this odd turning
up of a word.

November 30th

This morning a white valley, covered with hoar-frost. Up the
hill on the plateau the fields full of birds – seagulls, crows and
smaller birds. In one field of winter wheat I counted three
hundred plover sitting motionless. I suppose they are on their
way south. The valley is full of mist tonight. J. is hoping her
husband has leave tomorrow. He is a gunner, in the Midlands
now, and, shaken out of the life of an artist, moves from place to
place haphazard, without any privacy or freedom, among a crowd
of yokels. This living in a crowd, which I had some experience of
in the last war, is tiring to creative minds. It is often said that war
does man good. I doubt this very much. I cannot remember to
have seen any man improved by the last war. I saw many broken,
many incurable mentally, many permanently saddened or dulled.
War is entirely destructive by its very essence – it is killing,
raping, burning and plundering. Yet people uphold war and think
it leads somewhere and even say it is fine. If men would make
war on themselves, the world might improve. But no improvement of the world can be expected so long as people think that
improvement is external and consists in getting more for themselves. The other night I could not sleep and was looking up some

of the poets on 'sleep', 'beloved from pole to pole'. Here is
Shakespeare. The King, Henry IV, unable to sleep, is speaking:

> How many thousands of my poorest subjects
> Are at this hour asleep! O sleep, O gentle sleep,
> Nature's soft nurse, how I have frighted thee,
> That thou no more wilt weigh my eyelids down,
> And steep my senses in forgetfulness.

December 16th

Tonight cloudy and wet and quiet so far (nine p.m.). Plenty of
turkeys in Gloucester, I am told – but how can one buy a turkey
now? It will go bad by Christmas. I have never understood the
mystery. Soon the shortest day will be passed and this is such a
relief. Was reading about Glastonbury and St Dunstan's and have
learnt the meaning of 'peg'. I was always told that, in regard to
drinking, a *peg* meant another peg in your coffin. Actually, St
Dunstan who seems an unquestionably able man on the whole,
before his time, was at times virtually in control. Bringing in
many reforms, he found that people quarrelled in inns over their
drink, the custom being for many to drink out of one large
tankard. Dunstan got the tankards marked with silver pegs, so a
man drank a peg and handed the tankard to the next man.

December 20th

Such a strange thing – singing Christmas carols in the drawing-
room and the guns going outside in the wet misty night. I have
come to the conclusion that B.B.C. does not understand England
and gets its impressions of it from cocktail bars and odd freaks and
night clubs. They put some grand Christmas carols on last night
and the announcer was as flippant and imbecile as possible with
smart jazzy comments. Whereas these grand carols and Christmas
hymns, well sung, are very beautiful lovely things, loved by
everyone. But I am wrong. I remember a young spoilt American
boy in the flat above us, years back, flinging up the window while
the local and very good carol society was singing in the wintry
snowy street and yelling 'Curse you, curse you, curse you all,

12. Château du Prieuré

13. Tyeponds

14. Alley Cottage

15. Great Amwell House

etc. etc.' This is a disease of the mind, purely and simply, a horrible one, for which science is somewhat to blame, untutored slick unenlightened science, I mean. Without beauty, art, music, drama, literature and *belief*, how can the emotional life of mankind ever be lifted? I have heard that the earth is the only planet where the habit has been developed of mutual destruction. Hatred seems abroad today as the main emotional factor, in spite of all that has been done, and I am reminded again of the German boy at my preparatory school who spent all his spare time in drawing scenes of torture in hell, working the faces of the devils out with the utmost love and pleasure. There is pleasure in cruelty – and devils; and, although I am a doctor, I have come to think often that people are afflicted with devils and that the idea explains very much in pathological psychology – and the only remedy, if any, is through love, charity, affection, good manners, belief in the higher, and a fineness of the feelings, which lifts us above the power of lower things. When I imply that a man can be possessed by a devil, I mean that a personality can either form itself in him, or infest him, of such an order that it is sub-human, and can at times control him. Some people are definitely evil and only seek to harm or destroy. The idea of devils, I have read, is to destroy the human race and they can use any method, however vile, criminal, false and horrible, but the angels who resist them in a man cannot use violence of any kind. The idea is interesting, even reduced to ordinary terms of bad and good people. And this world was set going on that plot.

Boxing Day

Two quiet nights – and we all feared so much that England would have the bad taste to bomb Germany. A good Christmas – turkey, whortleberry sauce, and most of the etceteras and plum pudding and good claret and an amusing night, with charades, songs and good feeling. Christmas is a blessed time – a really wonderful good influence. And all the parcels and good-will and interchange so good for everyone.

I used to think how wonderful it was for a French *artiste* to speak English. Now, owing to our local fooleries here, I see it is quite easy to learn a part in French – and in fact, if one handles one's slight French to the point, everything is comprehensible to the audience. But the English require enormous encouragement before they speak another language and this is due to a very deep factor in them, which *may* have been useful, but I fancy is no longer so. Actually I believe if we began to speak foreign languages, it would assist the strange factors at work now. We never even tried to speak them out of a feeling that there was only *one* language.

Our Christmas gift from our nearest neighbours was a bowl of brown eggs and farm butter decorated with holly and mistletoe and a large basket of giant cabbages, leeks, parsnips, artichokes and potatoes.

New Year's Eve

Reading today of the Siege of Saragossa in 1808 or thereabouts – Napoleon and the Peninsular War. Horrible – the dead six foot high in the streets. Everyone underground in cellars because of the 'bombs' fired by the French. Heroism. Pestilence. Carnage. The same old thing. Nothing is new. Man revolves in the circle of his own nature and comes always back to the same point of horror and carnage. History has no meaning save that it is the recurring expression of *what Man is* in his nature. But I have never read a history book giving this as the main interpretation. History is *Man as he is* – and nothing else. Man, *as he is*, attracts what is called history. There is no other point of view – and that means that unless the forces that have been brought into the world that teach Man *to be different* are realized as essential to Man's development, nothing remains as regards the future. Our scientists are too narrow, uppish, and if educated, which is rare, too Alice-in-Wonderland folk to have the strength to tell people that everything is a mystery ultimately. A weak rather mealy and watery set and a bit silly, but good at inventing new bombs and new horrors and evils for man and new complications of everything.

A friend wrote me asking for a good 'diagnostic doctor'. Knowing them well, and what it would cost her (teeth out, tonsils out, guts out, ovaries out, etc.) I thought – *no* – and sent her a good prescription, old-fashioned.

January 4th   *1941*

All the valley covered with snow against which the gaunt woods stand out black and silent. Bristol got it last night, but owing to the winter murk in the sky we saw no flashes. We are trying to get chains for the cars as the hill is almost impossible.

January 6th

Talking of means of reducing weight – probably unnecessary now in view of the future – Miss K., a physical exercise expert, said that exercises do not reduce weight, but that dancing at *night* does so. Since I have taken to walking five or more miles a day I have gone up half a stone, although eating considerably less. The trouble about walking is that it leaves you pleasantly tired and inclined to sit about. From previous experience I know what brings weight down rapidly and that is continued physical work from early dawn till late at night, with a very simple diet and very little sleep. (Sleep is fattening.)

January 19th

A real blizzard raged all yesterday, a soft drizzle of snow falling and the S.W. wind blowing hard. Several Army lorries early in difficulties on the hill – spades, shunts, backing, turning, all morning. They all had to go down and try the other hill, by the 'Air Balloon' pub. In this snow, our barrage balloons are all floating tilted up. We got six rabbits with ferrets. Are cutting down trees for fuel. This house very cold – and the usual coughs and flu' – this *illness* called an English winter. But today everything is marvellous in the pale sunlight – the fir trees laden with snow, as I like them best, and that strange alteration in sounds. We tried yodelling. The two dogs, Chan the Chow and the poodle, both black, bounding in the snow and getting soon exhausted. Jane and John climbed the hill in the little Austin car on a private expedition and I could later see by the wheel tracks that they barely got up. Had to attend a Colles' fracture on an old lady in the village – over thirty years since I dealt with such things. Great shortage of water in Birdlip. Our ram still working to our surprise, so we can have baths down here. We got a ton of coal, luckily. This, with logs, keeps the fires going. Logs alone last no time. A whole big tree is consumed in a day almost. To me the message of the snow is always the same – rest, think, read, be calm, for this is the time of quiescence and peace – but the momentum of modern life drives through all these natural messages and ignores them. We seem long ago to have lost all harmony with nature – in fact, all harmony with ourselves – and live strange unreal existences.

January 21st

Have been reading the late Lord Riddell's *War Diary* (1914-1918). I read it some years ago and understood nothing. Whether it is due to 'growing up' more or to this war and the perspective it gives of the last one, I do not know, but every word I find interesting. If anyone wants to know what is going on in the Cabinet now, the Diary will tell him – the names merely are different – but one must have reached the stage of no longer being critical, having seen the difficulties of life for oneself. I remember he asked me to lunch after I came back from the Dardanelles. He gave me champagne – he drank nothing himself – and unless you are used to it, it excites the mind too quickly. I spoke in the usual way of officers at that time – why didn't Lloyd George do this and that and so on. Now looking back I can see he was trying to tell me something, that one so slowly understands. He said that L. G. was not quite like that, and that it was difficult to get things done, people in high places were jealous, new steps required long preparation, politics was the art of dealing with people, etc. I understood nothing at the time. Now I see better. I remember he said: 'People in high places are not friendly to each other, you know.' This surprised me. Why do we all live so long in the illusion that 'they' exist – a race of supermen who know everything? Actually, those in high office are more isolated and restricted and bound than any other grade of people are – and there is no master-mind who 'knows everything', as we imagine. Asquith knew only a little of what was going on, Kitchener the same, L. G. the same, and a Cabinet Meeting was not a meeting of super-minds, but an affair of intricate ordinary human motives and counter-motives, in which no one knew the whole situation but wondered if his neighbours knew something he did not know.

For instance, none of them seemed to know whether there was a shortage of shells or not until L. G. took over the Ministry of Munitions. Yet any artillery officer in the line could have told them. Kitchener was sure there was not and so on. And another strange thing that is merely human and yet not what we expect in high circles – General French rang up Riddell from the country on the eve of war and asked him if he knew whether war was to be declared and who was to be in command, etc. L. G. happened to be dining with R. so R. asked him and was told to tell French that war was certain to be declared and that French was in command and he was to come to London next day. French said he could come up to town next morning.

January 29th

A long lull in air-raids. The country under snow and mist and rain. This evening while still light and the valley full of mist and the drawing-room full of people talking over a bottle of sherry, sudden noises in the distance. I went out and saw a flaming mass dropping vaguely through the mist far away. Thought it was one of our aeroplanes caught in the balloon-wires – a too common tragedy. Then various bangs and we found ourselves in an air-raid. A bomb fell near us and broke the drawing-room window. It also felled some trees which we can use for fuel. All over in half an hour (so far at least) – and a strange experience, because owing to the mist, though still daylight, nothing could be seen of the enemy. A 'plane close over us twice, but we imagined it one of our fighters. We went and sat in the kitchen – the lights almost failed for some reason – Mrs B. sitting in the dog-basket belonging to the gentian-coloured Chow, Shan. I shewed her what Lord Dawson said of this dog's parents – in Riddell's Diary: 'He said that Chows are not really dogs at all. They are most calculating and carefully consider with whom they shall make friends and how much attention they shall pay to each.' They are more like cats, I think.

Madame R., one of our Russian friends, is with us, recuperating after an operation. She asks a great many questions. Russians have this habit. They fire a regular stream of questions, like a cross-examination, a feature of which they seem unconscious. She was a singer. I asked her about Bolshevik music. All she could say was that many extra verses had been added to the old tunes. Like all Russians one notices something very tough in her – perhaps this is not the right word. They are not easily abashed and often shew a sort of physical determination or insistence which is in complete contrast with their emotional melancholy and vagueness. They are crafty. They have more contradictions in their nature than English people have and are not easy to understand. But no one is. They seem closer to us, however, than the French are, and can speak our language nearly without any accent, and sometimes with nearly the same cadence.

February 1st

A diary depends only upon the freshness of the immediate record of things. So I record tonight – the first clear moonlight night for many days. It is seven-thirty p.m., a fresh west wind blowing up from the Severn, Orion blazing in the sky, and a distant dog barking in the now mist-free valley. Now the rumour of invasion grows on all sides – and I expect soon to hear the droning of 'planes. Many of our friends down tonight and a dinner preparing and some wine. We, I suppose, are in what is called 'history in the making' – only no one ever feels that. We eat, we drink, we talk – and our little soft bodies have to go to bed.

February 8th

After trying to draw and paint full-grown sheep in vain, I found some fifty new-born lambs in a pen up the road. Their legs are enormous. W. tells me they are born with the full length of leg and only their bodies increase in size afterwards. Their long tails and their great legs and small bodies give something to draw. W. tells me that in the case of sheep, the more a ewe bears at one litter the better but that in the case of pedigree cattle, if a cow produces two heifers, their value from the breeding point of view is more than halved, though the farmer can sell them on the basis of their pedigree without saying they are twins. Signs of spring vaguely in the air. A soft south wind and the jackdaws very happy in their volplaning over the edge of the wood. Snowdrops in abundance. We expected a raid last night – bright moon and calm

– but nothing happened. Benghazi has fallen. Food is on the short side and the shops have little to sell. Claret is locally unobtainable, save some vile Algerian stuff.

February 21st

A period of quiet here. Last night the guns sounded for a time. Someone said we are in for a hundred years' war – one which started in 1914. I think he is right. The French revolutionary and Napoleonic wars lasted some twenty-five years with a short interval of peace only it was in a way more endurable because distance was great owing to the slowness of communications. But we had bread-riots and starvation in spite of naval supremacy; and all Europe suffered horribly. Napoleon squeezed France like an orange of all its juice.

March 3rd

What is more difficult than to realize that national differences are real? One would like to suppose that all people are the same, particularly if one likes or loves a foreigner. But one thing is true, namely, that the best types, the highest types of all nations, approximate to each other and begin to have a common language. But this can only happen through the existence of such higher types. Otherwise our relations, in this respect, are scandalous – i.e. based on the common basis of most relationships which depend on unpleasant things, in fact, scandal and suspicion. A good aristocracy has its advantages. What on earth will happen when such slight possibilities of mutual regard and relation disappear completely? Well, they are doing so rapidly. There is no idea remaining of this biological necessity of castes, in order to maintain the slight degree of decent national relationship that is possible.

March 23rd

The local builder in the village asked me last night if I and my folk would attend a 'drum-head' service today. So off we went this morning, finding that it was a general day of Prayer called for by the King. I wore a town coat and gloves, and we all did our best. The local Home Guard and the R.A.F. detachment here formed up in the 'Royal George' yard. Two R.A.F. padres appeared who seemed to know all about drill, etc. and a procession was formed and we all – so to speak – marched down to a tin-hall at the end of the village and had a service, the chief padre, a nice enough fellow with eyes that could fight, telling us it was up to us to have a service by taking part. Behind him was a legend scrawled on a sheet of paper: 'The legion of the damned' – no one seemed to know why it was there – and to one side, in a kitchen, a meal of beef and vegetables was cooking for the troops with loud sizzles. The padre was gracious enough in his sermon to refer to the presence of soldiers, and sailors (one, aged about ten) and Air Force and so many civilians (our party of twelve came in here). No local gentry attended which I thought bad. He spoke of the King, of Prayer, and of Miracles – in fact, 'put it all across well', as someone said. I liked the man and sang heartily hymns long forgotten and which not having brought my glasses I could not read one word of. We told them all afterwards what a fine show they made and how steady on the march they looked and how well it went off, so we were of use. After all, everyone needs an audience to tell him how he did – and we acted as theirs – so if you come to think of it a king is *psychologically* necessary as the final audience under God. A good day. Some bomber came roaring over the tin-hut during the sermon, but everyone sat motionless and not a head turned. We probably all had the same thought – difficult to turn into words. The blue Chow-dog Chan came to Church with us of his own accord, but waited outside, not affecting the Christian religion as yet. There was a collection and we hastily raised what half-crowns we had about us. Then, immediately the Blessing was given, the piano struck up Mendelssohn's Spring Song and we tripped out, the troops formed up and the chief padre took the salute, and they marched up the village to the 'George' where they were dismissed and entered as one man into the pub, where our host Mr King awaited the Church-goers. How good Church would have been formerly if we all had had a good drink and talk after.

April 7th

I have been reading the *Life and Letters of Walter Page* – the American ambassador here in the 1914-1918 war. An extraordinary book.

April 8th

To return to Page's Life and Letters – the most extraordinary thing is that Page, as U.S.A. Ambassador here in the last war, could get no replies to his reports and letters either from President Wilson or the State Department in Washington. Nor was he told what they were doing. Naturally one imagines always that important people are in close touch. But this is not the case. Riddell's Diaries of the last war shew so plainly the same thing. This form of imagination must be destroyed in us – but not in the people, I fancy. Chaos everywhere. For example, Lord Kitchener, a popular hero, was in private a man impossible to work with. (Riddell's Diaries shew this well enough.) Page went to the funeral. (Kitchener was sent to Russia and was torpedoed on June 19th off the coast of Scotland in the cruiser *Hampshire*.) Page says, after attending the memorial service at St Paul's: 'There were two Kitcheners as every informed person knows, (1) the popular hero, (2) the Cabinet Minister with whom it was impossible for his associates to get along.' Yet Kitchener was the only man who saw from the beginning that the war would last for years. No one believed him. When told to go to Russia to link up with them, he said he was only going because ordered to. Page adds: 'There was a hope he might not come back till after the war.' What a subject for a *drama* – a popular hero, to be got rid of for very good reasons – and how to do it discreetly. All real 'theatre' depends on this basic situation – what *appears* and what actually *is*. I am going to quote from Page again. Today the glass is rising – fine weather – 'good bombing'. On the wireless tonight 70,000 tons of our shipping sunk last week – all that food, oil, grain, etc., down at the bottom of the sea, and worse still, those men on the ships who brave the danger of the seas, without escort. I suppose if we asked every individual Irishman if he wished to be under German rule he would say no. Yet Ireland will do nothing to help us or to make our attacks on submarines easier by letting us use her ports. Man as a nation is a fool. A psychology of *nations* would be that of idiots. A single man is *cleverer* than his nation and this should be taught in school-books. Look at all the nations fighting now and no individual man, save a few, wants it.

Midnight

A high three-quarter moon sailing in a dove-grey scalloped sky of thin cloud. In the valley the steady blare of 'all clear' sounding from Gloucester and the warning wailing sirens sounding from Cheltenham, round the corner of the hill, at the same time: and high overhead the faint grinding beastliness of a bomber. The cattle are uneasy in the field across the hedge. They know. Probably animals know now something of what air-raids mean. Horses look *up*. Dogs know it well – and I hear cats do. Now we are all saying Good-night and going to bed – to remain listening with that part of the ear that always listens unless we are dead-tired, or have been to the pub. Alas, the pub has little to sell now, and is keeping Sunday hours, and may shortly close for three days a week. Mrs M., recently from Glasgow, says they have plenty of cigarettes there. None here. She left with her children today for Glasgow. Have been reading Herman Melville's *White Jacket*. It was he who wrote *Moby Dick*, that obscure terrific hurricane of a book. He was a disappointed writer who was never recognized in his time – a marvellous, torrential writer, a painter in words, who could write about anything, so to speak, through the power of his colouring, but without any corresponding clear mind or direction, it seems to me. But very graphic – to use a word that totally belittles him. His description of rounding Cape Horn in an American frigate of last century – in '45 – is just as if you had seen in a gallery some wonderful paintings of the sea strung along the wall, without any catalogue to explain them – and without quite remembering where you saw them. He cannot bring his characters to life but his description of nature is sheer marvel. He has endless and tremendous words for the sea. Every storm he paints is different. His power is magical where wild stormy unleashed nature is concerned. I would say he is the best prose poet of the sea and he knows about ships. He was born in New York City in 1819 and went to sea when eighteen.

April 14th (Monday – Bank Holiday) 8 p.m.

A *black* Easter indeed: the Germans already in Egypt, and also sweeping over Greece.

A picture in the papers today of Lord Halifax with 'thumbs up' side by side with the Mayor of New York. The last thing he could do easily, I fancy. I am not sure if I have expressed in this diary how much I feel that America is not yet behind us. Today we hear that in 1942 everything will be different. We heard that in 1940 in reference to 1941. Are the Americans out for peace? I think so. They have their eyes on 'big business' with Germany. If we have to be blitzed by Germans for another year and are only capable of the slight air retaliations we are making at present, the outlook is not very good. Coventry, I hear, is literally gone. And Bristol is on the way to it. And Lt. D. who passed through the East End of London seemed very surprised at the desolation. People do not feel anything that happens to others easily, as long as it does not happen to themselves. There is no *consciousness* in man as yet – only of himself – that is, a very limited consciousness.

Tonight we had a party (Bank Holiday) and did some charades and our guitar and mandoline band did wonders with 'Juanita' and 'Billy Boy' and 'Sole Mio', etc. We had some chicken and macaroni for dinner and some sherry and claret. Not so bad. Afterwards we ate a chocolate *Easter Egg* given to me – a great luxury now – and a tin of Bath Oliver biscuits sent from Fortnum and Mason's by P. G. – very good of him, and we appreciated the old flavours. No one is exactly depressed, but all are strained. In the last war, towards the end, the American Ambassador, Page, describes how everyone looked so tired and exhausted. Napoleon said: 'Battles make people old,' or some imbecile and obvious remark. He was a clever, stupid, man, and an Italian; and in his child-heart hated the French because they laughed at him at the Military School, so he could use them and drain their blood with equanimity. He revenged himself on France. Hitler is an Austrian, and Stalin a Caucasian – and the Caucasians to Russia are like the Irish to us – so I suppose to be a real dictator you must not be of the same blood as the country you dictate to and must in a way hate it. Disraeli might have been a man to dictate to this country – he was badly treated not because he was a Jew, but because of his vanity and bad taste. But he was very successful at the Berlin Conference: in fact, Bismarck was tremendously impressed by him, simply because he could look coldly and objectively at Englishmen, I believe. When a man in power is not of the same blood he can look coldly and mercilessly on the people he controls. He has, to begin with, no relatives, no real connections with the people under him, and by feeling himself a 'foreigner' gains power and force, especially if the private *dossier* of his heart-memories is full of hatred.

April 17th

War is a disease, accompanied by the same symptoms. It belongs to the category of *collective* diseases not yet classified – to diseases not of separate people, but of nations. It is accompanied by the same words, phrases, accusations, slogans, repressions, distortions, lies, evasions, etc. In the first place everyone is invariably fighting for justice. This is the first symptom. Then there are the horrible words 'reptile', etc., and the police, and the cruelty and the signs of hatred: and all niceness vanishes. This is the second symptom. But it must be admitted perhaps that the disease of war has got worse this century. I have never been able to understand why possession by devils is regarded as an absurdity. All my experience as a physician has made me believe that at least certain abnormal people are possessed by something evil that overwhelms them at moments – and that most of us are abnormal at times. Nations also seem to get possessed of devils of a vaster order. Evil thoughts have their own life, it seems to me, and are clever. Take suspicion! Hate, lies and suspicion – are they not devils? Perhaps we shall have a revival of the *moral* idea of human life again and these things will be taught as *evil*.

A lot more churches in London destroyed, I hear. It is odd they get hit and it is a pity, for a fine church or cathedral has permanent value. A great cathedral is a scaffolding for the senses to mount upon, something to transform the impression of everyday life. And this side of human labours is surely evident to anyone with eyes to see? In every age there has always been something, whether in stone, sculpture or painting, in literature, poetry or music, to lift a man above sensual life. If art is not more beautiful than life, what is its significance?

April 18th

Primroses and violets carpet the earth.

April 20th

A large number of monotonous birds here now sing a steady *chee, chee, chee* all day. They are rather small and have reddish-brown breasts, and two bars of white on the wing and a trace of green. Another little bird says 'British Empire' as if a little drunk. It is impossible to reproduce many bird-notes in words. I try in vain to find a word for the jackdaws, who when at their favourite sport of volplaning against the wind on turning utter either cries of satisfaction or mutual criticism. It is not a hoarse *caw* like a crow, but a cheerful sound. Many birds who are not songsters make noises like a carpenter's shop or a machine, factory-plonks, kinks, conks, grating, sawing, tapping, or filing sounds, screeches, tapping, etc. The songsters sometimes seem to utter half-sentences as 'Oh, no, not at all,' etc.

April 21st

In Plutarch's *Morals*, in the essay entitled 'On the "E" at Delphi' the remark is made: 'For the god addresses each of us here, when approaching him, as if with a salutation, in the words: "Know thyself", which is neither more nor less than "Hail", whilst we, in requital to the god, say: "Thou art", recognizing in him the true possession of himself.' Such a 'Hail' as '*Know thyself*' would be certainly a little different from 'Heil Hitler' and with a little more meaning. The papers report it was Hitler's birthday yesterday – he is fifty-two – and the *Express* said we all send him a fervent birthday wish to the effect that it may be his last birthday. Rome sends him an odd greeting to the effect that Mussolini was and is the greatest statesman the world has seen but another one is coming on a bit. The terrible 'desire to be first' that all these dictators exceptionally suffer from – which we either get in the nursery or a bit earlier from Lucifer – seems something that can never be altered in humanity – that is, in us – unless it is turned to love of God. Larissa taken and our troops falling back towards Athens. A lovely spring day here and everyone feels the joy of it in spite of everything. This evening, Catherine, cooking in the kitchen with Mrs B., invited us all in to a bottle of sherry she had procured and we 'assisted', in the French sense, at the making of two excellent-looking game-pies. We found a good story on the back of a box of 'England's Glory' matches. I am always interested in match-boxes and their traditional labels and decorations. Has anyone made a collection of them? This brand has a fine old steamship on one side with high funnels and masts. On the back they have jokes. This one concerned a little girl aged four, who was playing at being a doctor. She took her favourite doll's temperature, walked to the window, examined the thermometer, walked solemnly back, shook her head and said in horrified tones: 'A hundred to eight.' Her house was near Newmarket.

We have landed again at Basra – to march up the Tigris and protect Mosul and the oil-wells. I remember very well landing at Basra in the last war. How gigantic the steamers looked in the flat country, dwarfing the palms. But of course they will have railways now running through those immense plains. But how will all those lines of communication stand the new warfare in the air attacks? I am not sanguine. Defence is impossible now, *almost*. All depends on attack – and we are going to defend the wells, primarily. I suppose H.Q. India is looking after the expedition, as last time. This will not be very inspiring to anyone.

April 22nd

These are sad days for this country. Spent most of this lovely day walking over the hills and valleys, visiting Cranham village, a beautiful tranquil place. Some girls riding horses over the grassy hillside followed by a string of dogs. A cuckoo calling and a west wind blowing. Larks overhead, and high above them barrage-balloons glittering, and above them aeroplanes – a modern spring.

April 23rd (midnight)

Planes overhead but no guns, as yet. A clear starry night. What is England: *agoraphobic* or *claustrophobic*? *Agoraphobia* is a very real fear of going out, fear of wide open spaces; and many people definitely and agonisingly suffer from it, so that they cannot cross an open space – as Hyde Park Corner – or even cross a wide street. They cling to railings, etc. *Claustrophobia* is an equally agonizing fear of being shut in – so that people cannot sit in a theatre or be in a crowd or in any confined place, and worry about coffins and death-certificates. Which is England? If you think, you will see she is both. She is violently afraid of being shut in, and so is a *claustrophobic*. At the same time, she fears going out and her timidity in this respect makes her land a spoonful of troops in Norway or Holland or Greece, etc. – which is quite stupidly inadequate, and here she is *agoraphobic*. She fears both confinement and extension – i.e. she is paralysed between opposite feelings. (I don't much believe in this argument but it looks fine.) Now the Germans are definitely *claustrophobic* and have no opposite action working as yet on them. They want to go everywhere. One side of them is active – i.e. they fear to be shut in, and have not the slightest fear of 'open spaces' (i.e. Europe and the East and the world). From this I suppose it should follow that, hating to be shut in, they will fight best if attacked and contrarily fight worse when attacking. But it does not seem so – and I would never try to argue now from such 'psychological ideas'. But the diseases are *definite*. I once knew a *claustrophobic* who could not endure a door being closed even in his own house and insisted on sitting in a draught. And I have known many *agoraphobics* who could not even bear a smooth wall, because there was nothing to catch hold of. How many people take their friend's arm across a wide road – because they want support and are really *agoraphobic*; or they hesitate to leave their companion for the same reason? And how many refuse invitations to the theatre and little night-clubs, etc., because they are *claustrophobics*. Once the *habit* (which is slightly represented in us all, both ways) is reinforced one way or another by custom, it becomes overpowering, and is scarcely curable; and then it enters into a man's calculations at all points. Strange behaviour is often explained on this basis. Most 'behaviour' is nervousness. My tendency is to *agoraphobia* in the sense that I prefer to stay in my room or where I am and I am reluctant to go even a walk. But that is all. It is a slight difference – a tendency – and so normal. Once I get myself walking – and what a job – I enjoy it. I have often said (even in professional lectures) that all 'insanities' are only exaggeration of what we all can know and feel and understand in ourselves, if we have any insight. For example, take the idea that people are unfriendly to you – and exaggerate it. Then what happens? 'Delusional insanity.' Yes, of course, but most of life is 'delusional insanity'. Still, a threshold can be crossed and it is fairly definite when a person does so – i.e he cannot correct himself. His mind has come to consent. Something *snaps* – and the man is useless – insane. What snaps is the man's power of distinguishing between truth and falsity and it is on this that man's mental life is based; just as his emotional life is based on the power of distinguishing between good and evil motives. And this signifies quite simply that man is a 'moral creation' intrinsically and to take him otherwise as *à la* Freud, etc., is to harm him to his very depths. When he no longer exercises his given powers, however small they are, of sifting truth from falsity, and good from evil will, he ceases to be a *man*, and breaks up and either becomes insane or a criminal or a fanatic. And, by the way, why all this worship of criminals today, so encouraged by our literary stars? I wonder if the latter even think what they are writing and what effect it has on others? The 'hero' must today be a sadist, a thief, a murderer, and so on. Shall I cite names? Personally, I think them, whether with titles or not, a filthy crowd. Perhaps the war will make them see what life is like and deepen their pain, delicacy and sorrow. But war never does anybody good! People kill and kill each other in the names of liberty, honour, and so on: what? Is there any example of war leaving the world better? People fight to the 'bitter end': and then nothing is possible except a laying down of new bitterly revengeful seeds of war – as inevitably today. Let me quote you this example from Thucydides. It concerns an attempt to *stop war while it is going on*. During the seventh year of the Peloponnesian War the following offer of peace was made by the Spartans to the Athenians at a time when both sides had won victories and the outcome was still uncertain: 'They indeed are wise men who cautiously regard their good things as doubtful. . . . Such men, too, while they meet with fewest failures, because they are not elated by confiding in their military successes, would be most inclined to bring the war to a conclusion during their prosperity. . . . Now (we) invite you to a treaty and conclusion of the war . . . thinking it better for both parties not to try the chances of war to the uttermost, whether they may escape by force through some accidental means of preservation, or be reduced to surrender, and be more severely dealt with. And we think that great enmities would be most effectually reconciled, not if one party, acting in a revengeful spirit, and after gaining most advantages in the war, should bind the other down by compulsory oaths, and make an arrangement with him on unequal terms, but if, when he might do so, showing regard for fairness, and conquering him by a display of goodness, he should beyond his expectations, be reconciled to him on moderate terms. For his adversary being now bound not to retaliate on him, as one who had been treated with violence, but to make him a return of goodness, is more disposed, for very shame, to abide by the terms of the agreement. . . . To come to terms then were good for both of us now, if ever, before any irremediable disaster overtake us in the meantime; in which case we must for ever feel a private hatred to you, in addition to the public one; and you must lose the advantages to which we now invite you.' These peace proposals were not accepted.

It is now two a.m. and all is quiet. No aeroplanes passing, but I fear for London.

April 27th

I call a country a *free* country when it follows externally the orthodox form of life belonging to it, and has at the same time its own 'secret' or rather personal private life, which is carried on independently. The history of England shews this rather remarkable capacity; and perhaps the history of France also. A country ceases to be free when its external, temporal orthodox forms completely rule it and have power over every individual. Then a man is the 'state'. Was the Sabbath made for man or man for the Sabbath? Then that country is in slavery – and then fear, suspicion and *police* are necessary to ensure its existence as such. Man is the state. In England people like the King to follow all the orthodox forms of state – and they like him also to have the private life distinct from it. They love him for his 'exception to the rule'. No country can be 'free', just as no individual. Freedom is not possible in the sense of everyone doing what he wants – and this, as a matter of fact, is not freedom, because a rich, idle man is more vexed by troubles, internal and external, than an active man. No one in life can be *free* – just like that. Everyone suffers, high and low.

April 30th

A gentian is out by the house. The bleak wind is softer today and I went a long fifteen mile ramble over the hills and dales.

May 1st

Tonight the young moon is high in a starry sky and all is quiet so far and the piano playing in the drawing-room. I spoke to our circle here of the necessity of creating one's life every day – doing things apart from the drift and tendency of life. Every effort made individually lifts us above the trend of things, the swing of good and evil, which is life. I finished today a painting of cream roses, but cannot deal with all the background yet and have painted it out several times in vain. The roses not so bad, but how much one must observe to paint – I mean *look at* what one is painting and follow it – and how little one does so, preferring to paint from one's own habit and idea. But all the history of Man is like that – tradition, habit, overrides observation – and we take in new impressions with great difficulty, preferring to think that things and people are like what we suppose them to be. Now, eleven p.m., the noise of bombers overhead. The searchlight searching in vain in the moonlight sky and every few minutes the grind-grind of these hideous inventions of science across the serene beauty of the night. And in a moment the crash of guns – and what is far worse, the thought of those people upon whom bombs are being rained. Would each man in each bomber had sufficient development of consciousness to be able to think of what each bomb will do to others – for to think of others is to be in a new state of consciousness.

May 2nd

The tulips are coming out. Soon we shall reach the real height of nature's beauty, when the trees are feathered with early leafage. the birds full of song, the flowers and hedges not overgrown and tangled together – in about a week or two perhaps. Then afterwards things become too green and luxuriant in England and to the artist's eye there is nothing to paint, for *green* is the most difficult colour to manage and in a way does not go with other colours – or with nature. But plants are green-blooded and I suppose this complex molecule 'Chlorophyll' which all plants absorb happens in the nature of things to give the colour green, just as our related substance 'haemoglobin' is red, and it cannot be helped.

I have finished the *Kilvert Diary* and enjoyed it. It was written fourteen years before I was born – what I mean is that it has been a favourite idea of mine for some years now that a man should study the period just before and after he was born. In this diary a robust set of people is described, who ate well and drank well and did not care too much, and were kindly. The ladies were not so modest and vaporous as is commonly supposed in Victorian times. A wonderful description of skating on the ice, with a band and quadrilles. Kilvert remarks he had 'the honour of being knocked down by Lord Royston' – who later conducted the 'Lancers' – on the ice, and being criticized by a young lady 'went and sulked on the bank'. Torches at night and everyone waltzing, carrying torches. A young lady hurls her torch on to the bank striking Lord X on the legs who exclaims: 'Why do they throw their torches at me.' At a review of the militia on a Sunday morning for Church service, 'most of the men were drunk' and were fighting all over the common. Yet no one was profoundly affected – at least, for long. A light lunch is 'roast mutton, followed by wild duck'. A bishop, shewing him his cathedral, remarks that a cathedral always attracts mad people, old ladies and men, who perform antics or stand on their heads or shout, etc. The bishop hints to him that the running of a cathedral requires secret and drastic measures. All this in the year 1870. As a novelist of the Hardy type, he would have written very well. His Christianity was external. He was simply a deist – a man of good feeling, taking religion as external observances and a reasonable charity. He has a great capacity for enjoyment and flirts with all the pretty women, who find nothing extraordinary. He had a fine square-cut black beard.

We received by post from a friend in London the wrapper of an orange, one of the oranges which a few days ago had their arrival from Spain sensationally discussed in the newspapers and most of which turned out to be bad! Amid a design of stars, moon and planets we were interested to decipher the name of our friend

C. R., whose activities since he went back to Spain we had been wondering about.

May 6th

I am interested in names of people in graveyards and also in names of English villages. In Painswick I found: Organ, Loveday, Vanstone, Ponell, Woolen, Pulling, Bliss, Skerrett, Niblett, Cutts, Pegler, etc. Some of these people are described in the inscriptions as clothiers. And here are some names of villages near Painswick, found on a notice at the police-station about foot-and-mouth disease: Redmarley d'Abitot, Fretherne with Saul, Awre, English Bicknor, Thrupp, Ruardean, Hemelsfield, Weston Subedge, Somerford Keynes.

In *The Trumpet-Major* Hardy describes (in the days when Napoleon was threatening invasion) 'extraordinary machines which had been invented for the conveyance of troops to any point of the coast on which the enemy should land: they consisted of four boards placed across a sort of trolley, thirty men of the volunteer companies riding on each.' He describes the King coming to Weymouth, which was heavily guarded by frigates in the bay and how His Majesty was rather venturesome and went to sea too far and was nearly captured. The Georges were all brave. The story ambles on. Hardy seems sometimes vague about his time-sequence – for instance, he says Mathilda is coming on Monday and in the next chapter her arrival on Sunday is described, etc. He is a 'scenario' writer but cannot link everything together with any absorbing interest. He describes a parade of soldiers in the words of one 'who thought of every point in the line as an isolated man, each dwelling all to himself in the hermitage of his own mind.' If only people could always think like that! Armies and nations would vanish and human beings would appear, each different and each with her or his own private sorrows – and no man could ever drop a bomb on a city. But individuals become the 'hated abominable enemy' for whom nothing is too bad.

May 6th

It must surely be the fifth raid on Liverpool and Merseyside running – and all last night the bombers were passing over until early this morning and round here guns shaking and roaring. Mrs M. was in a train yesterday crowded with homeless families from that area. The wind went round to the West for a few hours last evening and rain clouds gathered but this morning it is in the North-East again and very cold and makes me irritable. We don't seem to have got charge of the oil-wells Mosul way, and no oil is coming to Haifa by the pipe-line. We have had no real report of the evacuation from Greece and are unlikely to get one. Hitler made a special report yesterday and certainly not flattering to our fighting prowess or military genius. People sometimes tell me that the Germans are not having it their own way. I confess to thinking they are having it all their own way. American aid seems very tardy – we hear of only 1,000 aeroplanes having been sent so far – after nearly two years of war. She wants to eat us up – and so does Germany. Countries are like wild animals. And what have we spent all our credit in the U.S.A. on? A pity the veil is not lifted. Perhaps better not. Probably muddle and incompetence are such that the night bombing people would give up in despair. Hitler hits nastily at Churchill as 'paralytic' or 'drunkard'. Have bought a volume of Penguin short stories, but cannot get through it.

Pupil-Pilot H., in a letter today, gives an interesting description of his training experiences. He says: 'The piloting of a twin-engined, fairly heavy trainer is vastly different from performing on the very sweetly tempered Tiger Moth – my first training aeroplane. I did fifty hours' flying on this type at Birmingham and apart from the initial anxieties (shared in good measure by my instructor) of trying to make a not-too intimate contact with the ground on landing and of avoiding the particularly malevolent species of balloon barrage nearby, I enjoyed my flying there. . . . I am now managing to control the twin-engined trainers fairly well. In both the courses I had difficulty in the initial stages, in flying one so often works against the body's normal instincts, particularly those of balance, and it seemed to take me rather a long while to overcome these reactions.'

May 7th

I walk in vain to reduce my bulk. The week before last I walked nearly one hundred miles and found I was little less reduced than a few pounds, though I felt perhaps more braced physically, but tired mentally. Walking is pleasant if one walks alone and can idle when one wishes and does not have to consider. But it becomes a pleasure of simply going on and on – and to walk without aim is not good. I walk with a stick to deal with dogs, a book under my arm and a pipe and tobacco, though I smoke very little while walking. I love the air and wide views from the Cotswold uplands and get very mixed up after crossing a valley to trace the way I came. I read in Kilvert's Diary that Dorothy Wordsworth went 'silly' in her old age because she had walked so much – so Wordsworth said in his complacent way – she having accompanied him on his long walks. People say walking is the best of all exercises. This is true perhaps only it does not exercise one's arms or belly muscles. I read of a walk of sixty miles in a day. This seems very hard going. I walked eighteen miles or perhaps twenty next day, but felt blank as I neared home, and only a mechanical and small satisfaction of having done it. Anyone can become dogged like that – and go on and on from small motives – as those imbeciles who cycle round tracks or dance for days, etc. Still, walking is a fine thing and fills the lungs and ventilates the body and relaxes the face and makes you see things. But it does not reduce weight remarkably. I notice it deepens my voice and makes me more at ease. I heard a labourer in a pub saying he'd rather walk any day to his work than cycle because 'it made yer get there right'. This is a true observation. To walk two or three miles to your work settles you down and relaxes you, I can well imagine. It is difficult to *think* when walking. I find it difficult to think of anything requiring concentration, without slowing my steps. But I find it easy to imagine a story and, as it were, entertain myself or have amusing thoughts. Nature, on a fine spring morning is very wonderful and is the true musical accompaniment of walking. But one does not want to botanize, or find names for birds – but simply to watch everything, with a simple curiosity. Air, too, is wonderful – and what qualities the different winds have and the height of the skies and the touch of every soft breeze. I am constantly interested in dead leaves – how they dance, how they follow you along the road sometimes . . . but I loathe dogs that rush out suddenly. So I carry a stick. I see very few rabbits now but many green plovers tumbling in the air and making a strange note with their wings. I was watching a magpie – there are lots here – flying through a thin wood and I have never seen a bird looking so much like a *flying-machine* – its very long tail horizontal – just like a toy bought at Hamley's painted black and white and wound up to fly a short way. I saw a male and female hawk on an upland, hovering and diving for a long time and trying to get – I think – larks on the ground. When a lark comes down from song, he hops and bounces as if still full of ecstasy – and then seems to vanish in some hole or cover. Everywhere I see timber being cut – a fine avenue of pines, over a hundred years old, all coming down. The drought continues. These hill-farmers here seem to do without water. The chestnuts are in early leaf now, their young triple leaves now hanging down, very limp and dejected. But what a marvel their first budding is – so fine and strong. Is it the drought? We hope for a quiet night. The moon is about half and it is clear, so we will probably have another disturbed sleep. Although we have nothing comparable to Plymouth, Bristol, etc., the gunfire and the heavy drone all night exhausts everyone. We got a present of a leg of mutton, which we ate at dinner with cauliflower and actually – caper-sauce. And then some sort of synthetic cheese and pulled bread. Tomatoes are 7/- a pound, as I think I said before. We are already in May. Soon it will be June – and the shortest night passed and the darkness increasing again. How quick is a year. Our time is now two hours in advance – that is, ten o'clock at night is only eight normally – so we go to bed about nine or earlier.

May 9th

A happy night here – at what we now call the Knapp Cabaret – a dozen and a half of us – singing, guitars, impromptu acting – Mr C. and I doing our French Customs scene again – and I hope it was not too French. None of us knew whether bombers were overhead or no, nor did we care, and we went to bed in the early hours and woke to find a lovely day – so the party went on on the terrace and in people's bedrooms overlooking the ever-changing, ever-absorbing valley.

And here is a tragedy that I believe I have not mentioned – that in the last raid on Cheltenham below us, a bomb fell on Messrs Dobell's wine warehouse and destroyed 'thousands of bottles of claret, sir, and the funny thing was that there was no sale for it, and we had been wondering whether to give it away'. Two tragedies in one, so to speak. Is there any better wine, any more sociable and more harmless beverage? Or any drink that you wake up from with the same happiness in your head as you went to bed with? The Scotch in former days understood claret – and needed it. The civilizing effects of wine are not appreciated by historians. It is not only a question of *cherchez la femme* in history, but of *cherchez le vin*. Now no country ever becomes civilized on spirits, and France can well claim to be the old centre of European civilization because of her vineyards. I read in *A Newspaper Man's Memoirs* (Aaron Watson – a bore, it seems) that someone asked Marie Corelli, the novelist, why she had never married. She said that it was not necessary to her for she had three pets who took the place of a man – a dog that growled all morning, a parrot that swore all evening and a cat that stayed out all night. The Humber area raided last night, heavily, so perhaps there were no aeroplanes over here last night.

May 14th

An immense monotony pervades us all. What is more dull, more stupid, more monotonous than war? We create our good moments here anyhow. But often I reflect on my long periods of inexpressible utter boredom in the last war, sitting in tents under blazing skies, or in mess-rooms. Who are, I used to wonder, those men who sing war as beautiful and incite people to glorious deeds? Yes, there are glorious deeds, and I have witnessed them, but the young are wiped out in them and what comes of it save fresh wars and more glorious deeds, etc? In the last war people said openly that only those over fifty should be eligible for war – and a very good idea.

June 7th

Here now after nearly three weeks on my back owing to a vein that decided to cease work, I find the valley clothed in thick green and the chestnut-tree with its white candles – and also Crete taken, France ugly and Roosevelt thundering vaguely. A lovely thunder-weather day, the lilac in bloom through the garden, the apple blossom out and the lettuce, onions, spinach and so on growing hard. To be really ill is always a good experience. It withdraws a man from life and makes him think of eternal life, which is the whole thing. Do you wish to die as you are? And how much one thought important is nothing at all.

July 2nd

Have read several stories and novels. How strange some writers are – those who must *kill* the hero, so to speak. Very modern, this tendency. Shalimar's 'Windjammer' is excellent, save that he must kill off people we begin to like, and so it is not interesting to read further. I wonder what centre of gravity people find today. Many must feel as the ancient Greeks felt: 'It is better not to have been *born.*' That was the message of Greece on one scale: and on the other there was Socrates, thinking too that it was better not to have been born *if there were nothing to find out* – and he set himself to the task of interpreting life on another basis – in terms of a possible higher life – or rather, he knew it already. Yes, that is the only solution. Taking life as it is, the Greeks are right. But taking life as a training for a spiritual development – that is indeed the only message. It is beginning to *transform* it. And that is what Christ said. Only no one seems to understand either what Socrates, or Christ, or anyone else ever said in this respect and people find their solace in Woolworth's and the Sunday papers.

The peonies scattered over this hillside green, starting deep red, are all white now. The Roman snails are very active.

July 10th

Considerable snarling in the House of Commons yesterday – labour, absenteeism, muddled control, no tanks, thirty different kinds of aeroplanes being ordered from the U.S.A. etc., and every department jealous of the next and no one capable of looking at truth in the light of truth but only through their own eyes and self-interests. It reminds me of something reported of Wilcox, the government analyst, just died. Of Crippen he said: 'He made the greatest mistake of his life in burying his wife in quicklime as it helped us to detect the poison.' Yes – and that is just how everyone is looking at everything nowadays. Surely the greatest mistake was to poison his wife?

July 11th

A big thunderstorm is breaking over the valley after days of heat. Heaven's artillery is preferable to that of Hitler. The potatoes will now swell and the whole countryside will thank God. Have been reading D. H. Lawrence's *Twilight in Italy* written before the war of 1914. He foresees the terrible mechanization – the enormous new roads, the cement ant-houses, the loss of all local grace and custom. 'The new world', he said, 'that I see coming in on all sides terrifies me.' We are in it, worse than he knew – the world that science has made possible. I like his words on Switzerland, through which he tramped: 'this dead, uninspired, *neutral* country – of utter soulless ordinariness, something intolerable . . . all was the utmost level of ordinariness and well-being.' He tried to stay in Zürich: 'the place was soul-killing. . . . I found a steamer that would take me away. That is how I always feel in Switzerland: the only possible living sensation is the relief in going away, in always going away.' Lawrence had no *shoes*. He walked barefoot – in a bad world. He was tortured, and how rightly, by the unfathomable mystery of sexual union but did not see it is the type and reflection of another union, of that alchemical marriage, that union of all that, in oneself, is truth and all that is good. The whole of his writing would have turned into 'mysticism', as it is stupidly called, at a single touch. But all that came to him of intense meaning, he ascribed to himself, so his writing exhausted him: and one feels the exhaustion and wonder mingled. He could not get beyond woman. He halted at the threshold, at the first test.

July 18th

Dr E. from a London hospital tells me that the only disease that has increased notably since the war is duodenal ulcer. He thinks it is due to nervous strain. Young soldiers with it have to be invalided out of the army, otherwise they do not recover. It is not treated by operation but by milk diet and magnesium silicate. He says the wonder is that no epidemics have appeared. But I fancy that the quantity of pain and illness and suffering remains a constant factor in life and, if war is on, other evils are less. Hull bombed last night. Quiet here. Tonight very clear and fine though cold. A lot of rain has fallen and the flowers are spread on the ground. Yesterday H. R. H. came to tea and we were all pleased and flustered. He is too thin and gives an impression of being very tired, deep in himself. Asked about Japan, he said he knew nothing. He gets no special news apparently.

July 19th

All quiet last night, though we expected the old din to start and the meaningless seriousness of inane war to press on our souls again. Thought during the night very much of eternal life. What is there in ourselves that we would wish to be made eternal? How strange that people say it is egotism to believe in eternal life! This idea, taken rightly, is the reverse and very painful.

July 28th

The roses are lovely in the garden this evening after the rain. The barrage balloons are pointing in all directions as the wind has fallen. The evening is full of bats and owls. Chan met a fox, and suddenly became a thing of speed. As a rule his legs seem out of order. We call him Mr Maisky. A guitar is sounding from the drawing-room. Night is near – and blessed sleep, beloved from pole to pole. Already I can hear the beat of our night-fighters in the air to the south and over Bristol-way searchlights are playing on the dark clouds. There is a tramp of feet on the stairs. Doors slam. Everyone is going to bed. In a short time the house will be quiet and I will hear only the clock ticking and the mouse in the corner of my room and the occasional rush of a motor cycle down the hill or the scream of a car in low gear ascending – which still makes us at times listen a moment. A rising vapour in the dark valley – probably the smoke-screen.

August 2nd

The *Daily Telegraph* has produced now a map of the world in which America appears *East* of Europe. This gives rise to endless discussion like summer-time. People do not think easily in terms of the *roundness* of the world, but take West and East literally or absolutely – and no one can grasp the imaginary nautical line where in crossing it is either two days the same date, or a day is missed in going round the world. After all, people do not even realize that the sun does not rise or set, but the earth turns. All that sort of non-sensory thought is beyond mankind. Yet nature invites us to think beyond the senses, which is the only solution to life's meaning.

I find myself indolent, and disinclined to make efforts, save towards my writings. I am reading *The Land of the Blue Poppy* by the naturalist, F. Kingdon Ward, a good travel book, gentle, easy to read, mildly interesting. The Cambridge blue poppy with the corn-coloured corolla, *Meconopsis Speciosa*, grows up to 18,000 feet in Tibet. Is it not clear that to develop anything in oneself one must isolate oneself from collective influences? Ward felt this. Witnessing the second major war in my lifetime, now as a civilian, I realize this truth. But the dreadful atmosphere of war hangs heavily on me and one must make a special effort to over-come it every day – every moment of the day. Modern civiliza-tion is a burden if seen to lead nowhere. I suppose it is no use regretting anything or thinking of the young life being sacrificed every day. Yet there must be some right attitude which includes both the tragedy and the necessity of a future together. And I suppose this is everyone's secret problem. But I realize that one must not be afraid. As Dr Johnson said, one must be afraid of nothing on earth. Finding myself ridiculing someone, Plato's words came into my mind: 'He who ridicules another does so out of vanity and ignorance of himself.' No one seems able to put himself in the position of another person. If civilization today led in that direction and had a real teaching about inner development, it would be interesting and worth while.

August 5th

A mysterious thing is happening just at this moment – a clear tranquil sky passing towards darkness and all the barrage balloons suddenly being lowered. Overhead a faint pulsation of squadrons of aeroplanes, very high. Perhaps with the night-fighters as our main defence now, they take balloons down, to be out of their way. A light is twinkling far across the valley, reminding us of more gracious days, and of all the small things that made up the best of life. Suddenly it goes out. The little owl wheels and turns and alights on the wires carrying our electric current and looks round carefully. A glare of light over the woods behind the house. The full moon is rising. The smoke-screen is weaving up from the valley towards us.

August 10th

Double summer-time ended today and eight o'clock became seven o'clock. The fiery sickness of war seems about to extend over the whole world. Japan is threatening everyone. The Germans seem to do anything with our army. I was reading Eckarthausen's *Cloud in the Sanctuary*. In his first letter he addresses the generation of the French Revolution – the so-called Age of Reason which was to purify the world of all evil for the rest of time. Things are the same and worse today: 'Everywhere there is war between animal man and spiritual man. It is said we live in an age of light, but it would be true to say we live in an age of twilight. . . . Poor mankind! To what standpoint have you raised the happiness of man? Has there ever been an age which has counted so many victims, or one in which immorality and egotism have been greater? The tree is known by its fruits. Mad men! With your supposed natural reason, from whence have you the light by which you are so willing to enlighten others? Are not all your ideas borrowed from your senses which do not give you the reality but merely its phenomena? . . .' But truth today is *machines*. Truth is only a matter of sense. Alas, in consequence, men, having nothing internal to hold them, are seized by these machines and made to serve them. I see nothing that can really stop war in this century, such disintegration on all sides. Then perhaps man will lose his capacity to make machines.

August 13th

Yesterday my sister Mildred's birthday – grouse day. She is in Aberdeen, her husband back in the Black Watch, acting as liaison officer. I see Aberdeen is being bombed. Last night a wild S.W. wind and torrents of rain against the house here, and in the distance the sound of bombs and/or guns. What a strange life. It is stranger than can be imagined. We have got a small kitten for the mice. He is very fine and brave and stands up to the dogs and has chosen his special chair already and sleeps and plays without a thought. What strange charm very young things have – enough to make an atheist think twice. Innocence is a genuine quality – that is, they have no wish to harm, which is what the word means.

August 16th

A grand day of pouring rain. Tonight a good party with our friends at the house up the hill. Some acting. 'The Russian H.Q.', 'The British H.Q. in the Near East' and finally Roosevelt and his advisers. We all wore beavers and moustaches of different kinds and enjoyed ourselves, which is the great and most blessed thing. The one thing is: *enjoy yourself.* Try, and see how difficult this is! All of us spend most of the time in being unhappy, depressed, angry, jealous, sad, etc. That means that to enjoy oneself requires a lot of effort and conscious living.

September 21st

I find myself thinking of Mithraism. It was a religion that ran parallel with Christianity for a long time. All the Roman villas in England and Europe have Mithraic chapels, pointing to the East. It was military in character – commending the virtues of physical fitness and valour, but it had behind it something far deeper. Is it possible that the raw manifestations of Nazi-ism and of Russia are vaguely the first steps? We are weak and soft in this country and have no idea what we are doing or fighting for. Maybe we witness the 'end of the world' which in the Greek means only 'consummation of an age'. Christianity as commonly taken is so much Dickens' sentiment, in general, – i.e. in Dickens we have an example of the commonly accepted idea of a 'Christian' – not in his personal life but in his writings. The 'new god', therefore, may appear in a very strange form – born out of what we least expect: 'from the manger'. If you think of this, you will see it must always be so. A new influx of spiritual force cannot pass through what is outworn, and accepted as spiritual. Everything only lasts *for a time – including truth.*

October 21st

Read a fine sea-story *Hurricane Williams* by a Mr Gordon
Young to whom I wrote, congratulating him. He has the right
note for a fine sea-story, semi-mystical, strange, forceful, practical
and allegoric, the sea and a ship-full of men and women on it
being a profound, spiritual symbol that catches at the inner
thought continually while reading. His figure of the avenger
coming dripping out of the sea at night into the midst of the
mutineers and the account of the shark-fight are on the first level,
and all the sea-imagery is of a high order and the language
powerful and knowledgeable.

October 23rd

A true philosopher has always to deal with life first and unless
life is arranged and attended to he cannot go beyond it rightly and
become a philosopher – in the sense of a student and lover of
wisdom. Wisdom begins at home. I have been reading Dorothy
Wordsworth's colourless 'Diary'. She is tedious and thinly bright.
Her narrative is most real – as in the case of most women – when
she talks of unpleasant things, as the bad inns and the bad lectures
she and William received in these towns in Scotland – and
elsewhere. She speaks much of the dirt of the Scottish inns and is
contemptuous of them.

William remains a vague, weak figure throughout these Diaries;
Coleridge seems to be more tenderly treated, but one cannot see
him or anyone else. He was, of course, always 'ill' and disappear-
ing. Both she and William seem to be people who do not start
from the events of life. Life is an infernal nuisance to everyone. A
tolerant attitude gained by suffering is necessary before one passes
on to anything else. But I do not know either about Dorothy or
William. They sound like weak 'Yogis' – both of them – but I
catch no clear idea of William. I fancy Dorothy did not think
much of him at heart. Like a woman she does not mention anything outside her own small interests and actual sight. The period
was 1798 and so on – the aftermath of the French Revolution,
Napoleon and so on. But one never gathers any history from an
Englishwoman's Diaries as one does from those great diarists, the
French women. French women have brains and are 'wicked'. She

is occupied with neither history nor cookery nor knitting, but only with the badness of inns, the longness of the journey, and with the trees and flowers which touch her. 'A mild morning, the window open, the redbreasts singing in the garden. William went a walk. . . . Dinner was bad and the people uncivil. . . . At the inn they hesitated to give us beds. We were alarmed, supposing the inn to be filled with *tourists*. . . . We found nothing remarkable save the impertinence of the waiter . . . the house throughout dirty.' She and William go to see (Sir Walter) Scott. They arrive before 'Mr and Mrs Scott had risen' and all we hear is that 'they had a meal'. She says, however, that driving away a person hailed them 'whether an Irishman or a foreigner I know not. I suppose we were an occasion of suspicion at a time when everyone was talking of the threatened invasion.' In this meagre blind way we see 'Scott' and 'Napoleon' through tiny eyes. The Diaries are just barely worth reading – just barely words-worth.

October 27th

One of those special days in which normal accidents are, as it were, concentrated in one place. A vast Army lorry lying across the hill with two petrol trailers, a car on fire, a motor bicycle smashed, a car in the ditch – and a little girl goes and sprains her ankle. All this rather suddenly, within a short distance on the hill, just by our house. The day fine and dry and nothing to account for it. These packets of things happening together – or of the same kind of events – sometimes seem to be merely normal accidents concentrated in one place, and sometimes unusual accidents. We all know that if the train is late, then it is likely all sorts of other things will follow, such as that the expected telegram will be delayed, the guests will be late, and so on. But very unusual things happen sometimes together, as when one meets an old friend of years ago and, lo, another comes into view. Or sometimes the same odd word, in book, paper, talk, etc. But I will give a better example. I was washing and the soap jumped swiftly out of my hands. I could not find it anywhere. It had vanished. Later on, I found it was in a small jug some distance off. Then I got in the car, dropped the engine-key and could not find it. It had vanished. I took mats, floor-boards, etc. up. It was in the turn-up of my trousers. Then I could not find my fountain-pen. I hunted high and low. It was hidden in a book. All on the same day and all the same kind of thing. There is a time for everything.

November 1st

Col. B., back from London tonight, says the cold was very great and everything frozen and that people took the cracking of ice on the roads as an air-raid warning. Here is nearly full moon and white frost – and Russia is expecting a German gas attack. Have been in bed reading Andrée's Balloon Expedition (1897) and find some interesting accounts of *bear-steaks, kidney,* etc. Even a blood-pancake does not revolt me. This is because things go with the instincts when eating is limited. The whole expedition seems to me very unintelligent and Andrée very stupid, but the Scandinavians have made a tedious 'American-German' volume out of it, reporting everything – the remains found, their position, weight, etc.

November 14th

C. has sent us his impressions of his first week in the Navy. He writes as follows: 'Well, I've been a sailor a week now and have only seen the sea in the distance except for the ferry trip over from Harwich Harbour. And life is not too bad. Food is plentiful and good but nearly always cold and is eaten from aluminium crockery. However everything is clean and polished in true Naval Style. Dormitories are warm and there is an abundance of hot water everywhere for washing and drying when you have time for such frivolities. H.M.S. *Ganges* is an old established training place which used to train boys pre-war and is well equipped with libraries, likewise gym, etc. As a matter of fact I came here to swim some years ago, only on that occasion we were entertained in the Ward Room, which we now salute and go past at the double. Our draft numbered three hundred and from these nine of us were selected as Class leaders and have to stay behind for another week to look after the next week's draft. We go over with these to the main establishment with two leaders to each mess of about sixty men. . . . We have a draft of seventy New-foundland lads in our dormitory and had heard ghastly rumours of their toughness and filth before they arrived. . . . Now they are clean and in 'Square Rig' they look a first rate crowd of young animals and a good deal superior to the long-haired narrow-chested Cockneys who arrived at the same time, but are not now long-haired. . . . Of our crowd three are university men, one a theological student. The most striking feature about life here is that both Officers and Petty Officers are extraordinarily kind, although discipline is pretty rigid.'

If you consider the fact of service (we are all slaves) domestic service is the most real, for then a man knows what he is doing and whether he has done it or not. A butler knows if he has done his duty and he knows what his duty is. But a doctor neither knows what he is doing nor what he has to do, and still less a politician.

November 16th

J. C. writes as a member of the Home Guard at Bournemouth: 'I have qualified as a Lewis Gunner and am entitled to wear a badge, bearing the letters L.G., but as I have never fired the gun I feel this is a little premature.'

November 23rd

I read today that the tea-plant is not really a bush but a tree growing to thirty or more feet. It is pruned down so as to be easily picked. I also learned that the leaves are allowed to wither when plucked, mixed and rolled up in water, strained and allowed to *ferment* and then dried. The result is tea. It came from Tibet, where the leaf was used as a flavouring adjunct in frying. The Chinese found out how to make tea out of it. Trees are extraordinary chemical factories, making turpentine or camphor or rubber or tea or coffee, etc. Surely a man's mind must be half-dead who does not see some meaning in all this? Listened to the Brains Trust today – a parcel of able – if able – asses. Was glad to hear them quarrelling. All stumped by why a horse gets up on its front legs and cow on its back legs (the horse being accustomed to live in long grass, so looks up and around first for enemies, and the cow accustomed to live where grass is short).

November 29th

I was talking today to my wife about the point when tragedy becomes ridiculous. She quoted the story of the bus-load of children that fell over a cliff in France. Everyone felt the horror. But when a bus-load of the mothers arrived and also fell over the cliff, people could not help laughing. There is always behind the most awful aspects of life some odd feeling that it is all unreal. Even in really harrowing moments we feel this – and it must mean that we have not to take life too seriously. Daudet told a good story on this subject when speaking of the theatre and how tragedy can easily become ridiculous, if too much is ladled out in a scene. He said: 'It is like this. A woman in black gets into an omnibus: her mourning and her bearing force her neighbours to enquire into the history of her misfortunes. These she relates and all the occupants of the bus are moved to tears. She tells of the deaths of a first and second child, but at the death of the third, the interest of the omnibus begins to slacken and when she reaches the death of the fourth, devoured by a crocodile on the banks of the Nile, everybody bursts out laughing. Yes, whenever an author writes a play, he should keep in mind the story of the woman in the omnibus.'

CHAPTER TEN

Birdlip 1942

The Diary extracts which comprise the preceding chapter omit all reference to Dr Nicoll's two main occupations, both of which belonged to his private life, his psychological work with the group and his Gospel studies. The most important work of each day he was silent about. His psychological teaching was esoteric and could not be spoken of at that time to anyone outside the group; his private writing belonged to his inner life and was inspired by deep meditation. His Diary was written as light relief, generally at night, as a record of this strange war period.

His psychological work was continuous. We who lived with him were his pupils, gaining self-knowledge no less in Gloucestershire than in Essex. At the week-ends, however, a clear note was sounded when people converged upon the two houses from various directions. Every Friday the paper to be read and discussed during the week-end was gradually built up. Sometimes he would begin his paper on Thursday, but in that case he would be liable to change his mind and would find a new subject on Friday. Many of the papers were inspired by questions that came from Mr Bush. Many versions of each paper were written – in fact, the paper seemed to evolve. At the meeting on Saturday evening, when the people from a distance had arrived, I would read the paper aloud, and then Dr Nicoll would answer questions. The weeks took on a certain rhythm, working up to an intensity of effort on Friday, which was maintained throughout the weekend, to be followed by a period of relaxation when Monday came and Dr Nicoll would rest. I would be busy preparing the copies to be sent out, but on Tuesday I would go off into Cheltenham to find a new batch of detective novels. When he had rested he would turn again to his Gospel studies.

During 1941 Dr Nicoll had completed his chapters on *The Lord's Prayer* which were published posthumously in *The Mark*. The writing of the chapters which were eventually published under the title *The New Man* began in a curious way. We often had talks about the Bible characters. One day an idea came to

198

me. I collected from the four Gospels all that was said about St Peter and arranged the material, as far as possible, chronologically. Then I laid this document on Dr Nicoll's table with the tentative suggestion that he might like to comment on the character of St Peter and the part played by him in the Gospels. This experiment had surprising results, for Dr Nicoll was immediately interested and wrote with the utmost rapidity the chapter on St Peter which was later included in *The New Man* just as it stood without alteration. We little thought at the time that this was the beginning of a whole book. We read the chapter to the household and it was received with delight by all. Then I read it to the group assembled at the week-end. Dr Nicoll went on to make studies of John the Baptist and Judas, and to write whole chapters about the meaning of certain Greek words as used in the Gospels. For instance, the word φρονιμος proved to be most interesting to speculate on, and a study of its meaning gave the clue to certain parables. The word used to describe a man who was practical and awake to what was necessary for his own inner development, for his entry into the Kingdom of Heaven. A man who was φρονιμος was one who had presence of mind, who had his wits about him. As Dr Nicoll says in his chapter on *The Idea of Wisdom in the Gospels* the word has a strong, bracing, practical meaning and is used to describe the right action of an intelligent man seeking inner evolution. It is not the same as 'wise'. The man who founded his house on the rock and the five virgins who had oil in their lamps had a practical wisdom for which there is no word in our language. Thus Dr Nicoll stressed that Christ was always urging those whom He taught to be as practical in seeking the Kingdom of Heaven as they would be in seeking their life-goal. This word had deep meaning for us as it conveyed what was expressed in our own teaching by the term 'Sly Man' where 'sly' retains its original meaning. Then we studied the word δικη translated as righteousness, and understood its Greek meaning of balance, the righteous man being the upright man who is able to stand firm in the middle of the pendulum. This study led us to the Sermon on the Mount to investigate the words describing the new kind of righteousness exceeding that of the Scribes and Pharisees. Here we found much that was unexpected. For instance, the discovery that the word translated as 'meek', πραος, originally meant 'becoming tamed, as a wild animal is tamed' suggested that the word implied in itself a capacity for going against all natural resentfulness and passion and anger. A whole chapter about the Sermon on the Mount followed, making clear what these strange instructions are, the obeying of which can lead a man to a level in himself called the Kingdom of Heaven.

A chapter on the idea of prayer does not minimize the difficulties but gives the key to communication with a higher level which is how Dr Nicoll defines prayer. He collects the instructions given by Christ in the Gospels for the technique of prayer concluding with the startling statement that request always evokes its response.

Dr Nicoll now began to think of these writings as material for a book on the interpretation of the parables and miracles in the Gospels. He turned his attention to an introduction on the language of parables, which should give the key to the whole book. He felt that it was important to make people familiar with this language, and spoke of it as a language that could be learned which would contribute to the understanding not only of parables but of fairy tales and mythology, and dreams. A knowledge of this language opened the door to a world of new meaning, which has always been accessible to esoteric schools, being one of the vehicles in which age-old truths have been preserved and handed down by those who could memorize stories and value them for their beauty and interest even though unaware of their inner meaning.

It was his understanding of the language of parables that gave Dr Nicoll the clue to the meaning of the Miracle of the Marriage at Cana, the first of Christ's miracles as related in the Gospel of St John. Although the chapter on this subject was begun at this time, it was not completed for several years as Dr Nicoll continued to work over it many times before he had said what he wanted to convey. He thought that this Marriage represented a stage of Christ's own development, after which He was able to enter upon the period of His own teaching.

Dr Nicoll wrote finally about the Kingdom of Heaven, as a level within Man which could be reached by those who followed

Christ's instructions. He gathered together all the parables which speak of this.

Following the interpretation of Gurdjieff and Ouspensky, Dr Nicoll spoke of the Crucifixion as a drama prepared in the Esoteric Schools and enacted by certain characters who were trained for their parts. Gurdjieff and Ouspensky and Dr Nicoll all were in agreement in interpreting the part of Judas as consciously played by the disciple specially chosen to play the most difficult role of traitor.

As these chapters were written, we read them in the evenings to those who were living in the household and sometimes we read them at the week-ends to those who had come down, and we talked of them. They became a very familiar part of our lives and I think everyone gained a very intimate knowledge of the Gospels from reading these studies. The chapter on Faith originally belonged to the study of the Lord's Prayer, the remaining three sections of which, on Metanoia, Nicodemus and Truth, are published in *The Mark*. The commentary on Faith is very illuminating. He defined Faith as a living, active seed in a man, an awareness of scale, not merely passive belief, and showed how all was possible to one who possessed it.

Throughout the year the Diary continued, expressing Dr Nicoll's thoughts about the events of outer life with no reference to the private speculation of his inner spiritual life, or to all that he was teaching us and those of his group who were physically separated from us. He was awake to all that happened in the War.

Dr Nicoll spoke of Churchill as a man of destiny, kept alive to play the role of intermediary between Great Britain and U.S.A. The son of an American mother and a descendant of the Marlborough family, with his lack of bitterness, his power of impression and his courage, he suited the role well, but Dr Nicoll considered him unlucky and reminded us that Napoleon chose only lucky men. He was to change this opinion before the War was over. Churchill, he said, was a man of sudden impulse, brooking no criticism, overriding everyone. Turning the pages of Blount's Diary, he read out to us the entry for the 22nd October 1903:

Met for the first time young Winston Churchill. He is a

little, square-headed fellow of no very striking appearance
but of wit, intelligence and originality, a strange replica of
his father, Lord Randolph Churchill, with all his father's
suddenness and assurance and I should say more than his
father's ability. There is just the same gaminerie. He interested me immensely.

At this time, the Home Guard began to be armed with pikes,
to everyone's surprise. Jane now had her calling-up papers. She
put herself down for the A.F.S. and took a room in Cheltenham.
Dr Nicoll was charmed by Camilla Copley, now three and a half
years old, who came over with her mother. She asked Dr and Mrs
Nicoll if they were staying here. A good opening remark to the
hosts, he said. After all, that is what everyone is doing, staying
somewhere, staying in fact on this planet for a short time.

The weather was now milder and there were a few air-raids.
Dr Nicoll had toothache and went to the dentist. He found a
dentist called Mr Boodle with whom he discussed the connection
between earache and toothache, which are both so close to the
brain they are hard to bear. He said he found lying in bed with
toothache in the dark impossible and that a light helped, but
getting up and doing something was best. He was pleased with
two Valentines that arrived, one with a very nice line, he said.
'I am sorry that I am so old fashioned but I love you very much.'
He wrote in his diary:

> Snowdrops on my table and a gift of chocolates, but I have
> toothache lurking. Am afraid I am only reading detective
> stories, which do not refresh one, though they hold the
> attention. Have trapped a mouse that I had grown rather
> fond of, but it became a nuisance.

We were now having a cold spell and with hard frosts at night.
An owl nested in a chimney pot above Mrs Nicoll's room and
made weird noises at night. She called us in to hear it breathing.
For a long time we did not know what it was; it sounded like a
person breathing somewhere just outside the room.

On 3rd March there was a lunar eclipse which began about

eleven-thirty, the earth's shadow creeping on to the left side and the moon assuming shapes different from its phases. It was an evil eclipse, the malefics Mars, Saturn and Uranus being in conjunction in Taurus. Probably its approach was responsible for the horrible accident on the hill the day before. Seven guns piled up, ten men were injured and one killed. The artillery column took the hill too fast. They complained there were not any notices warning them.

A fortnight later there was another military accident on the hill. Mrs Butler said that the authorities had come to the conclusion that nothing could be done about military accidents because the Army had not learned to drive. She had heard that the Colonel had reached Cairo safely with his new royal boss, flying by Gibraltar and Lagos to West Africa and across to Greece.

Dr Nicoll read out to us a letter from Lieutenant Sam Copley written from on board his destroyer:

> As regards mixing with the crew, many jagged points have worn smooth now and I can be quite free with them as a rule. Going into action together breaks down a lot of barriers between people because in the height of the excitement quite impossible people become bearable and people for a while understand each other. There is a sort of joint fear and joint pride and officers, P.O.s and men fall into their proper relationships so all are friendly, but although much etiquette is dropped, there is no lack of respect.

Suddenly on 25th March we had the most lovely weather, although the glass was falling and hundreds of seagulls were wheeling high over Birdlip.

> 'It was 90° in the sun,' Dr Nicoll recorded in his diary, 'and fir cones were cracking up in the wood. Two silver butterflies were wantoning in the air and a lizard was standing on a bit of limestone as if it could not remember, or did remember.'

The gardener was now to be called up, so it was arranged to divide the garden work between the household. Potatoes, onions, beets, turnips, greens and beans – the care of those was shared. There were several local air raids and Dr Nicoll wrote to the Air

Ministry to draw their attention to the fact that the balloons on the ground marked the position of the factory. The factory was severely damaged in a raid, twenty-nine people being killed, a hundred injured.

The entry in Dr Nicoll's diary for April 16th was:

> Halcyon days. We swim in an ocean of light and air and bird songs. The women are all gardening. We went to Cheltenham to a cinema to see Walt Disney's *Fantasia* and were charmed by the baby Pegasus.

On 1st May Dr Nicoll wrote in his diary:

> It is night. The full moon is slowly rising behind the hill. In the valley there is mist. A few stars shine. In the distance there is the sound of an aeroplane. You look up and listen – is it one of ours? Who are in it? Where is it bound for and what will be its 'fate? One can tell nothing. One does not even know what will happen tonight here. Everyone is helpless, even those passing overhead in the aeroplane. Everything is moved and those boys in the aeroplane are being moved; they are under its laws. In their secret hearts they do not wish to be where they are. In their innermost hearts they do not wish to drop bombs, but everything is moved; everything happens as it must. Only one escape exists – for a man to become different. This is the teaching of Christ – rebirth; to become another man; to become what this innermost, secret heart faintly tells us; but how, with all this machinery that makes us obey it? Suddenly the searchlights blaze; they are looking for the aeroplane. It has gone.

A few days later he was delighted when the candles appeared all over the chestnut tree and he thought the leaves hanging down seemed to be clapping in the morning breeze.

On 20th May Miss Corcoran was bitten in the finger by an adder in the garden. Dr Nicoll applied a tourniquet tightly and opened the wound with a razor blade; then Dr Grove-Whyte came over from Cirencester and opened up the cut and eventually took her with him to hospital as the arm began to swell. She complained of local pain. We now recalled Mrs Hicks-Beach's warning when she called on our first day to tell us to beware of adders in the garden. We had forgotten all about it as no one had seen an adder until now.

Dr Nicoll painted several of the big snails with oil paint in different colours, hoping that we should recognize them the following year. He thought them a very strange experiment of nature, a ready-made house and double sex, so that each is the father and mother and so no inequality of the sexes can arise and so no bad feelings, and each has its own children.

Dr Nicoll enjoyed a visit from the village constable who called one day in his neat car. He described him as a kindly, large, earnest man with a comfortable soft voice. He came to speak of the mystery of some large stones which had been placed on the hill road. Dr Nicoll was struck that while he was speaking earnestly to him, suddenly looking upwards as if praying, he said, 'That's good', pointing to a painting of his of the local pub, and went on without loss of continuity. He thought that unlike a policeman, who can usually attend to only one thing at a time.

After three days Miss Corcoran returned from Cirencester Hospital cured. We heard that adders are most poisonous in July and August when the young are being reared and that the cock adder can jump up to the chin. Doctors seem to know nothing about them. Local folk said adders were common on the hillside and they were best killed with a shotgun. We decided to try the saucer of milk trick. Mrs Hodder was reading a letter from her husband in one of the fields on the hill and happened to turn round to see an adder with its head reared, only a few inches away. She said she was on the other side of the field in a matter of seconds.

The second anniversary of John's and Jane's wedding had arrived. Whit Monday was a wet day, with gleams of sunshine and a gale in the west. In the evening there was a rainbow in the east. The lilac was lovely. Jane came for the week-end in her dark blue uniform.

June brought the news that the greatest of all raids had taken place. More than a thousand of our bombers had gone over Cologne and the Germans retaliated on Canterbury. The raids continued day after day. We talked of Roosevelt saying that he often felt he had done it all before and that he was steering his country safely a second time. Dr Nicoll thought that possible. He said William James' twice-born man is nothing inconceivable. Napoleon had done it all before and remembered up to a point. Also he thought a man like Dr Johnson, with his extraordinary memory, was perhaps not memorizing it all for the first time. Many unusual facilities suggest previous experiences.

On 15th June Mrs Hodder had her baby in a nursing home at Cheltenham. He was tiny but everyone was pleased that he had arrived, even though he was premature.

On 19th July, Dr Nicoll wrote in his diary:

> Had a very blessed and quiet birthday. People very good to me. I was born so very far away psychologically in 1884 that my age no longer interests me. One begins to have thoughts that are no longer to do with time. Found myself amused remembering all the good resolutions I used to make on this date. Worked at a picture of double pink poppies against the sun. Had great satisfaction and found my mind and heart full of their beauty afterwards. Cannot understand people who paint ugliness. It must react on them internally. The poor dog, Shan, has to be kept on a lead for sheep chasing. He cannot understand and no one can explain. Just like us.

John was now a lance-bombardier in an anti-aircraft battery defending Birmingham. He wrote that his gun was a new device and had brought down four aeroplanes in a recent raid. Jane used to go to Birmingham to visit him from time to time. Our August weather was mild and stormy, with westerly gales. Both houses were full of friends snatching holidays. Some came on bicycles. We had an exhibition of paintings at the King's Head. All the paintings that we had done during the past year were shewn. Someone asked for a catalogue of the exhibition and Dr Nicoll and I amused ourselves by naming the paintings as in the *Punch* articles on the Royal Academy. The best paintings were those by Dr Nicoll himself – his poppies, his beautiful chestnut trees and his landscapes. He received a reproduction of Renoir's 'Les Parapluies' by post, which he liked very much. He said he was in love with the woman without an umbrella and hoped that the gentleman with the suede black ribbed gloves was not going to offer her his protection. He spent a long time and a very pleasurable time in copying this painting.

It was at this time that the Duke of Kent was killed when his aeroplane crashed. Dr Nicoll felt this very deeply as he had so very recently been with us.

There was an eclipse of the moon and the weather was hot. After a few days, Colonel Butler returned after working in the late Duke's office at Coppins. There had been thousands of telegrams of condolence to reply to and it was said that the aeroplane should not have started, the weather was too bad. All other 'planes had been cancelled. There was to be an enquiry as to why the Duke's 'plane was allowed to start. It had obviously lost its way – it ought to have been over the sea. The surviving rear-gunner was still concussed and could only mutter 'we're losing height'.

On 28th September, Dr Nicoll wrote in his diary:

> Though no one speaks of the war, all feel its drain continuously. One has to keep oneself alive by one's own heat, like those alpine flowers, Solanbella, that grow through the ice, melting a passage by their own heat of growth and emerge in flower above the ice to receive the first bees. Nature is always a lesson in effort, however bad the conditions. The old spiritual alchemists to whom man is the lead to be transformed into gold often said, 'study nature'. Saw a sunflower today over which a spider had woven its web.

A letter came from Lady Syfret describing the investiture at Buckingham Palace at which her husband, Rear-Admiral Syfret, was knighted.

October came in and the trees became yellow. The hawk hovered once again. Dr Nicoll remarked how lovely the hawk was in what it could do in the wind and the glint of sun, and said how lovely is anyone when he is doing what he can really do. In loveliness lies the power of doing.

On 9th October, he wrote in his diary:

> What a blessed thing it is to feel well again after a month of hoarseness and coughs and intervals of bed. Some illnesses awaken the spirit and some confuse it. A sore larynx seems

to attack the spirit and these days I have felt the nearness of
all those hells that surround Man and await the failure of his
spirit. We enter a winter that will press heavily on all people.
All are weary of war and action but no one speaks of it.
Stalingrad not yet taken.

Dr Nicoll was interested to read in Seneca that at one point he
discovered at last that this world, which in his insensate pride he
had believed to have been arranged in a manner hostile to himself,
was simply nothing more than ill arranged.

There was now a great shortage of everything. Edith had a
birthday and was given by a friend a box of matches and an egg,
for both of which she was very thankful.

We had a mild and sunny Christmas. Captain Hodder who was
staying with us with his wife told us of a private in his battalion
who threw his boots at his company commander. Asked why the
next day by the C.O., he said they were spoiling his feet as regards
his profession in private life. 'What is your profession?' he was
asked. 'A cat burglar' he answered with pride. 'Well,' said the
C.O., 'we cannot take action about your private profession but
we can about throwing your boots at an officer. Two weeks'
detention.'

On Christmas Eve Dr Nicoll wrote in his diary:

A fine sunny, sharpish day. We have only four or five
guests over Christmas. Jane is with us still and her John is
coming at New Year, it being forbidden for the military to
travel at Christmas time. They are singing carols in the
drawing-room, a very sweet thin sound in this hard, evil age.
Tonight we dine early and all go up to the 'Royal George',
as Mr King has promised us he has one or two bottles put by.
It is nearly impossible to get anything at the wine shops. We
bought port at 48/- a bottle, a little rum and two bottles of
white wine, all costing a lot. A white turkey came from
Chirk Castle to Mrs B. and Captain H. brought chickens,
and a duck has arrived and two geese are somewhere on the
railway, so we are lucky. The Russians are advancing still.
The aeroplanes roar overhead every night, but not enemy
ones so far. A bright moon is shining. C. is up tonight after

two or three weeks in and out of bed with a tickling throat. This laryngitis seems very common nowadays. Mrs King at the pub has lost her voice completely again, as she did last year. It lasts three months.

We had a gay New Year's Eve, inventing a haggis out of a sponge bag and bagpipes out of a small easel upside down in which a concertina was concealed. Three of the men walked in procession wearing kilts made of rugs.

One day Dr Nicoll was writing about the Miracle of Water into Wine. He picked up *Chambers's Journal* and found a reference to Cana of Galilee. Later, taking up one of the detective stories that I had brought him from the Library he began to read *Footprints on the Ceiling* by Rawson, and on page 24 found a drawing of two glasses labelled respectively 'water' and 'wine'. He thought that such coincidences, occasions when events happen together, are times when one is in a special state of attunement, causing correspondence between outer life and inner life as though for the moment one knows the time. Dr Nicoll preferred to call these coincidences examples of synchronicity, and believed that whoever experienced such synchronous events was temporarily above the ordinary laws of horizontal time. He was continually pondering on the cause of such an unexpected coming together of events that seemed unrelated.

As soon as we began to observe examples of synchronicity, we seemed to attract them. Not only did those of us who were in the household experience them, but people visiting us from outside to whom the subject had never been mentioned would relate similar experiences. For instance, Barrow's wife came to stay with him at the cottage for a few days and told us that on her way to work one morning recently she had noticed a torn newspaper of that morning's date blown about and trodden near some railings, and when she reached the place where she worked and tore off the Daily Calendar she read:

> Only a newspaper!
> Quick read, quick lost –
> Torn, trampled under foot,
> Who counts thy cost?

Many of our coincidences occurred in connection with the ordinary incidents of daily life. One morning I had noticed a picture of a rabbit and a stoat in the *Daily Express*, and on going into the garden very soon afterwards I met the gardener who was coming down the path carrying a rabbit in one hand and a stoat in the other. I had never seen those two animals together before, alive or dead.

Dr Nicoll had the experience, within less than ten seconds, of reading the words 'cork' and 'bottle' from entirely unrelated sources, about which he said that the point was that the words 'cork' and 'bottle' had entered his consciousness twice within a brief time and it was this bringing together, without apparent connection, into one's own experience of two related things that we had to reflect on.

I was chiefly interested in synchronisms which consisted of request and response, or question and answer, the answer following hard upon the question. One evening at the pub at about eight o'clock someone asked the question: 'What is the difference between a butterfly and a moth?' Someone began to explain but no satisfactory answer was given. Dr Nicoll went home and soon afterwards began to read in bed *Country Life* which I had left in his room while he was out. He opened it at an article called 'Some Day-Flying Moths' which began with the words: 'The dividing line between a butterfly and a moth in the general sense is very hard to define . . .' and went on to define it.

We were talking with Dr Nicoll in his room one evening, and he read to us (as he often used to) a passage from the *Evening Standard* from an article by Dean Inge which interested him because the Dean spoke of a model of a mouse placed in a church. He was writing of the unpopularity of British Officers in Germany after the previous war: 'An Englishman, visiting the treasures in a German Cathedral, asked the meaning of a silver mouse. "There was a plague of mice which was suddenly removed in answer to our prayers." "Do you really believe that?" "If we did we should shew you another silver object – a British officer." '

Mrs Currie exclaimed that she had been reading the night before a passage in Herodotus (Vol. 1 Penguin). She fetched the book and we read the following passage about Sethos, King of

Egypt, who was outnumbered by the invading army of Senna-
cherib.

On this the monarch greatly distressed entered into the
inner sanctuary, and, before the image of the god, bewailed
the fate which impended over him. As he wept he fell asleep,
and dreamed that the god came and stood at his side, bidding
him to be of good cheer, and go boldly forth to meet the
Arabian host, which would do him no hurt, as he himself
would send those who should help him. Sethos, then relying
on the dream, collected such of the Egyptians as were willing
to follow him, who were none of them warriors, but traders,
artisans, and market people; and with these marched to
Pelusium which commands the entrance into Egypt, and
there pitched his camp. As the two armies lay here opposite
one another, there came in the night a multitude of field
mice, which devoured all the quivers and bowstrings of the
enemy, and ate the thongs by which they managed their
shields. Next morning they commenced their flight, and
great multitudes fell, as they had no arms with which to
defend themselves. There stands to this day in the temple of
Vulcan a stone statue of Sethos, with a mouse in his hand, and
an inscription to this effect – 'Look on me, and learn to
reverence the gods.'

Dr Nicoll was delighted with this example of a synchronism
in which the statue of a mouse in a temple turned up twice from
independent sources within the space of twelve hours. He commented on it: 'The idea "image of a mouse in a sacred building"
is the typical ingredient – the curious ordering force that we can
see in coincidences. It may be "the great characteristic of a wise
man to see events in their causes", as Dr Johnson said, but I look
at the event itself and what is the common thing in it to another.
The thing itself is important as it stands. The modern tendency is
to explain one thing by another. This leaves out the thing itself,
as, for instance, when a man is explained by his organs, his parts,
his atoms, this leaves out the man. Certainly events have causes,
but similar coincidental inner or outer events – as this *idea* of a
mouse in a sacred building – being registered in two minds from

totally independent sources cannot be explained causally, so far
as we know causes. But it can be explained by *time*, a tendency to
similar events – a time for things.'

Two days after I had begun to arrange in order the material
for this chapter, which I had not looked at for several years, I
called on my bookseller in London and asked if he had any
interesting new publications. He shewed me *The Interpretation of
Nature and the Psyche* by Dr Jung and W. Pauli, which contained
Jung's Essay on 'Synchronicity: An Acausal Connecting Principle'.
This I bought and took home with me. Early in the Essay an
example of a meaningful coincidence is given which I quote:

> I noted the following on 1st April 1949. Today is Friday.
> We have fish for lunch. Somebody happens to mention the
> custom of making an 'April fish' of someone. That same
> morning I made a note of an inscription which read: 'Est
> homo totus medius piscis ab imo.' In the afternoon a former
> patient of mine, whom I had not seen in months, shewed
> me some extremely impressive pictures of fish which she
> had painted in the meantime. In the evening I was shewn a
> piece of embroidery with fish-like sea monsters in it. On the
> morning of 2nd April, another patient, whom I had not seen
> for many years, told me a dream in which she stood on the
> shore of a lake and saw a large fish that swam straight towards
> her and landed at her feet. I was at this time engaged on a
> study of the fish symbol in history. Only one of the persons
> mentioned here knew anything about it.' (*The Interpretation
> of Nature and the Psyche* by C. G. Jung and W. Pauli: Rout-
> ledge and Kegan Paul.)

Later in the evening I took out the folder containing the MS.
of this chapter and glanced at some odd pages of typescript which
I had included some time ago as they seemed to have some bearing
on the subject. I had received them among some papers belonging
to Miss Hoffman, who had died shortly before Dr Nicoll. I had
forgotten their contents. My eye fell on some familiar words: 'I
noted the following on 1st April 1949. Today is Friday. We have
fish for lunch. . . .' The whole paragraph was there. Dr Nicoll

having been a student of Dr Jung in the past, must somehow have received this extract from his MSS. before it was published. But why should I have had my attention drawn to it on this particular day? And why should I have had the opportunity of buying the book containing the quotation while I was in process of writing this particular chapter? I recommend this Essay on 'Synchronicity' by Dr Jung to all those who seek further enlightenment on this subject. It would have been stimulating to our conversations with Dr Nicoll if it had been available at this period of which I am writing. Dr Jung gives the reason for his choice of the word 'synchronicity': 'I chose this term because the simultaneous occurrence of two meaningfully but not causally connected events seemed to me an essential criterion – I am, therefore, using the general concept of synchronicity in the special sense of a coincidence in time of two or more causally unrelated events which have the same or a similar meaning. . . .'

I quote an interesting example of an extended coincidence in which an event experienced in 1941 was linked with an event in 1948. While we were living at The Knapp in Birdlip Miss Kemp, who was staying with us, was given by Mrs Nicoll a recipe for a pudding, blackberry roll. This was, except for milk puddings, the first that she had made, so she was pleased when it turned out well and copied the recipe into her diary on the same page on which she had written down the name of a piece of music which had taken her fancy. Seven years later, at Great Amwell House, where since her marriage she had been living with us, she was asked for the recipe, as the conversation had turned on puddings, and the incident was recalled. She went upstairs to look for it and idly turned on the radio before beginning her search. A tune that she knew and liked was being played but she could not recall its name. The announcer gave out the name at the end – Elgar's 'Lullaby' from Three Bavarian Dances. Mrs Streatfeild found the old diary with the recipe which she had not used since 1941 and there on the same page was the name of Three Bavarian Dances. The curious link in time between the tune and the blackberry roll is a mystery which we have never ceased to ponder over, but it is surpassed by the example of a triple coincidence, quoted by Dr Jung from Flammarion's *The Unknown*.

A certain M. Deschamps, when a boy in Orleans, was once given a piece of plum pudding by a M. de Fortgibu. Ten years later he discovered another plum pudding in a Paris restaurant, and asked if he could have a piece. It turned out, however, that the plum pudding was already ordered – by M. de Fortgibu. Many years afterwards M. Deschamps was invited to partake of a plum pudding as a special rarity. While he was eating it he remarked that the only thing lacking was M. de Fortgibu. At that moment the door opened and an old, old man in the last stages of disorientation walked in: M. de Fortgibu, who had got hold of the wrong address and burst in on the party by mistake.

CHAPTER ELEVEN

Birdlip 1943-1944

MAN

Man is so created
His body is a little world,
The ether is stored in his eye,
The air is in his ear,
All movement in touch
And in internal sight
The mind of God.

To begin anew,
To be re-born as an infant,
To learn what is evil and false,

To receive a new will
Is to become Man.

Maurice Nicoll

In this, the fourth winter of the war, Dr Nicoll was concerned with the power of evil which seemed to be at its height. Everywhere there was evidence of Man's degeneration. He wrote on 10th January:

> I find myself more and more convinced that the age of good men is over. Our last good man was Neville Chamberlain. He was not a great man, but he was a good man. Churchill is now the intermediary. The subsequent history will be the rise of bad men – men who use others' suffering for their own purposes. Miss M. here today tells me that her experience at the Ministry of Food shews her that it is a far more evil cut-throat age than when, many years ago, she was in life – on the stage. She says people used to have some kindness and decency, but now they have none.
>
> The Russians advancing to Rostov. The Caucasus German Army may be cut off. But I don't think so. I still think that no great victory is possible on either side. It is going to be stalemate. One reason I have for saying this is that mankind is degenerating and passing into regimentation and so there-

fore leaving individuality and personal freedom. Man is doomed to slavery – more than he is by nature. This is the Flood – of falsity and evil. There have been floods before. The question is – to find an Ark, to ride on the waters of evil and falseness.

With this idea of the new Flood in mind, a flood of falsity and evil, of materialism, he began to interpret the Genesis story. He wrote:

The Flood, understood in its internal or psychological meaning, is not a flood of water, drowning the earth, but a flood of evil. The Flood refers to a period when all right understanding was dying among a particular division of humanity. Violence and evil were in the ascendant and everything to do with truth and good was being lost sight of. Humanity, left to itself, is barbarian. Only teaching given over a long period can raise mankind to the level of culture and civilization. But every teaching sown into life has its period and loses force and dies. When a teaching loses force and dies, a flood of violence and evil and falsity arises. The story of the Ark refers to such a period, occurring amongst a part of humanity, situated perhaps in what we call the Middle East. All this part of humanity, all this 'earth' was flooded with barbarism and all teaching was being lost sight of. But teaching always starts again and where such a flood of evil arises it must preserve itself and wait until the time comes when a new form of the same teaching can begin. Understood psychologically, therefore, the Flood is a flood of barbarism, of evil and violence, and the story of the Ark is a story about how esoteric teaching preserved itself during that flood.*

In 1923, on his return from the Institute, Dr Nicoll had spoken to Mr Kenneth Walker, whom he met by chance, of a small group of people who had begun to build an Ark. It was now twenty years later and the disasters prophesied by Gurdjieff had occurred, even to the destruction of many buildings in London. The Ark was now in existence. Just as a school called Noah,

* *Commentaries on the Teaching of G. I. Gurdjieff and P. D. Ouspensky*, Vol. V.

having eventually three branches, gathered together everything that was valuable and preserved it until the time came when a new teaching could be given, so the System was being preserved intact within those groups who were practising it. Dr Nicoll showed us that a teaching could only be preserved by being lived.

During these cold weeks in January he worked out his interpretation of the story of the Ark and it was read to the group on 18th January but not published until after his death when it was included in an Appendix in Volume V of the *Commentaries*.

On 29th January he wrote in his diary:

> We seem committed by our notable folk to endless war. Formerly it was war until the Nazi Party in Germany was destroyed. Now it is – for ever. There is no *light* anywhere. In the last war Grey said the lights of Europe were going out one by one. Well, today there seems no trace of light – only violence which breeds only violence. Churchill has no light in his speeches. He is the equivalent in this country of Hitler and Mussolini – a hoarse shouting adjectival voice. Of course he is much saner and better, but yet. . . . It looks as if Vansittartism is in the ascendant – kill, exterminate, castrate. Yes, but what if Germany were destroyed? What about Russia? Germany is an *organ* of Europe – like the kidney in a man – and Germany has stood between us and Russia. The Bishops continue to make a fuss about the treatment of the Jews. They have just heard of it. But what problems exist! And there is no solution. 'Do not pray for the end of strife' – for that is the end of life.

10th February was hailed in Berlin by Goering as the tenth anniversary of Hitlerism – there was no speech by Hitler, but a message affirming the mystical mission of Germany in the future as the redeemer of Europe. Dr Nicoll said that to see everyone as criminal and oneself as guiltless, as Hitler did, was the state lying at the root of paranoia. He had written in 1939 the following note on the character of Hitler:

> Hitler is an emotional man. What Neville Chamberlain has done is to act as a psychologist. Because he is fundamentally

a *good* man he is naturally a psychologist. All real and true *psychology* in practice depends on fundamental goodness of being.

Hitler is an emotional man. His being is wrapped up in his earliest impressions. He is exquisitely sensitive to the injustice of the world, as all emotional people are. The world is unjust. He had his own example of injustice, in his personal life. He saw Germany in its terrible suffering after the war.

To deal with him is not a matter of cunning politics. It is personal. Only a deeply honest and understanding man, a man who believes in human goodness, can deal with him. That is why he responded to Chamberlain. Hitler is not a sick man or a pathological man. He is not a cruel man. He is above all things not a dishonest man. He sees clearly his side of things. No one else sees as he does, because no one else has felt, experienced, as he has done.

Today, for the healing of nations, psychology is necessary, not politics. Hitler is not cynical. He is not idly playing with power. He is quite genuine. And unless he is taken sincerely, unless an attempt is made to understand him, only catastrophe can result.

Chamberlain 'made an attempt to understand him. The result was an incredible relief of tension. Far more than that, for people feel a new influence at work, a new hope of a better way of dealing with national problems than the way of political manoeuvring and, let it be added, the totally imbecile way of standing on points of honour, and self-interest and self-liking. The danger is that Hitler, feeling that no one understands him, and acutely sensitive to criticism (he desires love) goes to lengths that would not only destroy him but destroy Europe. And in this question of understanding another person it is useless to employ the attitude of high contempt as if a mad dog were the source of trouble – Hitler is no mad dog – but might be made to become one. That would not be his fault. What will give him peace and internal freedom is an understanding view of all that his nation has endured since the last war.

Chamberlain is really our premier psychologist. He feels

the deep importance of personal contact and explanation. He does not enter into such discussions charged with ridiculous ideologies – what he looks at is the man himself and the actual situation, knowing that he, also, is a man easily upset and wounded. This is when a new interpretation and arrangement of life begins – when we see the other person as like ourselves. Look at those who recently showed they were only interested in their personal self, their honour, their theories, their own self-wills. One saw in their speeches no trace of any attempt to understand Germany, her wars and terrible suffering, and the significance of her hero. Their speeches were nothing but the result of purely selfish feelings. There was not a single phrase that pointed to an *abnegation* of self in view of the terrific world issues. The central motive in them was *vanity*. In order to understand another person, vanity and personal opinion are the worst instruments. To take an aggressive person in terms of what he says is the worst way of dealing with him. The hurt is deep in Germany, but the possibility of healing it and making the forces acting on that nation, which spring largely out of bitterness, change into reasonable forms is not a political but a *psychological* task. People try to pin a man down to what he said when hurt. Ease the hurt, accept the other person's point of view a little, and he will no longer hold to what he said. Why? Because the forces acting on him are changed thereby. Everyone knows in personal life how a word rightly said at the right moment from understanding totally destroys malignant feelings. It is this that counts today. Hitler is an ordinary human being, acting as we all do, from what he sees as right. He has effected a marvellous regeneration of a stricken suffering country. No one does evil wittingly – everyone acts always from what he sees to be right. This is the only formula that will give peace to mankind. If we attempted, following on this lead, to understand Hitler and Germany, we would lead the way to a new orientation of Europe. It will be quite surprising to everyone to find what *real difficulties* existed once we dropped suspicion, fear and hatred – hatred understands *nothing*. Real difficulties would certainly remain, but the basis of the discussion of them would be reasonable and war would at least become very rare as a solution.

It is a question of a man who feels with the deepest emotions he is capable of, that he is right, and when in personal life a matter of this kind arises the first thing to do is *to feel the other man*, to enter into his views and motives and become aware of the innumerable causes that have led to his attitude. If this is done sincerely the other man is already helped. He is helped simply by feeling he is understood and, feeling he is understood, he no longer has to emphasize to the point of violence. Nothing is more productive of violence than complete lack of understanding, and nothing is more easy to take as violence, as criminal intent, than violence that arises as a result of no one's understanding the situation. This is the curse of things – no one sees where the real source of the trouble lies – then the usual epithets are hurled – 'viper, snake, malignant, criminal, dog, swine, filthy beast and so on.' This language is an old one. It blossomed in Cromwell's days; it is almost the ordinary language today between nation and nation and it is the language we find at hand when, feeling the justice of our cause, we are completely ignored by someone more powerful.

Such was Dr Nicoll's psychological interpretation of Hitler's character, and subsequent events did not lead him to change it.

The last two years of the war brought him much weariness of soul. He had now in 1943 completed his Gospel studies and had ceased to write his Diary. He turned his attention to a task which Gurdjieff had recommended to him in the early days of the teaching – this was to connect Gurdjieff's System with science. He had always believed that in the new age which was approaching science and esotericism would once more be conjoined as in the school of Pythagoras. His scientific training gave him the ability to make certain connections and he began to work on these lines. He began by giving blackboard lectures to us at The King's Head in Birdlip, first during the week and later also at the week-ends. We now had the privilege of attending lectures on many branches of science – neurology, physiology, biology, chemistry, physics.

In these talks the fundamental ideas were reduced to the utmost simplicity and correspondences were found between the ideas of the System and each branch of science. I quote Dr Nicoll's introduction to a lecture on chemistry which was afterwards formulated in writing.

> In view of the fact that I was taught that one of the objects of this Work was to unite the science of the West with the wisdom of the East, and that G. used to emphasize this many times and sometimes look at me when he said it, it has seemed to me good to write introductions to the different sciences that exist today in the Western world. For a long time I have cast about for suitable books to recommend people to read dealing with the different branches of science and I have come to the conclusion that it is necessary for us to write our own introduction to the subject.

He began with chemistry, his first love among the sciences, which he called the science of transformation. Here there were many analogies, for alchemy, the Hermetic Art, had long been the symbol of the regeneration of Man. He recalled how in his boyhood the discovery that every substance was composed of combinations of the ninety-odd elements led him to feel that he had a key to understanding the mystery of things. He remembered as a result of this vision at school regarding the masters as merely combinations of different elements and when he informed his stepmother that this was how he now regarded her she responded with her usual politeness, expressing surprise but not disbelief. This vision had given place to wonder at the mystery of differences in quality and he had much to tell us of the relationship of quantity and quality. What I remember most vividly are the talks about the brain. Text-books are difficult to read but as Dr Nicoll talked the structure and function of the brain and the central nervous system were made clear. Dr Nicoll had been deeply impressed by the teaching of Mr Wilfred Trotter, the brain surgeon. I quote what he said to us about him:

> I remember very well how he often used to say how the brain was so utterly different from the rest of the body that it could only be understood in terms of quite different

concepts from those applying to the bodily organs. He used to say that no one understands the brain because everyone still takes it in terms of the body. Many times when I was assisting him he used to say on exposing the spinal cord lying in its delicate and silvery flexible box of boxes: 'Look, that is something utterly different from anything in the body. Look how it is guarded, look how it is preserved, look how isolated and remote from everything else it is. Think how everything depends on it, how the slightest injury would paralyse the body. Think how everything in the body has to serve it with food and think how utterly unknown it must be to the organs such as the liver or stomach which are working for it.'

Dr Nicoll had found inspiration in Hughlings Jackson's vision of the central nervous system – the brain and spinal cord – as built on the principle of hierarchy, the whole nervous system representing the different parts of the body at different levels. This was in correspondence with the hierarchical principle on which the universe is framed. Hughlings Jackson had observed that the highest level was not the most organized, but the reverse, i.e. the more highly organized a level was, the more mechanical its response and the less choice it has. He defined evolution as the passage from the most to the least organized, the least organized being at the same time the most complex, and the most modifiable. We were able to study these principles in detail as Dr Nicoll disclosed to us some of the wonders of the brain. The existence of silent areas in the brain remained a mystery. He thought these represented vast latent possibilities awaiting perhaps Man's spiritual awakening. He condemned the operation of lobectomy which was at that time beginning to be practised, as he had reason to believe that the result of cutting the frontal lobes of a patient was likely to cut him off from his spiritual memory. We knew of certain cases where this had apparently happened. It was while Dr Nicoll was writing papers on the subject of the brain that a most interesting article on 'Brain Rhythms' was published in *Nature* (25.3.44) in which Professor Adrian (now Lord Adrian) gave a résumé of what was known about electrical charges in the brain. He quoted the findings of Professor Hans Berger, of the

Psychiatric Institute at Jena, who had recorded by means of an encephalogram the changes in electric potential in the brain during a certain period. Study of these recordings showed that the changes in potential took place rhythmically, and it was possible to learn from the analysis of the various underlying rhythms whether the brain was working normally or not. What Dr Nicoll found so interesting was that the rhythms varied according to the amount of attention that was being given by the person under investigation. A certain oscillation, known as the alpha rhythm, appeared only when the subject was at rest with attention released and eyes closed. What was surprising was the discovery that there was a regular rhythm, a uniform pulsation, shewing that large numbers of brain cells must be working in unison at the same time. The statement that the electrical activity of the brain could be recorded through the skull suggested to Dr Nicoll the hope that 'brain events connected with consciousness' might be detected. He was, meanwhile, interested in what could be discovered about attention. As far as vision is concerned, what really determines the presence or absence of these alpha waves is not whether visual messages are or are not coming into the brain but whether we are or are not attending to them – whether we are looking at anything.

It was thus ascertained that the alpha rhythm detected was found to be a rhythm of inattention, a positive activity filling those parts of the cortex which are for the moment unemployed. The rhythm disappeared when the attention was directed, for instance when the eyes were open and looked at something.

Dr Nicoll thought that there was much to support the view put forward that there is a deep-seated part of the brain containing the mechanism by which attention is directed one way or the other and that the rhythm is under the control of this region if it is not directly produced by it. Attention is the beginning of consciousness!

This was one of the traces, for which he was always looking, of an understanding in the mind of a scientist of the relationship of psychology and science. He found an example of what he sought when Professor Erwin Schrödinger's *What is Life?* was published towards the end of 1944. This proved to be an event of some importance for us. The book consisted of a series of lectures which the author, a distinguished physicist, had given the previous year at the Institute of Advanced Studies, Dublin. Dr Nicoll welcomed the book as the first attempt of a physical scientist to connect with biology. He recommended us all to read it and talked about many of the ideas contained in it. He was most interested in Schrödinger's discovery that whereas the ordinary physical laws are based on statistics, on the average behaviour of the atoms, molecules, etc., the molecule responsible, so to speak, for life, the seed, does not obey statistical laws but works in a rigid way, *according to laws unknown to statistical physics*. The central idea in the book was the idea of Entropy. The word, Entropy, was new to us. It was defined as *increasing chaos*. Schrödinger had observed that the molecule of life resisted its entropy – he realized that there must be some force behind this which he called God or Consciousness. Here was a scientist who had connected a spiritual idea of God with biology. The living organism was able to feed upon what was called negative entropy. This process was described as 'sucking orderliness from its environment', in short, eating, drinking, breathing, assimilating by metabolism.

Dr Nicoll now began to use the term 'Entropy' in his psychological teaching, and shewed us how Man's natural tendency to chaos, or disorder, in himself could only be arrested by means of effort which would decrease entropy – for instance, the effort of forgiving one's neighbour was given as an example of a means of decreasing entropy. How refreshing Dr Nicoll found this scientist with his sense of wonder. In his final chapter Schrödinger expresses his amazement at the new type of physical law which he discovered in the structure of living matter:

> The physicist and the chemist, investigating inanimate matter, have never witnessed phenomena which they had to interpret in this way. The case did not arise and so our theory does not cover it – our beautiful statistical theory of which we were so justly proud because it allowed us to look behind the curtain, to watch the magnificent order of exact physical law coming forth from atomic and molecular disorder; because it revealed that the most important, the most general,

the all-embracing law of entropy increase could be understood without a special assumption ad hoc, for it is nothing
but molecular disorder itself. (*What is Life?* by Erwin Schrödinger: C.U.P.)

We studied the chapters on the chromosomes and eventually
Dr Nicoll arranged a dance in which we enacted the stages of
development of the chromosomes in both their mitosis and meiosis.

Schrödinger pointed out the danger of mutations induced by
X-rays or γ-rays and explained very clearly how this danger arose.
Mutation or ionization, he shewed, was a single event, occurring
in one chromosome during irradiation. He concludes his chapter
with the warning:

> Any possibility of gradually infecting the human race with
> unwanted latent mutations ought to be a matter of concern
> to the community.

The first atom bomb was to be exploded two years after he
wrote these words.

CHAPTER TWELVE

Quaremead

Beyond my window
The poplars bow,
Assuring one another
And laughing.
In their branches
I see sudden faces.
How pleasant poplars are
In the early sunlight,
How friendly and communicative.
They never seem bored.
They are so alive.
Their moving thumbs and fingers
*   are covered with golden leaves.*
With their beautiful manners
They bow and smile
As the butterflies pass them.
They must love each other
To be like that.
            Maurice Nicoll

As 1944 drew to a close the end of the war came in sight. Dr and Mrs Nicoll had now decided that the time had come to look for a house within reach of London. The Farm in Essex was uninhabitable. Mrs Nicoll acted with her usual sense of immediacy and took steps to find a house which would be suitable for a headquarters for the group.

On 4th November Dr Nicoll wrote in his Diary, 'C. looking at new house with Goodman.' The result of this search was that a house was found at Ugley on the border of Hertfordshire and Essex, a few miles from Bishop's Stortford.

We now spoke often of peace and all that it would mean for us and for the world. Dr Nicoll gave his own definition:

Esoterically, peace is not being not attacked by enemies. It is not the opposite of war, but a state in which the whole being is filled with an uncritical tolerance so that whatever one sees it does not strike inwardly unpleasantly even where

226

it previously did, so that there goes with the state a surprising freedom, as if escaping from a prison.

Now that our departure was decided upon we made the most of our last weeks at Birdlip. New Year's Eve, 1944, was memorable, one of the most festive and interesting evenings that we ever had. For us it marked the end of a stage. We had a party at The King's Head, acting, and then feasting on cold goose. After dinner our band played and Dr Nicoll talked to us. It was a clear and lovely moonlit night and at two a.m. we walked down the hill to The Knapp, playing our guitars and singing songs with the utmost joy. I recall that Miss Stella Kent was with us. We really ushered in the New Year with new thoughts and feelings.

We were now very busy packing ready for our impending move. Once more I packed Dr Nicoll's books and manuscripts. The weather was very wintry and in the middle of January I was called away to nurse my aged parents who were both ill at the same time, one of them very seriously. After three weeks they were convalescent when I received a telegram from Birdlip confirming the imminent date of the move and I managed to leave in order to get back in time to complete the necessary packing. Several of the household had already returned to London.

26th February was the date fixed for our departure. We were to give up the tenancy of The Knapp and Dr Nicoll was to move to The King's Head and to join us later when we were settled at Ugley. In the end we did not leave on the date arranged, but on 26th February there was a farewell party for us at The King's Head. I recall the bowl of snowdrops on the polished table at which we once more dined festively. Afterwards the Guitar band played through its répertoire, ending with 'Goodbye and Farewell to you, Birdlip Ladies,' a parody on the song with which we always broke up a party. Two days later we prepared to leave. I travelled by train with Mrs Nicoll and her sister and we were welcomed by Mr and Mrs Wilshin who were doing the housekeeping. Miss Corcoran was delighted to be allowed to drive Dr Nicoll's little car across country. I think we were all very pleased to be going to a place where Dr Nicoll could take his full groups again.

The house was well-built, half-timbered, of the period 1902, with the rather unattractive name of Gaul's Croft. It was set in a pleasant garden and had about eight acres of land, one field being let to a local farmer for his wheat. We never fitted quite harmoniously into that house, although it had many good points. The dining-room was pleasant to come down to in the mornings with a coal fire, but it was L-shaped and when we were a large party at the week-ends some people were out of sight. The large room where we had our meetings and parties was too big to heat adequately. It was a disadvantage that we had our own electricity, as the plant would not stand many electric fires, and the lighting had a tendency to become faint, and would sometimes unexpectedly fade away if it had not been charged. My own room was tiny, and I had a coal fire and an oil stove. We were all interested at that time in the idea of keeping pigs and I said I would look after them. We bought four pigs. I liked them. They behaved rather like children and seemed good-tempered and happy. We also had chickens which I looked after, and some ducks. At that stage of the war we were all eager to produce as much food as possible. But I liked my charges for other reasons.

Dr Nicoll was still at Birdlip for a while and there was a good deal of long distance telephoning between us. No one liked the name of the house so we tried to think of a new name and it chose itself in an odd way. Dr Nicoll thought that we might name the house after one of the meadows on an old map of the land. He had asked me to find out the name of the largest field. I wired to him on the telephone: 'Name of field is Square Mead.' The telegram arrived: 'Name of field is Quare Mead.' Dr Nicoll rang up in great delight as this was a name after his own heart which he thought suited us exactly. So the house was named Quaremead.

We organized meetings at once. Dr Nicoll would send me papers which I would read to the group. Inspired by Schrödinger, he was now writing about psychological entropy. People soon began to flock down from London and we all appreciated being together again.

We were most interested to hear of the war experiences of those who had been in occupied territory. Miss Keane's brother and sister-in-law had been in France, with their children, and they had strange tales to tell of secret radios, and tobacco growing. I remember the day when they arrived and the picture of restricted life at the village of Pontoise which Mrs Keane described.

Dr Nicoll did not join us until after Easter. I remember the first morning after he arrived. He asked me to come to the summer-house in the orchard to work with him. We were surrounded by apple blossom and sat at peace in the spring sunshine listening to the birds – a halcyon morning. On Sunday, 15th April, two days after his arrival, he wrote to Mrs Hodder and the other mothers who had stayed behind at The King's Head as follows:

Dear All of you,

I arrived at six p.m. on Friday, after a smooth, somewhat sweaty journey, in which I scarcely saw a dog. This place is a good place – I have not yet seen all of the house as I do not like to be shown around. But I found myself descending the grand staircase yesterday, and, quite lost, opened a door and found myself in my room again. I was very pleased to think how clever I was. My room is really nice and I am surprised about all the books in it. I do not know who collected them. Today we are on the lawn and Mr Taylor is trying to get the lawn mower going – he is always trying to start motors. We had a good brisk talk last night, followed by Chinese Magic (those dice and card games) and charades (acting Quaremead as queer) and some guitars. . . . The cuckoo is at work.

My love to you all,

M. N.

Dr Nicoll's own room, once more on the ground floor, opened on to a verandah from which he liked to watch the birds. After the rain the lawn would be covered by a remarkable number of spotted woodpeckers who flew down from the elm that they inhabited to look for leather-jackets. We thought they were a whole family that had quickly grown up. There were also green woodpeckers who would flash to and fro among the trees. The house was well set back from the main road to Newmarket. Its long drive bordered by rowan trees remains clearly in my memory. There were fields on either side of the drive. There was a pleasant little pub called 'The White Hart' near the gate where we used to foregather, and we soon became friendly with Mrs Pitter, our hostess, who did not drink herself but kept a wonderful stock of all the drinks that had become unobtainable in Gloucestershire. There was a very quiet atmosphere in this pub (except when race-goers looked in on their way home) and we were able to sit round a table and talk without being disturbed.

We did our shopping in Bishop's Stortford where there was a very good bookshop but not much else attractive. It was at this time that Dr Nicoll had the idea of revisiting his old Cambridge tailor as he needed some new suits and those of us who accompanied him on various expeditions had the opportunity of being conducted by him to Caius and shown his old room on the ground floor. In the summer the corn in the big field was cut and we all helped with the stooking. I soon left the workers and did a rapid oil painting of the scene which was so full of light and life and warmth that I had to try to put it on to canvas. Dr Nicoll said: 'I like that, but you cannot draw tractors.'

Our livestock was now increased by the addition of eleven Muscovy ducks and a drake, also some bantams, all of which gave me great pleasure as they were in my charge and I grew to know them. The bantams flew like wild birds but at the same time they were more friendly than the chickens. I have always been interested in cocks as solar birds and one fiery-coloured bantam cock was the epitome of pride and dignity in his bearing and behaviour without the arrogance of the Light Sussex and Black Leghorns three times his size. He greeted the dawn on a sweet, clear note which I loved to hear.

In the summer of 1945 Dr Nicoll began to be interested in toy-making, and soon this became one of the group activities. I remember a miniature caravan, made by Mrs Keane, gaily painted, correct to the minutest detail, with chicken coops and buckets hanging on behind. Dr Nicoll installed electricity in this and other toys. This was followed by a merry-go-round with music, an Italian organ grinder, a hansom cab, and a model of The White Hart. Later Dr Nicoll returned to snowball making. He had not yet discovered the secret of sealing his snowballs, which were glass balls containing a solution which when shaken, produced snowstorms. These had been popular in Edwardian times.

All the same we never felt that we really belonged to Quaremead. Dr Nicoll did not make much use of his room for entertaining. He simply worked and slept in it. It was at this time that he began to dictate walking up and down the room instead of writing. On Saturdays we would talk at supper. I remember our gradual return to normal life after D. Day and V.E. Day. It was possible now to go up to London occasionally. I went abroad that summer of 1945 for the first time for many years and enjoyed driving through Belgium and the Ardennes although we came upon much devastated country. When I returned it had been arranged for Dr Nicoll to hold a series of meetings in London for new people. Many people attended these, and he reformulated the ideas from the beginning. The influx of new people that he had always foreseen was now increasing our numbers.

In the autumn of this year Miss Corcoran died. She had been in the group almost since its inception and had lived with us since 1940, always taking a very active part in things, a tireless driver and very good cook, and a fine painter. She was devoted to Dr and Mrs Nicoll.

Mrs Nicoll went away in September to have an operation. It was now necessary for the household staff who had looked after the house and garden to leave us so that Dr Nicoll could transform the running of the house into that of an Institute. He could only do this if all the work was done by members of his group and used as material for psychological work. The household was reorganized as it was arranged for the mothers and children who had stayed on in Birdlip to join us and to take over the work of the household and cooking. The advent of these families brought new life to the house. They had their rooms on the top floor. The children, Richard Hodder, Sheila Elliott, Zette Barron, and Merelina and Tessa Kendall, were to be closely associated with us for some years to come. One morning soon after their arrival Zette who had never seen Dr Nicoll before, as she and her mother had only recently arrived from Scotland, looked out and cried, 'Mummy, there's a man in the garden.' This pleased Dr Nicoll very much as he liked the simple objectivity of her observation – she saw him without associations.

Some of the impressions recalled by Mrs Elliott are as follows:

The mothers and children arrived at Quaremead in September 1945. After living in the centre of the village at Birdlip with the Cheltenham and Stroud buses stopping outside King's Head Cottage, and the village life flowing by, Quaremead seemed to us isolated and cut off by comparison. At the end of the drive was the main road to Newmarket and Cambridge and cars continually whizzed by (with an occasional rural bus), sometimes stopping at 'The White Hart' (a few yards from our main gate) to disgorge bookmakers or racegoers. Apart from the one or two local people who frequented the pub, we were cut off from the communal life to which we had become accustomed at Birdlip.

The families who now joined us, except for the Barrons, had become accustomed to a kind of family life with Dr Nicoll when he stayed behind with them at Birdlip for a time, just as we had at The Knapp, and now they entered a community which was beginning to be organized as an Institute. It was clear that Dr Nicoll was preparing to continue the work begun at Lakes Farm which had been cut short in 1940. He had written to Mrs Elliott in August as follows:

> We shall of course have to run things ourselves and take our own rotation of duties here. I want people to live here and help to run the place. In this way we shall get the whole establishment under Work discipline and a Work atmosphere.

The Kendalls went off to a convent school each day in Bishop's Stortford. Dr Nicoll himself took over the care of the motor engine that supplied the electricity. He fired it twice a day.

We now began to become more closely associated with the kitchen which was the warmest room in the house. Mrs Elliott eventually took over all the cooking and worked wonders with the 'Esse' stove which could produce everything except toast. Dr Nicoll took to having talks there late at night. There were now many more people at the meetings. Among the new people who connected with us was Vincent Stuart who was later to become Dr Nicoll's publisher. He said afterwards that his visit to Quaremead was a great shock to him but he nevertheless came again and was with us almost every week-end afterwards until Dr Nicoll's death.

We rejoiced when Mrs Nicoll was well enough to return to us for the rest of the winter but she was restless and felt crowded, as we all did. She already had a vision of a larger house giving us the space that Dr Nicoll needed to expand his work. The first eight months of 1946 are best represented by entries from his Diary.

1st January 1946   Last night we sang and were gay. Writing about Water into Wine.

5th January   Good talk at noon on how fully conscious man would not be on this planet but that we can only have partly conscious man, partly awake, on earth. Also about shifting feeling of I – not to be one's jealousies. Also about God being *Purveyor of Meaning*.

6th January   Spoke of first step in this teaching – to observe and make conscious the 'other side' that we project and see in others.

12th January   Spoke of visualization: Don't kill people in your thoughts; Let them move about; Don't fix them by some opinion: Converse with them; Otherwise their images harden. To hate another will make a hard place and perhaps an illness.

18th January   Ill. Read Bates' *Amazon*.

21st January   I said in regard to 'Should a doctor tell?' that he should not if the patient has no spiritual side but should if so.

22nd January   Icy roads and fog.

26th January   Reading Darwin's *Life*. What are these movements? From Darwinism came Communism. Are the archetypes in opposition?

27th January   In the spiritual world thought controls matter *directly* – but here only indirectly, with the hands and apparatus.

28th January   Sing-song. Talked after in kitchen about gloom and ugliness of Presbyterianism – also how people think the Pharisees were people who lived *long ago*. How the artist in me hated the Scotch religious atmosphere.

2nd February   Every time you feel 'I' through a superiority you miss the mark. Also, every time you justify – yes, every merit too, every reasoning you trust in. Yes, and all these feelings of 'I' prevent you from being conscious of the *other side*.

9th February   Reading Darwin's *Beagle*. Through privation we approach one another – through plenty we attack. p. 132.

19th February   Making snowballs – read *African Queen*.

22nd February   Yesterday finished the *Beagle* – re-read the Autobiography. It is very clear he was *directed* – just as was W. C. Strange he studied as a clergyman at Cambridge. He was two years at Edinboro' as medico and like Paley – his logic, etc. A figure of destiny – clearly prevented from this and that and able to be with far older men and to pick up things and keep the mind fresh and observant.·

6th March   Snow still – N.E. wind. Made lighthouse snowball. Difficulty in sealing snowballs. Cotton wool and oiled silk seal. 'If I could be sealed, then I could seal.' Sealing – or The Mirror – the wetless hands, a highly polished metal may be immersed in water without becoming wet. It is covered by a thick layer of air which adheres. Air is spirit! Hand covered with spirit.

12th March   Universe exists through effort. It is built on that principle.

18th March   Bryant walking with his May
and Edgar with his Swan –
Hark! is demobbed
Marshall shooting in the snel groves?
No prisoner of war, but now
a freeman, hardy,
And Willis with him,
Taking liberties with jays.
Lo, there is Bryant walking with his May
And Edgar with his Swan.

28th March   Yesterday went to Great Amwell. House taken.

20th June   The Muscovy ducklings appeared this morning with their mother on the lawn! A symbol. She has been sitting several weeks and the last three days she did not emerge for food. She felt the miracle of new life under her and became quite passive, without personal desires.

Objective consciousness must be the opening of the interior sense as distinct from the literal. Then one sees what things mean, that everything is spiritual – representation. The interior becomes exterior, as it were. Yes, a reversal takes place at the level of objective consciousness.

13th July Saw a big owl dancing and squawking in the oak behind the Lab Hut just before wind changed.

19th July *Early morning* – my birthday. I have been thinking that I have been very blessed in many ways, one in that I have always had friends at school, Cambridge, hospital, abroad in my travels, in the war, and how many I have now! And how supremely blessed that my wife and I met this work, which is Light. I hear her moving about in the room upstairs. B. has done good painting of garden – portraits and roses. It is west windy, rainy and the crops are getting beaten down. The model of the 'White Hart' is now painted outside. I wrote on 'ascribing to oneself' at ten p.m. after talk.

22nd July *Freemasons*

> They march off tuning their guitars.
> They did not love one another –
> They did not like one another –
> They *were* one another.

27th July

> What is this sweetness in my heart
>   That is not me?
> This bird that sings within my heart
>   Hath visited me.
> Blind scientist – can you
> With scalpel or microscope detect it?
> Science that made Man blind to God,
>   Can you see this sweetness?

14th August *Coincidence. Sockets*

(1) Thought of socket on waking: re painting class and big shed – for easels – to take up less room. How many sockets in floor possible.

(2) Looked up Old Testament quotation in *Times* Personal (13th August 1946) Exodus Ch. 34 V. 6 and read on.

(3) Came to sockets for tabernacle (Ch. 36 V. 24) 'And forty sockets of silver made he under the boards,' etc. Here the word *socket* turns up from two unconnected lines of cause and effect. It is not a word one uses often.

28th August   Painted rowan trees in drive.

CHAPTER THIRTEEN

Great Amwell House

Greek in beauty,
A yellow crocus
Rises from the lawn,
Gift of Persephone
From the world beneath,
Sign to Demeter
That she still lives,
And in the sunlight
A small bee,
Sent by Melissa,
Becomes attendant.

Maurice Nicoll

All decisions made by Dr Nicoll were most rapid. Once the idea was put forward that we should find a larger house nearer to London in order to have room for all the new people who were eager to come to Dr Nicoll's meetings, Great Amwell House was discovered. This was in keeping with what he always taught, that the Universe was response to request. As soon as right request was formulated there was bound to be response in exact correspondence with the request made. In the spring of 1946 a friend had pointed out to Mrs Nicoll an advertisement of a house near Ware and she drove to look at it the next day, and came back with the report that the house was perfect for our needs. Thereupon Dr Nicoll set off at once to see it for himself, taking three of us with him. We drove to Great Amwell House, which was a mile or so beyond Ware, in the tiny village of Great Amwell.

The entrance was most unexpected. We suddenly drove into a big square courtyard with no gateway, the entrance being simply a very wide space between two pillars. The general impression was altogether very grey and austere. It was a cold spring day and we found the effect of the grey stone walls chilling. But when later we came round to the other side of the house the difference was amazing. A Georgian house of noble proportions faced on to

237

a long terrace with crocuses gaily peeping up all around, and below the terrace was a large expanse of lawns sloping down to the trees in the distance. Our inspection of the house itself was an unforgettable experience. Dr Nicoll acted with his characteristic rapidity. He positively raced through the house with the owner, his cloak flying out behind him, and we came scurrying after him. Then we raced through the grounds having en route a wonderful impression of the neatness of the walled vegetable garden which was entered from the courtyard through some beautiful wrought-iron gates. In half an hour we had virtually taken the house. Dr Nicoll simply said: 'I think this will do,' and gave instructions to Mr Goodman to make an offer. Meanwhile, we waited at the 'George IV', a few minutes' walk down the hill, and made the acquaintance of the licensee, Mrs Veltom, a unique character who was to become a very good friend. The price was agreed upon and the deposit was paid then and there. We moved in on 3rd September 1946, and seven years later Dr Nicoll died, on 30th August 1953. Thus we spent a complete seven-year period there.

I cannot say much about the move except that it took place on a wet day. We went over early in the morning and Dr Nicoll arrived during the afternoon whereupon we all drank to the house, having unpacked a case of claret in the kitchen. I remember that we unpacked steadily until evening, and I was very pleased to have been able to have my bed put into place. At ten o'clock we had supper in the kitchen. I remember being too tired to eat, and I remember also the odd experience of sitting at a table much too high for me. The kitchen table was a feature of the house – colossal in size, oblong in shape – and we had supper at it, but it stood very high off the ground having doubtless been used for other purposes than having meals served on it, and some of us found our chins level with it. After some weeks the legs were shortened. This experience made us wonder at the patience of children who often find themselves in such a predicament and seem to accept it as a necessity.

The next morning we had great difficulty in getting out of the house, as all the doors seemed to be locked and double-locked in most peculiar ways. I remember my impressions of the walled garden in which the trees were laden with fruit – beyond it the

flower beds were a mass of golden rod and Michaelmas daisies –
on the lower slopes we picked mushrooms, the supply of which
continued for some weeks.

On 4th September 1946 Dr Nicoll recorded in his diary:

> We moved here yesterday in fine rain – organized the
> rooms and so far things have gone aright. We supped on
> some of the Muscovy ducks and potatoes and coffee round
> the great kitchen table. This morning it is fine and dry.

After our first day I think it rained for six weeks and the
garden paths were thick with mud. I remember ploughing my
way twice every day through the beautiful but now overgrown
garden to the distant chicken runs where the chickens were quite
miserable and of course did not think of laying as their feet were
always wet. Some of the bantams soon flew away – they flew like
the wild birds that they still were and some did not return – but
the Muscovy ducks settled down well and my special bantam cock
returned with his two hens. We settled into our rooms. Mine was
a very pleasant one overlooking the terrace with a view of the
elm trees where a family of spotted woodpeckers lived which we
grew accustomed to see on the lawn digging for leatherjackets,
whenever we were not about.

It took some time to unpack the books and papers but eventually
all was arranged in Dr Nicoll's large room on the first floor, from
the wide bay windows of which he could look down on the
rose garden which was just below, and also view the terrace and
the gardens and the meadow beyond the ha-ha, stretching away
to the distant trees. Almost at once we procured some geese, three
geese and a gander, which were supposed to eat the grass. They
lived in a small hut under one of the beech trees and, like the
beeches which were now turning gold, soon became part of the
landscape. The two noble beeches were to be a source of the utmost
pleasure to those of us who had rooms facing the garden. In spring
they came out successively, and in autumn one turned golden and
when it began to shed its leaves we still had the beauty of the
other. The geese, like the other livestock, became my charge.
We could not leave them to subsist on grass only, but decided
that they should be fed once a day. Two were white with blue

eyes; the third was grey like the gander. They were extremely clever. The ha-ha separated the meadow from the garden and it could only be crossed by a narrow plank, but the geese soon discovered this and negotiated it. In spring when they knew that the young vegetables were at their best in the walled garden some distance away nothing could keep them out of it.

Mr and Mrs Edwards and Hilary now moved from London to live with us at Great Amwell House. The Hodders settled in what had once been a gardener's cottage which they made into a very attractive pink-washed house with a blue door. It had its own garden with fruit trees and was in the spring surrounded by blossom. There were now only two children resident with us, Richard Hodder and Hilary Edwards, who were now old enough to go to school. The war being over, Mrs Barron had been able to join her husband with Zette, and Mrs Elliott and Sheila returned with Dr Elliott to their flat in London. Michael Streatfeild, who had been in London during the war in the fire-fighting service, had recently married Cecily Kemp and they now came to live at Great Amwell House. Mr and Mrs Currie also joined us. Lesley Coad gave up her job at the B.B.C. in order to become resident and also later Florence Holmes was able to give up her work in London when her mother died. Thus we had a nucleus of thirteen people with Dr and Mrs Nicoll who were permanently in residence. Jane and John Mounsey were sometimes with us, and John prepared a studio for pupils and began to teach drawing and painting.

There was now a period of great activity at the week-ends and Mrs Nicoll was in her element arranging for fruit-picking and jam-making. The grapes were gathered but they were not very sweet. The wide lawns had to be cut with motor-mowers. Dr Nicoll was able to cover most of the activities from his windows, except those of the kitchen garden and the distant orchards. All the tools had to be unpacked and the apparatus set up in the old stables. There was a place for toy-making, a carpenter's shed, a room in the stables set apart for a studio, a place for modelling. At last it seemed that there would be scope for all that had been cut short when we left Essex. Our two wooden huts had been brought over in sections after being dismantled and it became a week-end job for the men to set them up again. So 'scurries' took place in the manner of the Farm 'scurries'.

We soon organized week-end work with meetings on Saturdays and Sundays. On Fridays people would ring up to ask if they might come and I would allot the rooms and put up a list of names and the housekeeper, having arranged for the catering, would write on a large kitchen blackboard the jobs to be done. Some of the cooking would be carried out by those who were visiting for the week-end and there were many jobs such as woodcutting and bringing in kindling to be done by the men. Some people would arrive at tea-time and Mrs Nicoll would be there to see them but Dr Nicoll was nearly always writing in his room preparing the meetings for the next two days, which he was never able to do till the last moment. However, he always used to wander into the kitchen before people arrived in order to see from the list who was coming. The first arrival was generally Winifred Park who would open up her hut under the tree and then go along to see Dr Nicoll. Later Miss Humby would arrive.

Friday evening was always my busiest time because he would be experimenting with ideas, trying this and that, and I would type what he had written at intervals during the evening. Sometimes by the time we went to bed the paper was finished and sometimes it was not. A few people would arrive for supper, among them Mrs Sandheim who would want to be gardening by seven o'clock the next morning. Outdoor activities continued as far as possible into the winter. The gardener whom we employed at first looked after the walled garden only – later we looked after the walled garden ourselves.

On Saturdays Dr Nicoll would see people at the village pub where he found it possible to talk more easily. He had made Mrs Veltom very happy by giving her a parrot. I cannot remember whence the idea originally arose that she would like a parrot but one day urgent messages were sent to Mr and Mrs Gloster to find a parrot immediately and bring it down to her. With their usual resourcefulness they were equal to this sudden demand and a very beautiful green parrot was soon established which became a good companion to Mrs Veltom and an entertainment for us when we were there. In the pub Dr Nicoll always occupied his usual window seat with a view of the door and a good view through one of the windows of the hill outside, down which everyone arriving had to come. Thus he was able to observe people for some minutes as they were on their way and sometimes surprised them by referring to their state. He liked his first meeting with those who were coming for the week-end to be at the pub where it could be informal. We would then go up the hill for a rather late lunch.

In the afternoon people worked in the kitchen or the garden but during the winter music became the chief indoor activity. At supper in the big square dining-room Dr Nicoll would talk late.

Many of the group learned to play the guitar. Miss Humby was so skilful in making it possible for beginners to be familiar with the chords of certain keys at a very early stage that she eventually conducted a band of thirty guitars and three mandolines although many of the players had only been learning a few weeks. All of us who were resident played the guitar, or mandoline, or both. I remember that Mrs Nicoll was soon able to be in the band although she did not know a note of music. People would practise privately at any time during the week-end but the band practice was on Sunday mornings.

On Sundays we would have a meeting in the afternoon as many people would have to leave after tea. Half past three was not the best time for a meeting but this custom continued during the time we were at Amwell. On Sunday evenings Dr Nicoll would talk to a few people in his room, those who were able to stay later and those who were able to stay until Monday. On Sunday evenings we would be relaxed and informal and sometimes we would have our own friends in our rooms for quiet talks. At Christmas we would have a festival, as always, a real feast, followed by dancing, music and singing. Dr Nicoll's presents were piled up in his room and he often did not open them until some days later. I would receive a sudden message – 'Come down, the presents are being opened', and we would all gather together to help him to open his presents. He received his presents very simply, like a child, and would immediately give away all those that were not essential to him. He would keep notebooks, pencils, marrons

242

glacés, wine and foie gras and would hand most of his books to Mrs Nicoll to read first – chocolates and sweets would be given to the younger people. I would make a list of the absent donors to whom we would write some time later.

On Boxing Day or New Year's Eve we would often dine in fancy dress. Dr Nicoll used to shew us how people revealed their psychology in their choice of what they wore.

The central heating being adequate, winter was not so severe as it had been in the other houses where we had stayed. During the week daily life arranged itself very much as before except that we were now so near to London that we were able to go up for the day for shopping or a theatre or to meet friends.

Dr Nicoll's favourite newspaper was the *Evening Standard* which was posted to him so that he received it with the morning papers. He liked to discuss current affairs after tea and would read to us anything he had found interesting. In fact, as in former years, we seemed to share all that he read. He was still reading all good biographies that were available and books which contributed to biographies. I remember how he was delighted with *A Distant Summer* by Edith Saunders because of the realistic picture that it gave of Queen Victoria's visit to Paris and he dashed off an impulsive note to the author in his own handwriting:

Dear Edith Saunders,
        Thanks for the 'Distant Summer' – an excellent book. Do please do some more – with more illustrations.
                                        Yours sincerely,
                                        M. Nicoll.

He was able to give a most vivid impression of a book such as Darwin's *Voyage of the Beagle* or Colonel Jim Corbett's *Man-eaters of Kumaon*. He requested Colonel Corbett to write another book about further experiences and asked Colonel Humphrey Butler to call on him in Africa. He corresponded occasionally with Major Jarvis, whose articles in *Country Life* were a source of great interest to him. He discussed with him Mirages, Coincidences, the Binocular Vision of Owls, the Luminosity of Fish, and methods of keeping undesirables from the bird table.

When we were reading Harold Nicolson's *Congress of Vienna*

(Constable) Dr Nicoll was much struck by the following passage which he read aloud to us:

> Nobody who has not actually watched statesmen dealing with each other can have any real idea of the immense part played in human affairs by such unavoidable and often unrecognizable causes as lassitude, affability, personal affection or dislike, misunderstanding, deafness or incomplete command of a foreign language, vanity, social engagements, interruptions, and momentary states of health.

Dr Nicoll's favourite biography was Boswell's *Life of Johnson*. He never wearied of reading it, or rather, to use a phrase that pleased him, he never wearied of reading in it, and sometimes he would read to us. One reason why Boswell gave him such pleasure was probably because he was fond of good talk and Dr Johnson has fittingly been described as 'incomparably the best talker of whom the world knows anything'. In some ways Dr Nicoll resembled Dr Johnson. He also was a brilliant talker who could hold his company spellbound for hours. He also had a cutting wit and a directness of speech. He loved Johnson for his warm heart, and humanity, and would often remind us how he kept old friends in comfort in his house although they had no claim on him. Johnson once said of Wesley: 'His conversation is good, but he is very disagreeable to a man who loves to fold his legs and have out his talk, as I do.' Many times has Dr Nicoll echoed such a sentiment. He liked to settle down and talk until well through the night and nothing irritated him more than if one of his companions said he must go, thereby perhaps breaking the octave. He admired Johnson's power of good formulation. One day, when we were talking of wine, he read to us the following passage which pleased him. It is a dialogue between Dr Johnson and a guest, Mr Spottiswoode:

Johnson: I require wine only when I am alone. I have then often wished for it, and often taken it.
Spottiswoode: What, by way of a companion, sir?
Johnson: To get rid of myself, to send myself away. Wine gives great pleasure; and every pleasure is of itself a good. It is a

good, unless counterbalanced by evil. A man may have a strong reason not to drink wine; and that may be greater than the pleasure. Wine makes a man better pleased with himself. I do not say that it makes him more pleasing to others. Sometimes it does, but the danger is, that while a man grows better pleased with himself, he may be growing less pleasing to others. Wine gives a man nothing. It neither gives him knowledge nor wit; it only animates a man, and enables him to bring out what a dread of the company has repressed. It only puts in motion what has been locked up in frost. But this may be good, or it may be bad.

Spottiswoode: So, sir, wine is a key which opens a box; but this box may be either full or empty?

Johnson: Nay, sir, conversation is the key; wine is a picklock, which forces open the box, and injures it. A man should cultivate his mind so as to have that confidence and readiness without wine, which wine gives.

On another occasion Dr Nicoll read a passage in which Dr Johnson reproves Boswell for complaining of his melancholy, saying that he must be attached to this melancholy of his or he would not continually speak about it. Dr Johnson advises Boswell most strongly to be silent about these things so that they may have a chance to diminish. Dr Nicoll drew the parallel with the advice given in Ouspensky's teaching not to express negative emotions. He also read out Dr Johnson's advice to Boswell, adapted from Burton: 'Be not idle if solitary.'

One day I returned from London to find that Dr Nicoll had moved from his room on the first floor to the room below. There had been a terrific upheaval and all the furniture and hundreds of books had been transferred downstairs. In his new room he had a French window through which he could step out on to the terrace, so he once more had the private means of exit that he valued. The move was completed in a day. He now asked Miss Lord to paint diagrams on the walls. On one wall the Solar System was represented, on another, the Universe as Vibrations, on another, the Table of Elements, and so on. Later Mrs Edwards painted a symbolical diagram from the *Liber Mutus* on the wall behind his bed. This depicted Man asleep on the ground while angels descending a ladder sought to wake him with their trumpets.

During our first five years at Great Amwell House the pace gradually increased as the numbers of those joining us at the week-ends grew. Mrs Currie once more taught the Movements which were new to many. Dr Elliott was asked to give courses of lectures on physiology as a continuation of the scientific talks which Dr Nicoll had given to a few of us at Birdlip. He had not had time to write the book linking science and the System which he felt should be written. His immediate work always lay in personal work with his group. He liked to feel that the house was full of activity during the week-ends, to watch the log-sawing and gardening, to hear the band practising on Sunday mornings, to see and hear the two motor-mowers speeding across the lawns until they stuck, and then he would remark later on the hours of time spent by the electrically-minded in apparent communion with those intractable machines. In the rose garden beneath his window Winifred Park and one or two others might be clipping the borders. We were very rarely able to have meals out of doors as in Essex – the terrace did not get the morning sun – but we would sometimes have tea out there in the afternoons.

Plays and Gilbert and Sullivan operas were rehearsed for Christmas and Easter or perhaps a variety show. I recall Obéy's *Noah*, scenes from *The Yeoman of the Guard* and *Trial by Jury*. Everything that took place was connected with our training in the teaching. Birthdays were always celebrated with cake and wine and sometimes a special party, and they were occasions for informal talks during which the person concerned might receive some valuable information about himself or herself at the cost of some pain.

Sometimes Mr David Blackhall would drive over in the afternoon from Elstree with his red-haired rat-catcher to rid us of our rats and mice. While the rat-catcher was roaming through the outbuildings laying his poison Mr Blackhall would be beguiled into conjuring for us in Dr Nicoll's room. Word of what was happening would go round and all the household would assemble and enjoy the display. Mr Blackhall has now become blind and it is a long time since he conjured for us but he has been no whit daunted by his limitation and his talks and readings from his poems on the radio have a wider audience than his sleight-of-hand ever had.

Dr Nicoll delighted in good conjuring, and when one day at the pub he witnessed certain feats of skill performed by a stranger known as 'Eric', he invited him to come up to the house to entertain us. It had been whispered that Eric was hiding a name known to fame and that he had appeared at Command Performances. Whether this was true we did not know but his skill was outstanding and the brilliant display that he gave us was memorable. Dr and Mrs Nicoll recognized his power to control matter. He could change cards in mid-air. We could see them in the process of changing.

One day someone said that if a new-laid egg were thrown over the house on to the grass it would not break. This was the kind of experiment in which Dr Nicoll delighted so we all foregathered on the terrace and I fetched some new-laid eggs for Mrs Streatfeild to throw over the roof of our three-storey house. She threw from the courtyard facing the kitchen while we waited on the terrace the other side. An egg came hurtling through the air and fell at our feet unbroken and then another. Several were unbroken, the only casualties being eggs which fell on the gravel walk instead of the grass. For a time this was a new game for us to show to people at the week-ends. We were fortunate in having a natural thrower among us and chickens to lay enough eggs for these experiments. It was only a new-laid egg that suffered no harm and Dr Nicoll said this was because the new life in it was protected.

We all appreciated a lantern lecture which was given by Winifred Felce who had been in charge of apes at the Munich Zoo from 1931-9. She spoke very simply about the work of the keepers there and showed some remarkable slides. I recall one of elephants gambolling in snow – a phenomenon hitherto unknown to them. She spoke in a very matter-of-fact way of certain dangers which all those in charge of animals had to meet. I heard Dr Nicoll say, 'You must be very brave.' He had always the greatest admiration for physical courage.

Miss Humby arranged for Julian Bream, who was at that time about twelve years of age, to come down to play the guitar to us. Dr Nicoll was most interested to observe how he played with infinite skill, and yet with great simplicity and lack of affectation. We have listened to his playing of the guitar and the lute many times during recent years but this first impression remains.

These examples shew how Dr Nicoll appreciated anything done well with skill and affection.

Ouspensky died on 7th October 1947. I was in Paris at the time and received the news on my return. Dr Nicoll simply said to me: 'Ouspensky has died.' There was no more to say. I knew that he was deeply moved, but he had been prepared and was only thankful that he had sent to Ouspensky his two paintings of Sidlesham while he was still able to appreciate them and to be reminded of the place that he had loved. Those who were close to Ouspensky in his last months have described the efforts that he made to revisit the places where he had lived in order to impress them strongly on his memory. He gave them an example of what it was to die consciously.

A few days after his death Dr Nicoll spoke to us of Ouspensky. He told us of a dream that he had had of him a fortnight after their first meeting. Ouspensky appeared in the dream as a bird which, when someone fluffed up his feathers and otherwise annoyed him, remained quite still. Dr Nicoll now read us the following Chinese Parable by Chishengtse:

THE FIGHTING COCK

Chishengtse used to raise fighting cocks for the king. After ten days had passed, the king asked if his cock was ready for a fight.

'Not yet,' he replied. 'The cock is still very impulsive and haughty.'

After another ten days, the king asked again, and Chishengtse replied, 'Not yet. He still reacts to noises and shadows.'

After another ten days had passed, the king asked again and he replied, 'Not yet. His eyes still have an angry look, and he is full of fight.'

Another ten days passed and he said, 'He is about ready. When he hears other cocks crow, he does not even react. You look at him, and he appears like a wooden cock. His character is whole now. No other cock will dare to fight him but will run away at first sight.'

We all delighted to think of Ouspensky as a 'cock of wood'. Thus with a kind of joy in our sadness we paid tribute to his memory. Dr Nicoll had once more made what was serious comprehensible through what was laughable.

Ouspensky's death was a very great shock to Mrs Nicoll who felt that she had lost her teacher. This event, however, was important for the group as a year or so later a number of people who had been working with Ouspensky now came to us, many of whom Mrs Nicoll knew well, and she eventually found herself surrounded by old friends. This influence further had the effect of strengthening the group.

The first to approach Mrs Nicoll was Mrs Beatrice Mayor who came down to Amwell with her sister, Mrs Warre-Cornish, and both found Dr Nicoll's practical teaching a new source of inspiration. Others followed, and I quote an impression given by one of them of his first visit.

More than a year after Mr Ouspensky's death I consulted B. M. who had taken me to Warwick Gardens so many years earlier. 'Would you like to meet Dr Nicoll?' she asked. 'He gives out the pure Work teaching. If you are interested, I hear that a new sub-group is about to be formed under Mrs Nicoll's supervision.' And so it came about that I met Mrs Nicoll at (I believe) the first meeting of Mr Sam Copley's sub-group for new people. The teaching was given to me all over again, under a new impact – the same teaching in its purity, but with a difference: a difference of emphasis, perhaps; also a greater flexibility in applying the ideas – or so it seemed, but maybe, after the enforced abstinence, I was putting better efforts into directed attention. There was no pressure on new people (or on old, for that matter) to come to Amwell, and, as an old Ouspenskyite, I felt a certain inhibition, not shared by my son M., who beat me to Amwell by several weeks. Reacting sub-logically ('There could be only one Ouspensky'), my first impressions of Dr Nicoll in action inevitably reinforced a kind of dogged determination not to find in him a substitute for the revered 'dead shepherd'. Separate identities were in fact preserved by marked differences of 'type' – the difference in manifestation between a Professor of Philosophy and the ideal Family Doctor. What I did find in my new Teacher – and came more and more thankfully to acknowledge – was a being of similar rock-like integrity, catholic and encyclopaedic in mental range, radiating wisdom with gaiety in a setting starkly at variance with ordinary life-conditions, yet oddly simple and what might be called Plain English. The ritual 'At Homes' in the local pub, for one who could not even imagine Mr Ouspensky resorting to such places, remained for some time a kind of Holy Mystery. I could sense the scope for self-study in the resulting 'loosening up', while vaguely resenting that the exercise should be so much pleasanter for some people. Later I came to accept it as a lightly imposed discipline – which could be as compelling as any of Ouspensky's Rules – against the temptations of careless talking and uncontrolled behaviour. Dr Nicoll was uncannily present at all times (not least when absent in the body). On one remembered occasion, arriving at the 'George the Fourth' on a broiling day, I tossed my hat at a hook on the wall, missing it and involuntarily grimacing. Dr Nicoll's voice reached me from a distant coign: 'Don't be angry, dear' – spoken so softly that, turning to acknowledge the reproof, I became aware that no one else had heard him. He had an eye on everyone. Not only in the pub. On Bank Holiday week-ends, I usually inhabited a portable wooden hut in the grounds, visible at an oblique angle from Dr Nicoll's window. It was unusual for a day to pass without his commenting on some circumstance attending my passage across the lawn before breakfast. As one came to realize that there was method in every whim and idiosyncrasy – not to mention all manner of 'fun and games' – Amwell became increasingly meaningful as well as joyful: the axis about which one's whole life revolved. The memory comes back of a journey from London in a fog, gradually thickening, until, as our car crawled into the highway before Hoddesdon, it began to lift: the one thing that could not have occurred to any occupant of the car was the possibility of turning back.

With the issue, privately, of Volume One of the *Commentaries*, Dr Nicoll's stature underwent a kind of illumination. The appearance in the following year (1950) of *The New Man* – an 'eye-opener' into deeper regions – carried the process further. Many besides myself, discovering these books, must have experienced what Keats felt 'On First Looking into Chapman's Homer'. Given such meat to digest, with the opportunity to practise the Three Lines of Work under the direct tuition of their provider – with that, added to all the other items, cups, in truth, were running over.

In December 1948 a daughter was born to John and Jane, and a great welcome was given to Dr and Mrs Nicoll's first grandchild. We all went up to the christening in St John's Church, St John's Wood. This child gave us all very great pleasure. She was brought often to see us and while she was very young she had an air of patience and wisdom and understanding, which is one of my most vivid memories.

In May 1950 Mrs Nicoll started a new group in London which meant that she would go up to her flat there for a day or two in mid-week. She had great wisdom in her manner of presenting the System to new people and many of those who are with us now say that they owe much to their first clear introduction to the ideas in her meetings. One of the group has described her memory of Mrs Nicoll's way of teaching:

> The main impression that remains with me is of the warmth of her meetings. The meetings were formal, simple and direct – she gave the Work formulations in a more direct way than anyone I've heard since, with very little personal elaboration. She was very insistent on our getting the principle behind a Work diagram and not arguing with details. She would also answer questions so many times from a Work formulation directly – 'Well, you see, dear, the Work

says. . . .' I can hear her voice saying it. Her affection for the Work came over very strongly – she appeared to take pleasure, for example, in putting a Work diagram on the blackboard – she would put it up almost proudly sometimes. She gave the impression of steadiness, confidence and stability to me. I remember what a shock it was one day and how affected I was emotionally when I noticed her hand trembling.

We were predominantly (at the beginning exclusively) female and her examples were often feminine. I remember the low chuckle that came so often.

During these years at Great Amwell House Dr Nicoll was thinking and speaking of the mystery of time, the Fourth Dimension. It was then that he began to practise being conscious in different points of his life. In connection with this idea he wrote to Mr J. B. Priestley as follows:

> Now, could you write a play of a man, say of sixty, visiting 'himself' as he was (say) a lad of twenty at Cambridge and seeing what he could advise this lad to do? To move through 'Time-Body' was one of the exercises I was taught by Gurdjieff. Only you, with your fine dramatic sense, could do this play.

Many of us had appreciated Mr Priestley's Time-Plays before the war, but the idea suggested by Dr Nicoll was not taken up.

In speaking of the life as a whole he emphasized that there are blank periods which are comparatively unimportant and nodes which are very important. Being conscious in a certain place in the Time-Body demanded far greater effort than remembering an event. Memory of an event was usually distorted – a certain reversal was generally necessary in that in our memory of ourselves we appear to advantage and see others to their disadvantage. To replace this distorted memory with true memory it was necessary to be conscious in the past and, by virtue of one's increased knowledge of oneself in the present, to be aware of one's true state in the past and to see the other person as he or she really was.

After the age of five his life had seemed to divide itself naturally into periods of seven years. What he remembered of his childhood has already been described in the first chapter. Now in his sixties he experienced once again many of his early pleasures. He began to take renewed delight in birds and flowers, in feeling the ground beneath his feet. The Crocus poem was a spontaneous expression. He reduced his life to the greatest simplicity, dispensing with all luxuries, giving away expensive presents that he received, enjoying talks with the villagers, and, above all, through being freed from the requirements of personality he was able to speak quite simply and truthfully of what he felt. He was free to be direct with people.

The second octave covered his early school days of which he recalled very little save his own inadequacy in the presence of schoolmasters and of his father and his father's friends. He did however recall most clearly the enjoyment that he gained from using his hands, setting up bells and telephones in the early days of electricity.

Of the third octave in his life, the period of his more advanced education, there is again a double memory. The suffering through his feeling of inadequacy had continued and he now transformed his memory of his father's domination through his later understanding which made it possible for him to put himself in his father's place and see what a nuisance he must have been as a son. This was how he described the necessary transformation. This was how the situation appeared subjectively. I have already referred to the different view of the same situation given me by his stepmother and sister.

With the fourth octave his life took on a greater intensity, bringing his meeting with Dr Jung and the greater psychological freedom which resulted from it. This was followed by his unforgettable war experiences in Mesopotamia and Gallipoli which he had re-lived during the 1939 War when we were at Birdlip. The constructive work in the treatment of shell-shock at the Empire Hospital which occupied the last year of the war was already preparing the way for his professional career in Harley Street as a neurological consultant – and this seemed to offer a remarkable future.

The period which followed however brought new and un-expected experiences of great intensity crowded together within an incredibly short space of time. Marriage, the birth of a daughter, the meeting with Ouspensky and breaking off of all connection with Dr Jung, all these events occurred in rapid succession, culminating in the meeting with Gurdjieff and the giving up of the Harley Street practice for the purpose of training at the French Institute. Here again the unexpected intervened in that Dr Nicoll was called away by his father's death and shortly after his return to France the Institute was closed. Shock had followed shock, each one opening new doors and revealing new possibilities. As he talked to us of these things he shewed us how the shocks that he had experienced had been transformed by his later recognition of their importance in his life, leading him on to further necessary stages in his destiny. The personal suffering under Gurdjieff's discipline, had made it possible for him to train us.

The return to England, when six months' rest made it possible for Dr Nicoll to begin to re-establish his professional life and to continue to study the System under Ouspensky, was the beginning of a new phase which was ended in due course by yet another sudden break, for almost from one day to the next Ouspensky banished him to the responsibility of establishing his own group, with its accompanying difficulties and a minimum of assistance. Eventually, after some years, as the group increased, the building of Tyeponds gave him opportunities for the practical work that he had in mind to develop and it seemed as though the future of an Institute shone clearly ahead. Once more he was checked, this time by the 1939 War, which made it necessary to abandon the Essex Headquarters at a day's notice and to seek a new home for the Work. Thus he was offered one more test of sudden renuncia-tion and repeated the experience of seeing that one door closed only to allow another to open, as the period of writing began, presenting him with a solace in those days of war.

The final octave of his life at Great Amwell House was one of completion. He was established in a beautiful house, fit dwelling for the Work, where he was able to expand his groups and teach all who came to him, and where opportunity was now given for all that he had written to be published, thus extending the influence of the teaching to a wider circle. This last period, during which he had, as always, a sense of urgency, was used by him for the recognition of the meaning of his life, as he saw how at each sign-post he had received unmistakable directions of the way to follow.

CHAPTER FOURTEEN

Publications

I put on record that of all the books I have read on the mind and the teaching of Jesus, I have read none more valuable than this. . . .

It will take its place at my bedside with the New Testament, the Bhagavadgita, and Patanjali. I bespeak for it the widest circulation. No book I have acquired for years has given me more instruction and pleasure. If readers think this extravagant praise I beg them to get a copy for themselves, and then disagree with me if they can.

DIOGENES in *Time and Tide*. (On *The New Man*.)

One autumn evening in 1948 Dr Nicoll said that he felt he would not live much longer and that Mrs Nicoll was to carry on the Work after him. He said that those of us who were with him must be able to teach the Work.

Awakened by these words to a sense of urgency Mr Bush was inspired to lay before Dr Nicoll the suggestion that the Psychological Commentaries which he had written during the previous seven years should be printed privately for the group. I quote a letter which he wrote to me after Dr Nicoll had agreed to the suggestion:

> *98a Redcliffe Gardens,*
> *London, S.W.10.*
> *9 . 10 . '48.*

Dear Mrs Pogson,

Publication of Work Papers

I understood that Dr Nicoll wished me to go ahead with the idea of publication for private circulation, but I gather from Mearns on the telephone this morning that the present idea is that Mrs Nicoll and you will form a Committee with a view to the publication of 1500 volumes. Of course, the greater the number the greater the cost but the less the price per volume. My plan was to contact some of the group members who would stand the original cost and recoup all or part of that cost by sale to those of the group prepared to buy at whatever figure is necessary to cover the expenses. However, I think, having made some enquiries, I had better await your news as to formation of a Committee, etc. It would be a great help if you could let me know how many there are in the group now all told. I think it is about 100?

I am all for this publication, whether for private or public sale; at a rough estimation I should say the number of words is about 500,000.

Mrs Nicoll and I went up to London shortly afterwards to settle details of the matter with Mr Bush at his house. It was decided that 200 copies should be privately printed in three volumes and that subscriptions of £9 9s. 0d. for a set of three volumes should be asked for. Preparations were now quickly made. I prepared the typescript for publication and Mr Streatfeild took it up with him. Mr Bush had meanwhile arranged with the printers, Messrs Kitchen and Barratt, to present estimates and a sample of printing.

Dr Nicoll approved the quality and size of the paper. On 2nd November Mr Bush wrote to me to say that the printers now had their complete instructions. For the sake of speed he suggested that there should be no re-editing of the text. I quote from his letter:

> My idea was and is that the papers be printed as they were written – to conserve a wonderful series of irreplaceable literature for sale and issue to members of the group or groups. When the question of issue to the public has to be considered it will probably have to be reviewed from many different angles. It is also my wish that Mrs Nicoll, you and I are put in charge in order to save Dr Nicoll from frequent queries, etc. and I think we can take all responsibility. I am prepared to be 'shot at' from every quarter. There is bound to be any amount of criticism. 'Why didn't you do this, etc.?'; that is inevitable. The three main points were stated by Dr Nicoll in five minutes – to get the book (or books) out as quickly as possible, as cheaply as possible, and he selected the print. All other details he left to us. Please have no

hesitation in telling me where I am wrong, or anything else that you think I should know.

Within three weeks I had returned the first set of proofs to the printers. I recall now a period of steady activity as the proofs came regularly and were speedily returned. It was wonderful to feel the volumes growing. Galleys were followed by page proofs. The whole event of this private publication was completed with the usual speed of anything done at Dr Nicoll's wish. Once more I found Mr Bush admirable to work with. He always responded with the utmost speed and courtesy to any instructions that I sent up in Dr Nicoll's name.

At last, on 15th June 1949, the printers wrote to say that they had sent off to us a complete set of flat unbound sheets of Volume I of *Psychological Commentaries*. This was a great moment for us all. Dr Nicoll's papers were now in print.

In due course the whole bound set of Volume I arrived. Each volume was numbered. Dr Nicoll had Volume 1, Mrs Nicoll Volume 2. I remember that I chose Volume 33.

Mr Bush lived to see Volume I printed and bound, but died a few days later. The sense of urgency which had prompted him to ensure that the publication of the *Commentaries* went forward with all possible speed was a true intuition. It was the last service that he rendered to Dr Nicoll whom he had so greatly venerated as a teacher and whose right hand he had been for eighteen years. He was irreplaceable.

Now Dr Nicoll was able to make gifts of this volume of his papers to his close friends and this was the occasion of many letters of appreciation which came to him. I quote Miss Hoffman's letter which was one of the first that he received.

146 Harley St., W.1.
June 27th, 1949.

Dear Maurice,

Now, more at my leisure, I want to thank you for your beautiful book. It will enrich my life for the rest of my days. I hope to always have it by me. And it shall not leave this house without me.

16. With the author, 1949

17. In his study, Great Amwell House

18. In the 'George IV'

It will help me so much in my review of the Work and to correct and add to my knowledge.

It is a book for us in the Work to treasure amongst ourselves and it provides a link amongst us.

Thank you, dear Maurice and Catherine.

Old time affection from

Joan.

Hitherto the teaching had been esoteric but at the beginning of 1949 Mr Gurdjieff announced that the time had come for it to be made known to the world. During the past ten years he had been writing steadily in Paris completing the three books that he had set himself to write. Now it was important for all that he had written to be given first to his groups and then to all who could read it. The future was uncertain and mankind needed all possible help. We had always been told that the teaching which had existed underground for long periods would come out into the world when extra spiritual help was needed by mankind. Ouspensky spoke about this in his early meetings; his words, quoted in *The Fourth Way* (Routledge and Kegan Paul), are as follows:

You see, we live in a very peculiar time and the work is very important, in that, apart from other points, it gives the possibility to remain sane – or to become sane. The further we go, the more we talk about these ideas, the more we are apt to lose sight of the meaning of the whole thing. We take for granted that we have these ideas, we talk about them, we want to get something from this teaching, but we do not think about why we are able to have these ideas and speak about them.

The teaching itself, certain kinds of teachings, certain kinds of ideas become accessible to people only at certain moments, at very difficult periods. These are not the ordinary kind of ideas that you can get at any time and any moment. Quite the opposite, the very fact that we can have these ideas shows that it is an extremely difficult time. It would have been much easier to work with these ideas, say, thirty or forty years ago, but in reality one thing depends on another, for if times were not so difficult we would not have had them.

Accordingly Dr Nicoll received a circular letter from Mr Gurdjieff in Paris which stated his intention of publishing in four languages the first series of his writings in three books under the title of 'An Objectively Impartial Criticism of the Life of Man' or 'Beelzebub's Tales to His Grandson'.

Dr Nicoll called us into his room the evening after the arrival of the letter which was read aloud. He then gave me a cheque for £100 to send in payment for the book. We were able to read Dr Nicoll's copy in advance of the issue that came out in the following year.*

On 29th October of this memorable year Gurdjieff died at the American Hospital.

1949 had been a year of preparation for making some of the ideas contained in the teaching of Gurdjieff known to the world. The real teaching in the background could never be otherwise than oral, but the books when they were available could stir their readers to new thinking. 1950 was an important year for us in that Routledge and Kegan Paul published *All and Everything* by Gurdjieff and *In Search of the Miraculous* by Ouspensky in the spring and simultaneously Vincent Stuart brought out *The New Man*. In some of the weeklies the former two books were reviewed together, and *In Search of the Miraculous* was thankfully hailed as providing a clue to Gurdjieff's allegorical work. I remember one meeting taken by Dr Nicoll at which *The Times Literary Supplement's* review of the two books was read and we examined its accuracy. Dr Nicoll recalled that Ouspensky had been given by Gurdjieff the task of formulating Gurdjieff's System in writing, a task for which he was very well fitted. The reviewer began by commenting on the number of 'teachers' who had appeared in Europe during the early twenties, last of which were Gurdjieff and Ouspensky who came from 'the Slavonic depths'. Here Dr Nicoll interjected that Gurdjieff was not Slavonic but Caucasian, Georgian. Dr Nicoll approved the summary of the main ideas

* My impression of this book, and the gradual unfolding of the inner octaves of meaning, is reserved for a later volume.

which were pointed out as important but we were all amused to see that by the end of the review 'the Gurdjieff-Ouspensky doctrine' had become in the reviewer's mind 'Ouspensky's system'. What chiefly interested Dr Nicoll was that the reviewer thought the book would be important both for scientists and religious people. This link between what is called Science and what is called Religion which Dr Nicoll had been awaiting for years was at last beginning to make itself apparent.

Many of the chapters from Ouspensky's book had been read to us in groups during the past ten years or so. Now it was interesting to find these chapters in their rightful place in Ouspensky's clear formulation of Gurdjieff's System. This was a turning-point in the development of the teaching. Both the original teachers were now no longer with us in the body but we had a text-book. C Influences had become B Influences. During the years that followed it was going to be possible for us to see how inevitably this must happen. Those who read the text-book without having had the oral teaching understood it quite differently from the way we understood it. New people who joined us now had an entirely different introduction to the System for in many cases they read the book first, and thus made it impossible to have the experience that we had had of having the System gradually unfolded, which made every word precious, demanding an effort of registration and memory so that the essence of what was taught at each meeting should be preserved in our minds.

The publication of *The New Man* had come about in this way. In the spring of 1949 Vincent Stuart asked Dr Nicoll whether he might publish his Gospel Chapters. I gave them to him to read and he wrote to Dr Nicoll on May 5th as follows:

Dear Dr Nicoll,

I have now read your 'Parables and Miracles of Christ' and have found them particularly clear and valuable – as they are they will make an excellent book. In the meantime I have given them to Richards to read and am waiting for any comments he may have. When he returns the essays I shall send you a proposed order for compilation.

I would like to know your wishes for the title of the book

– 'The Parables of Christ: an Interpretation', 'The Parables in the Gospels', 'Christ's Parables: an Interpretation'?

May I please have a short note about yourself to include in the catalogue announcement of the book?

Yours,

Vincent.

I propose to publish the book by Easter next year.

I well remember Dr Nicoll's humble amazement at the idea of having these chapters published. He chose the title, *The New Man*. This was the beginning of a series of publications, which had never been anticipated. I remember how interesting I found it to prepare these chapters for the printers, to correct the proofs. In the spring of 1950 *The New Man* was published, and then there was the pleasure/pain of reading the reviews. It was through *The New Man* that Diogenes of *Time and Tide* began his allegiance to Dr Nicoll which continued until his death in 1960. He wrote a most sincere and intelligent review which compensated for some of the rather odd criticisms that appeared elsewhere.

It was startling to read in one review that Dr Nicoll had made Jesus into 'a model psychiatrist'.

This book had been written not for Dr Nicoll's pupils only but for all those who loved the Gospels and sought new meaning in them. It was later translated into Spanish, and the Spanish version published by Ediciones Sol was read by many Catholics in Mexico and South America.

The publication of *The New Man* gave pleasure to Dr Nicoll. The mail was now enriched by letters from a variety of readers of whom a few only were in Orders. Most of his correspondents welcomed his interpretations of the parables and the new light which he shed on the Gospels. Members of his groups were already familiar with the material and were thankful to have it incorporated into a book that could be kept at hand. Diogenes writing in *Time and Tide* acclaimed it as a Bedside Book to be placed beside the Bhagavad-gita and Patanjali. He read all Dr Nicoll's published writings as soon as they appeared and frequently quoted from them.

Dr Nicoll had hoped that his interpretations would be interesting to the Clergy who might perhaps quote them sometimes in their sermons, but very few comments were received from that quarter. When a rather caustic review would arrive by post we would read it aloud when we were with Dr Nicoll in his room. We became accustomed to hearing that the allegory was obscure and the symbolism carried too far, the terminology inadequate. The *British Weekly* welcomed Dr Nicoll as a stepchild of the paper, being the distinguished son of its first editor, but thought the portrait of Christ far from satisfactory. Well, all this was received with the salt of amusement. At the same time there were comments shewing great appreciation.

Mr Rom Landau, writing in the *Nineteenth Century*, reviewed *The New Man* together with *All and Everything* and *In Search of the Miraculous* and linked it with them in several ways. He found it a coincidence that *The New Man* contained many parallels with Ouspensky's ideas, and himself made the connection between the awakening of which Ouspensky speaks and the inner transformation without which a man cannot enter the Kingdom of Heaven. He came to the conclusion however that the Churches would be likely to criticise *The New Man* and Science would disregard it, whereas the other two books would be dismissed by Church and Science alike.

In July Dr Nicoll received a letter from Madame de Salzmann who had been with Gurdjieff since the earliest days at the Institute and was now his successor in charge of his groups. She wrote as follows:

I happen to read two of your books, 'Commentaries about Mr G.'s teaching'. I give them a big value as the ideas are exposed in the genuine order in which they were given out with the exact formulation without any distortion. The ideas-system appears so clear and understandable for everyone. For me, it goes side by side with Mr Ouspensky's *Fragments*.

I will be very grateful to you if you could let me have your books so that I could read them to the group in Paris. I understand that the number is limited and I will be too happy to contribute to the expenses.

I am in London for about ten days. I wish to shew to a

certain number of persons the movements Mr G. has given in the last two years. They are really very exceptional. If you will be interested to see them and if you wish to bring some people with you, I will be very glad to see you. It takes place at Colet Gardens, the 10th of July, at 8.30 evening.

Sincerely yours,

J. de Salzmann.

This acknowledgement from the successor who was continuing Gurdjieff's teaching of the accuracy of his presentation of the System gave Dr Nicoll very great joy. This had been his aim, to transmit the ideas as they had been given him without distortion and to make them comprehensible to all who could understand them. He replied with an invitation to Madame de Salzmann to come down to Great Amwell House which was accepted. The memory of her visit is very clear in my mind and it gave us very great pleasure to have her with us, leaving us with an impression of her beauty and spiritual strength.

During the spring months of this year I was myself completing an esoteric study of some of Shakespeare's plays in the light of the psychology of the System. The publication of this was delayed until just before Christmas. I remember that it coincided with my father's death. It was when I returned to Great Amwell House after attending my father's funeral that I found awaiting me the advance copies of *In the East my Pleasure Lies*. This brought me much interesting correspondence of my own and as Dr Nicoll's mail had increased to a considerable extent letters took up a good deal of time that winter.

In the Spring of 1951 arrangements were made for *The New Man* to be published in U.S.A. I quote a letter from Mr Gorham Munson on behalf of Hermitage House, Inc., New York:

Dear Dr Nicoll,

A contract for an American edition of *The New Man* was sent to you via your agent a few days ago, and by the time you receive this letter I suppose that the signed contracts will be on their way back to us.

I am very happy about the acquisition of your book for our list. Like you, I had the good fortune to know A. R.

Orage and I became greatly interested in the ideas that form the background for *The New Man*. Naturally, I shall take a great personal interest in the promotion of your book here.

I enclose our Author's Publicity Questionnaire. Please fill out answers to such questions as apply to the English author of a book published in America. We need quite urgently a photograph of you.

Faithfully yours,
Gorham Munson,
Editor.

The demand for a photograph caused consternation as no photograph of Dr Nicoll could be found except the usual rather misleading passport photograph. However, eventually something suitable was procured. The American edition did not come out until 1952, which was the year the public edition of the first three volumes of *Commentaries* came out, heralded by Kenneth Walker as 'the fullest and most penetrating study of Gurdjieff's and Ouspensky's teaching that has yet appeared'. The impact of these volumes on the public will be described in the following chapter as it had a remarkable effect on the group.

The last publication of Dr Nicoll's work during his life was *Living Time*, which had been completed twenty-three years previously. Vincent Stuart read the manuscript early in 1952 and on 22nd January wrote as follows to Dr Nicoll:

> Having finished reading your book on *Living Time* I formally request your permission to publish it. The ideas in the book are, for me, an extraordinarily valuable under-mining of sensual thinking and have given me much aid to particular self-observation.
>
> While reading the book it has been curious to find how your present papers are linking with its theme: it is as if the present is opening the door for the 'past' to manifest itself. So that all you wrote in the book is being proved as living in the Now.

Living Time had been completed before the war. At that period it was not permitted to publish anything about the System but

Dr Nicoll had gathered together in this book all the thoughts about Time and Eternity that had come to him from Hermetic literature, from the Greeks, the Neo-Platonists, from the mystics throughout the ages, and from Ouspensky whose Theory of Recurrence was not part of Gurdjieff's System. These thoughts, on which his mind had played, were transformed into this clear conception of the nature of Time as *living in new dimensions*, not as an abstract idea but as a truth which can bring the sense of living life into every moment, making possible an eternal creation in Man.

Living Time was published at the end of November in the same year and was received with acclamation by an entirely new public. I quote an extract from a letter received by Dr Nicoll from Kenneth Walker on 8th December.

> My dear M.,
>
> I am barely one third through *Living Time* but I cannot wait till I have finished it to tell you that it is the best thing you have done. You may deny this and explain why it is not so, but your words will have no effect. For me this is the best thing you have done and the words, which irritated you in my letter to Annie Swan many years ago, to the effect that, in my opinion, you had never produced anything adequate to your genius, are no longer true. This book is, for me, your masterpiece. As you know, I thought highly of *The New Man* but I had to make certain inner reservations about it. . . . Here, in reading your last book, there has been no need for inner reservations. You carry me with you the whole way. I can remember your lending me some chapters of a philosophical work you were writing many years ago, when I was living in Boundary Road and you were living in Hampstead. It dealt with the invisible inner world of Man but what I read did not please me because I felt that Greek philosophy was not your line of country. I was wrong. Your handling of Plato is very skilful and very helpful to me. But I need not continue. *Living Time* is your *chef d'oeuvre*.

Kenneth Walker's review of the book duly appeared in *The Sunday Times*, early in January. This was concise and appreciative, describing it as 'one of those rare books which may have a lasting effect on the reader's thinking and give new meaning to the Universe, to himself and to human life in general'.

The Times Literary Supplement reviewer had more space and referred to the breath-taking vision that Dr Nicoll made possible to his readers so that they might think of their life-experience in a new way and understand what lay beyond their intuitions on the line of Eternity. The letter which came closest to his heart, however, was from a clergyman in the Church of England.

> Dear Sir,
>
> I have just read with extreme interest your book *Living Time*, and I wish very much to write and thank you for it.
>
> I have been familiar with Ouspensky's work for some years, but I think you have taken me a considerable step further towards the actual application of the principles he enunciates. The technique you suggest would seem to lie within one's reach, and I have every intention of putting it into definite practice. It should, I think, take me considerably further than any of the techniques I have so far pursued.
>
> May I thank you very much again for the book and for the invaluable light you have thrown on some of these abstruse problems.

Here was response from a stranger who through his spiritual understanding recognized Dr Nicoll's message. However, at this stage Dr Nicoll had come to receive reviews and letters from readers, new and old, very quietly. We would read them aloud when we were all together in his room. His own private reading was Swedenborg and the Gospels. The papers that he was still writing, week by week, many of them written in bed, were not published until after his death, and his further Gospel studies, also to be published posthumously, were not completed.

CHAPTER FIFTEEN

Last Years

(II CORINTHIANS XII.9)

In the dead of night,
In the dark of the Moon,
I beheld Thy Might
And craved a boon.
Not in thunder nor in storm-wind
Did'st Thou answer
But in the stillness of pure meaning.
Then I knew if the boon were granted
I would die comfortably
The most terrible death of all
Which is spiritual death.
Like a single chord of vast music
Containing all inexpressible divine truth
It entered the limitations of my language.
It became words – as once before:
'My grace is sufficient for thee
Because my strength is made perfect in thy weakness.'
So I understand that when a man can do nothing
And when he comes to that far knowledge
Only then is Thy divine power recognized
And his soul freed to turn to Thee.

Maurice Nicoll

In the summer of 1951 I had been unwell and was recuperating in Brighton when I received the news that Dr Nicoll had been taken to Guy's Hospital for a sudden operation. The first reports said that a startled nurse who had left him sleeping, as she thought, on his return from the operating theatre, found him sitting up, spectacles on nose, placidly reading the *Evening Standard* which he never liked to miss. He seemed to be recovering well but several days later, when I was with Winifred Felce in Wiltshire, a letter came from Mrs Nicoll to tell me that cancer had been diagnosed and the doctors gave him three to five years. She wrote:

> Maurice himself is being very brave and cheerful – laughing and saying 'what is the flesh anyway? and today is only *Monday.*'

Mrs Nicoll had sent this news to the older people in the group. A day or two afterwards he sent me a message to look up some Greek words for him – he was going on with his work – the new phase had now begun.

When he returned home, daily life continued as usual, but after convalescence he still continued to spend his days very quietly in writing, reading and resting in his room and sometimes he would come out on to the terrace and stroll a few paces, or sit in his big chair near his French windows. He had little physical strength, as was to be expected, but he drew on an inexhaustible supply of spiritual energy. His aim was clear now – it was to go on teaching and writing, to use to the full the few precious years that remained to him. He wanted to finish his work.

He had completed most of the *Commentaries* that have since been published in Volume IV. The last papers in the volume and the whole of Volume V except the Appendix were written while he was facing the certain approach of death. It was an illuminating experience to be in daily contact with one to whom the invisible world was more real than the material world. It was possible to talk about death quite simply. Dr Nicoll said at one time he hoped that after death he would be given the work of being an invisible guardian who could protect people from the dangers of their negative emotions. When the time came for him to return to earth his first care, he thought, would be to gather together all those who had helped him in his work, who had served the teaching. He had always believed that groups of people, working together, came into incarnation together in different periods of time to play a part in developing a culture. His group had a part to play in the regeneration of the age. Those who had worked together on Monday would meet more quickly on Tuesday.

Readers of Volume IV of the *Commentaries* will have noticed that there is a gap between June 16th and August 14th 1951 which was the date when Dr Nicoll began to write papers again for the week-end meetings. A deeper note was struck – he was speaking of more interior thinking, and during the two years of his life which followed his thought expanded and deepened. It was at this time that he had the dream of transcending violence, described as crossing a ditch of prehistoric bones, which meant so much to him in that it shewed him the necessity of not working for results but simply doing a higher will, and then going on to the next task, regardless of success or failure. He called his dream THE NEW WILL. It seemed to represent a stage that he had now reached, although in the dream he had felt he could never reach it.

In this dream of mine, what is this ditch? What are the bones? To have crossed this gulf would mean that I would have overcome everything prehistoric in me. What is the prehistoric part of a man? Look at the Liber Mutus. You see a picture there of a man clad in skins lying dead. The violent prehistoric man has given place to the Man and Woman. The man is with his soul. The Man and Woman are in contact with God who comes down. I do not cross this gulf myself. Some dreams are prophetic. You may have a dream that is beyond your level of being and you may see things that you are not ready to have. When you have transcended the prehistoric man in yourself you will come to a country like this. As long as your will is based on self-love it is based on violence too.

This dream does not mean that I have transcended the prehistoric man in myself. When you have overcome the prehistoric man you are in quite another country in which people do things like this teacher, this man, who seemed to me to be wasting a lot of time in training troops and not showing violence, and I, as a spectator am very surprised that he could do such a thing, and feel that I could never will myself to do it. So this shews you what it is to have a will not based on violence or self-love, and without negative emotions. Negative emotions all lead down to violence. This man, the whole thing, is a symbol of what a new will would be like. As I said yesterday, the new will would be something like this – if you cooked the lunch without losing your temper! The new will would mean going in a different direction. When you meet a real esoteric teaching like this Work you are astonished to find that it is so ordinary – and yet it is quite extraordinary.

He began to come in to meetings again and the group came

down in great numbers at the week-ends to see him and to hear him talk.

After his return from hospital Mrs Currie gave all her time to looking after him and continued to do this until the end. She cooked his meals and looked after his welfare with the greatest devotion. We had expected that he would regain his normal strength and once more take part in daily life, but this did not happen. He rarely left his own room. *The New Man* had been published in U.S.A. by Hermitage House and his books now brought him correspondence from all over the world but he began to leave more and more of his letters to me and to conserve his energy for writing and for taking the week-end meetings. When he felt equal to it he would still gather the household together after tea to talk informally; as of old we drank his claret while he ruefully sipped Ribena. All those of us who were privileged to be part of the household at that time were given something of priceless value. We all knew that we were present in the final act of the drama of Dr Nicoll's life.

Mr Kenneth Walker came down at intervals to see him as friend and surgeon and gave him all possible support at this time when he found that he was not regaining the strength that he had hoped for. I know that he advised him not to expend his energy in writing if he wished to prolong his life, but Dr Nicoll made a conscious choice here, electing to use all his available energy in order to make full use of the limited time at his disposal.

The publication of the *Commentaries* in 1952 brought him letters from readers in all parts of this country and later from abroad. People wrote with requests for personal contact. Many wanted to join his school. A question would be put: 'Is it possible to achieve much in the Work – as you say – by simply trying to apply what you write about in your Commentaries to yourself?' The writers of such questions would come great distances to see Dr Nicoll. There were many enquiries as to where study groups could be found, but some people simply wrote thanking him for shewing them the way to a practical understanding of the System. The kind of letter that he really enjoyed was one such as the following, from one of his contemporaries in the medical world:

MAURICE NICOLL

Heathcote, Redbridge, Dorchester, Dorset.

Sept. 2nd, 1952.

Dear Dr Nicoll,

I was house surgeon to Wilfred Trotter for a short time in 1916 and in the course of an operation to fill in a gap in a skull I was given a bone graft from the shin to hold, which I inadvertently dropped on the floor. Without the slightest hesitation, annoyance or resentment Dr Trotter said, 'some people would just dust it and carry on – but I think we'll have another piece.'

This was the first shock that made me realize that things were not quite what I had assumed they were.

I have read your *Commentaries* with great interest and instruction. I feel I owe you and O. and G. and others a great debt of gratitude which I shall try to repay by hard work.

I have retired from medical practice and now live a very isolated life – nearly a mile from the nearest neighbour – and this I assume is my right setting at present.

Yours sincerely,

Charles R. Smith.

One result of this publication was that new demands were made on Dr Nicoll by interviews with strangers seeking help and also by the increased attendance at his meetings. However, he was not always well enough either to see people or to take the week-end meetings. It was interesting to us as onlookers to observe what different experiences his visitors attracted. Some went away perforce without seeing him at all, never to return; some would return again and again until they did see him, persistence being inevitably rewarded in the end; others would depart having been enlightened or shattered by a few quiet penetrating words from Dr Nicoll. I quote an impression of one correspondent from the country who followed up the above question with a visit and afterwards came to Amwell with his wife as often as distance and his exacting professional work allowed.

We were late for the meeting. However, there were notices telling us to go straight in when we arrived, and this we did. We went to empty chairs in the big room, and the first strange thing was that nobody turned round to see who we were, no idle curiosity, just space made for us, without any fuss. I suppose that this sense of *appropriateness* was one of the most striking things about the house. There seemed to be nothing that did not need to be done, and yet everything that should be done, and more, was done. So that there was still the feeling of the individuality that a house should have, in spite of the large numbers of people using it.

Of the meeting, I cannot now recollect the details, but I do recall on another occasion the opening part of the meeting being taken by one of the group who talked quite sensibly about the questions that were asked. However, when Dr Nicoll came in the whole atmosphere was different and as if electrified. He made everything that had been said before seem quite trivial and beside the point. Here was someone who *knew what he was talking about*.

The same quality came out when Dr Nicoll invited us into his room after the meeting, which he always did. This was surely external considering, as he was far from well, and knew that he could not expend more than a certain amount of force in this way. We had come from Liverpool, and always hoped to see him, though never daring to *expect* to do so. Although the subjects of his conversation sometimes seemed to be rather trivial, I believe that everything that he said was deliberate. I remember him being delighted with a little clockwork toy mule which he had been given, as its actions were so like those of the real creature. He talked about mules and their characteristics, and I much later thought that what he had said then had been aimed at me, though of course I did not recognize it at the time. He liked to try to draw people out on their identified topics of conversation – such as antibiotics with me, and saying 'Dr' not 'Mr' when he addressed me. But if the fish would not rise he dropped it immediately and went on with something else. I recall his commenting on Christie, the murderer, and saying that it would be better for him to be hanged than reprieved, as it would give him a chance to start his life again, and not go on repeating the same thing. This struck me as a wonderfully true and just thought, though one could hardly imagine anyone using it as a plea for the retention of capital punishment! It was things like that which gave one the knowledge that here there was someone who really did believe in Scale, as we are taught in the Work, and who had the very best of reasons for doing so, in that he really and practically understood it. His conversation seemed at first to be very short and almost gruff. If a topic was leading nowhere it would be dropped immediately. Ordinarily we tend to carry on, round and round in the same circle. About detective stories – 'Do you imagine that I am poring over enormous learned volumes all the time?' – to one who had a bad back – 'Why do you do all that stooping and bending in the garden? You ought to have more sense.'

Altogether, I had the impression that I had met a *man* for the first time. Yet he had a very ordinary exterior, and a strange mixture of fierceness, humour, leg-pulling, relaxation; but nothing of what we would call earnestness, or piousness.

In the house on a Sunday it was not always easy to know how to behave, probably because the usual outlets of gossip and boasting, however mildly, simply did not seem to be possible. Of other aspects of the party I will mention simply the great feeling of pleasure at being one of the men who did the massive washing up after meals, and the lack of any comment or recrimination when a pint of beer was spilled over us at a crowded little table at the pub. Unnecessary emotions again did not seem to be allowed – what bliss it seemed to find that what one really knew inwardly to be true was so, and that there was a teaching which explained why it was, and how it might be achieved.

During 1952 Dr Nicoll had been writing chapters for a second book on the Gospels for which there was already a certain amount of unpublished material. He had been in doubt about the title of the book but eventually received inner prompting to call it *The Mark*. We had already spoken much of the word ἁμαρτανω trans-

19. 1953

lated as 'to sin', whose true meaning was to miss the mark. Many of our conversations were about this. I quote from one that took place on Dr Nicoll's birthday in July 1952. He said:

About this book that I propose to write, I shall read parts of it occasionally. The idea of the book is at present 'The Mark'. You cannot have an aim without a mark. I think you should have a mark. Man is created a self-developing organism. There are four ways to the development of Man. This Fourth Way is the way of Consciousness. Certainly the Mark is Consciousness, as someone pointed out in a letter. The aim is to establish consciousness by means of Higher Centres. There is only so much consciousness but the quantity of consciousness available is far greater than the consciousness sought after, so there is no deficiency. If everyone on earth were seeking this Work no one would get anything. Only certain people are allowed to awaken.

The Mark is the Kingdom of Heaven. Everything that Christ teaches is how to aim at the Kingdom of Heaven. For instance we are asked to try to be meek. This aim does not mean that you must be meek in our sense of the word. (Dr Nicoll acts looking meek.) The Greek word, πραος, means absence from resentment. You can see that the wrong translation is given. If you practise absence from resentment, you then come to the next stage which is κατανοια – considerateness. If you are always resenting everything you are not externally considering. You are laying up thoughts in the mind which are mere pus. You should not go on like this. You should try and see the same thing in yourself. It is all to do with this. If you resent everything you will not be able to have κατανοια, which leads to αγαπη – conscious love. Christ taught that you must love your enemies. When you say 'I love everybody' do you think that is conscious love? There are three kinds of love in the Work, physical, emotional (which always turns into its opposite) and conscious love. In Matthew ch. 19 the rich man asked Christ what he could do to inherit Eternal Life. Christ answered, 'If thou wilt be perfect, go and sell that thou hast, and give to the poor. . . .' Notice he said 'perfect' – τελειος. This means complete. Man No. 4 who has illuminated his life with sufficient consciousness has the choice of getting in contact with No. 5 Man, and through him to No. 6 Man. But if a man has no photographs at all he does not perfect himself. He perfects himself in relation to life, but does not do anything extra. This is what Christ means when he says, 'If you would perfect yourself.'

It was during this summer that we received the shock of Mrs Nicoll's announcement that she was about to go into the Royal Northern Hospital for an operation for cancer of the breast. She had known for some time that this was pending but had kept silence. Dr Nicoll felt her suffering very deeply. It was always the thing that he found hardest to bear. The operation was successful and Mrs Nicoll went away for a long convalescence from which she returned in time to be with us for the winter. She was very precious to us – it was wonderful to see her well again.

1953 was an eventful year for us all. The octave spent at Great Amwell House was drawing to its close. For our country also it was an important year, the year of Queen Mary's death and the Coronation of Queen Elizabeth. For Europe it was made memorable by the death of Stalin.

In January there were floods and disasters at sea. Dr Nicoll had of recent years found the winter months difficult and now his strength was failing. He felt deeply the death of Colonel Butler. I remember the bleak day at the end of February, when Dr Nicoll, from his bed, asked me to ring up the London Clinic for news of him – the only information available was that he was in a uraemic coma. Dr Nicoll's comment was, 'It is an easy death – so I should like to die.' (His wish was fulfilled.) Colonel Butler was greatly beloved and many of us mourned him. This was the first of a long series of bereavements which the Group suffered during the year.

At Easter Dr Nicoll recorded in his diary a prayer that if he were granted some more months of life he would not misuse them. He felt he had still much more to teach, much more to write. His prayer was granted and he continued to work with all his remaining strength during the spring and summer in spite of

Mr Walker's advice to spare himself in order to prolong his life. Spiritual energy flowed through him as he cheerfully went on unfolding new and deeper meaning in a sustained effort to give us everything he could before he left us.

I quote a conversation recorded by Mrs Beatrice Mayor at this time:

> I last saw him a few months before his death. He was smiling, carefree and radiant.
>
> 'Cast your burdens upon the Lord,' he said, with a light gesture. 'That's all.' 'Stop thinking.' 'Cast your burdens upon the Lord!'
>
> Earlier he had mentioned his illness, and that he would die before long.
>
> 'You are not afraid?' I said.
>
> 'No,' he said slowly and with great serenity, 'I am not afraid.'

In April Dr Nicoll received news from Mrs Jung that Dr Jung had been unwell throughout the winter. She commented in her letter on the coincidence that Dr Nicoll and her husband had been independently thinking and writing on parallel lines. She expressed her appreciation of *Living Time* which they had received as a gift from Dr Nicoll. He wrote back with the warm feeling that he always had for them both. This was his last communication with them. A contract was now signed for the publication by Ediciones Sol of a Spanish version of *Living Time*, *The New Man* having found many Catholic readers in its Spanish form in Mexico and South America.

Mr Mearns had instituted an intercom to make it easy for Dr Nicoll to speak to anyone in the house from his room. He had beside his chair the small switchboard connecting him with Mrs Nicoll's room, with mine, with Mrs Currie's and with the kitchen. He who had all his life disliked speaking on the telephone, and had limited his part in any telephone conversation to a brusque minimum, now began to enjoy sounding his buzzer and making remarks to startle the cooks, to amuse Mrs Nicoll, or to ask one of us to come down to his room.

After the meetings on Saturday and Sunday he would like to

relax in his room talking to a few people and he liked then to have the young about him – David Wynne and John Pettavel, with their clear minds – and those who had come from a distance to be with him.

The month of June opened with the splendour of the Coronation and the glory of the ascent of Everest. It was a new beginning for me personally as on 8th June I went down to Haywards Heath by request to start a group there. It was our first experiment of a group in the country as hitherto all study groups had taken place in London. The rainy period of the Coronation had given place to the most delightful summer weather and I have clear impressions of the sounds and scents of the Sussex lanes and gardens. Dr Nicoll gave his blessing to this new venture which eventually expanded and has continued to the present day.

On 16th June I went with Mrs Nicoll and Mrs Wilding to see the play, *Out of the Whirlwind*, produced in Westminster Abbey. One of the group, Diana Wilding, was acting in it. I remember how gay and pleased Mrs Nicoll was. She loved to have a day in London. We visited Mrs Butler for drinks on our way. We were delighted at the prospect of being inside the Abbey which still retained many traces of the Coronation ceremony. We sat in the chairs which had been arranged for those entitled to seats. I remember walking down the lane from the Green Line bus in a fine rain as we returned later. Although we did not then know it this was the last time that Mrs Nicoll was to go to London for pleasure. On 28th June she became ill. Her arm and shoulder began to pain her. This was a recurrence of her illness although it was not recognized as such for the time being. We had now entered a sad period of illness and bereavement. On 20th June we had news of the sudden death of Miss Maud Hoffman, Dr Nicoll's old friend, whom I had visited at intervals for the past three years so that by now she had become my friend.

On Sunday 26th July, I remember that a swallow came into the room where we were having the meeting. Dr Nicoll smiled and said: 'You all think it a bad omen' – there was an eclipse of the moon that day.

The following day Jack Edwards died in hospital where he had been taken some weeks previously. This was a bereavement that touched us very closely as for nearly seven years he had been one of the household. Mrs Nicoll's doctors now diagnosed a return of cancer – she had been in pain for many weeks and on August 14th she went into the Royal Northern Hospital for deep X-ray treatment. This was a very great shock for Dr Nicoll, who once again had to face the fact of her suffering.

On Sunday 16th August, a fortnight before he died, Dr Nicoll took his last meeting. He had written a paper on 'Observation of Attitude to the Work' which Mr Stuart and I had read to the Group. Then Dr Nicoll came into the room and began to answer questions. He talked to us for a long time, very quietly. After a time we became aware that he seemed to have thrown off his illness altogether. His voice had changed, his face had changed – it was Dr Nicoll as we had known him of old who was sitting there talking to us. He spoke very simply with a deep note of urgency about the need of humility, the Sermon on the Mount, the danger of vanity, of resentment, the need of valuation which was the way towards service. At one moment during the talk I had an inner intuition, which I afterwards found had been shared by others, that this was his last meeting, and that this was the last time when he would speak to us as a group. He was stressing with a quiet intensity the same truths that Christ had stressed when teaching. I quote his final words:

> About this inner and outer happiness. The gratification of your conceits gives you outer happiness, and going against your conceits gives you inner happiness – that is called work on yourself. To go against the gratification of your conceits would be to go against your mechanicalness, and to go against the satisfaction of your conceits would be work. If you annoy me very much and I can see myself in you and you in me as a result of long work of observation, what then?
>
> I am trying to make you see what the Work is, and contrasting it with your ordinary conception of life, with your vanity and so on. Some of you are no good because you do not do the Work from your understanding, you seem to think it is something on the board, and so I cannot use you. Or else you lose your temper, so I cannot use you. Also,

you get rude, but you don't notice it. You will not be able to teach this Work if you do not notice these things because you do not know enough about yourself. If you lose your temper, it will not occur to you to see that you lose your temper, and see what it is that causes you to lose your temper, so, therefore, I cannot use you. Now, when you satisfy a form of conceit it has this peculiar taste about it which is utterly different from this inner taste which has to do with going against your mechanicalness.

It is a very curious thing that Work happiness does come to you sometimes when you have done nothing. It is usually because you have seen through something. Ordinarily our happiness gets coarser and coarser, you may take more and more gin. People without knowing this Work do work on themselves; there is a better side in us and a worse side. There are 'I's that understand more without having got the Work, but to hold the Work in you, you require an organized thing like the Work. Even if you cannot believe in anything, people must admit that there are better states and worse states. It is so. And when this Work does shew you a little bit it leads right down to the bad states in you. You have a map in your own psychological country and you will know that you should not go down that road because you know what will happen, so after a time you will avoid going down certain roads. Just to get to know a little about this map is a great advantage. You are always in some country. There is always some place where you should not go. If you have not learned this at all then it is a pity. But people do not see that they are down on this planet for some reason. We go down the same road time after time, and after a time you just go down to the slums, and then things are getting worse and you are lost. Some people think they have not much to do in this Work, that there is no special task, but of course you have, you have Chief Feature for one thing; there is always something to work at. I think it becomes plain that there are some things that if you had started working on earlier, it would have been a good thing. I am speaking to those who know there is something wrong with them.

The more you value the Work, which is called Esoteric Christianity, the more room you have for it. How would you have liked to play the role of Christ and have to be a failure? He was tempted on the side of power and that had to be given up. He explained to his friends that to fulfil the prophecy He had to fail. To get anything done He had to fail. How could He have expressed what the Work meant, how else could He have expressed the Beatitudes if He had not been a power man? And at the same time there would not have been any work if He had not wanted power. If you work on yourself you give force to others, not only to yourself. When people are not working it is a very great drag on me and Mrs Nicoll. But when anyone works on himself it gives force to everyone. That is why it is important to remember that. But if you have no place of reception of the force that you get from the Work and treat it scurvily, the force will be lost. One of the causes why the Work seems some distance from you is that you are resenting something. You make accounts about everything, some of you, very quickly. Read the parable that Christ gave to the disciples when they said to Him: 'Increase our faith.' (Luke XVII, 5-10). Esoteric Christianity, as G. called the Work, is not religion, but it is the inner meaning of what Christ taught. In this parable the servant has to understand *that he is serving*. Some of you seem to freeze when I talk about the Gospels. It is nothing to do with religion, it does not make any difference whether you are a Jew, or a Christian, or anything else, this Work is about Esoteric Christianity, and about a certain development which Man can undergo; if you do not understand this it means you have a wrong attitude to the Work. Some of you even think it is good of you to be here. If you are going to *serve the Work* it is no use standing on your rights. This parable shewed that the disciples were putting too much value on themselves and they became resentful and lost their feeling of faith. You can read about this in the Chapter on Faith in *The New Man*. Man is a failing experiment, but if sufficient people try to awaken it is some good. You have to have a big background for this Work, not a little mean background.

He had raised the consciousness of the meeting so that all who were present had an experience they never forgot. A few days later, a week after Mrs Nicoll had gone to hospital, he fell in his bathroom and afterwards seemed to have no further will to live. He knew then that he was dying and we knew it too. The shock of Mrs Nicoll's illness seemed to have loosened his hold on life. The day before his fall he had written the beginning of one more paper, which was never finished. He had been writing about how to become free from the illusion of the senses, how to become conscious of one's neighbour as oneself. One day as he lay in bed I drank to him and said, 'your health', but he replied, 'my *spiritual health*'. Several days afterwards he fell into a coma and died on Sunday 30th August.

The last words recorded in his diary were, 'I would be pierced and I would pierce.'

'Mortal things are fatal to the flow of God.'
The spiritual man stands over all things of earth.
The Divine light reaches only the highest love.
May my soul transcend my daily anxiety!

'The work of God is the noblest product.'
So my outward life is dead. Prayer,
Sorrow, anxiety, do not redeem it.
The highest love alone meets God.

There is daily suffering and daily suffering,
But only right suffering releases.
There is a place within to suffer rightly
And when found, God enters in.

All riches, virtues, and suffering from the loss of them,
All wishes to be unchanged by sin,
Unchangeable, respectable, liked,
Is not suffering. To suffer is not merit.
Suffering is to know God.
Only to know God is suffering.
For if we know God is,
We know within what we are and only thus.
To know what one is is to suffer, and this is to know God.
To know oneself is to call helplessly on God,
Self-love wanes, God enters.
Self-knowledge is knowledge of God.
If God is not, self-knowledge is not.
Knowledge is to love the unknown.
Without God we cannot know more,
All knowledge passes into love of God.
'Nothing makes a man so like God as suffering.'
To suffer is to know one's fault, not to complain,
To lose oneself in the emotion
of self-knowing, and know God's knowledge.

Why does suffering free from lust?
Because lust is self-will, and right suffering
is another's will, so infinitely greater
That all self vanishes in freedom.

Maurice Nicoll

Index

Adams, Bill, 11
Adrian, Lord, 222
Agoraphobia, 176, 177
Aldenham School, 11
Amwell, Great Amwell House, 16, 25, 73, chapter on 237-55
Ark, symbol of esoteric teaching, 132, 217
Asquith, 166
Atkins, Basil, 11, 12

Barron, Mrs, 240
Bart's Hospital, 5, 20
Bay Tree Lodge, 1
Berger, Professor Hans, 223
Birdlip, 17, 42, 138-47
Blackhall, David, 246
Blue Germ, The, 61, 62
Bookman, The, 2
Boswell, 27, 28, 244, 245
Briitsh Weekly, The, 2, 6, 33, 59, 263
Bream, Julian, 82
Bush, Fulford, 105, 108, 110, 113, 120, 124, 126, 147, 256-8
Butler, Colonel Humphrey, 137, 144, 195, 207, 276
Butler, Mrs Humphrey, 131, 141, 144, 146

Caius, Gonville and Caius College, Cambridge, 11, 13, 14, 230
Casswell, Thomas, 113-14, 120-1
Chamberlain, Neville, 132, 215, 218
Champion Jones, Miss Léonor (Mrs Nicoll's sister), 73, 80
Champion Jones, Catherine, *see* Nicoll, Mrs
Château du Prieuré, *see* Institute
Chishengtse, 248
Chorley Wood, cottage at, 63, 66, 69
Churchill, Sir Winston, 25, 149, 201, 217
Claustrophobia, 176-7
Coad, Miss Lesley, 240
Commentaries, Psychological, 146, 251, 256, 258, 263, 265, 269, 271

Constance Nicoll, *see* Miles, Mrs Elystan
Copley, Sam, 156, 203, 249
Corbett, Colonel Jim, 243
Corcoran, Miss Dorothy, 110, 140-1, 144, 204, 205, 227, 231
Craig, Dr Maurice, 57
Currie, Mrs, 126, 135, 138, 144, 145, 210, 240, 246, 271
Currie, John, 135, 240

Darlow, T. H., 29, 33
Darwin, Charles, 23, 234
Demery, Miss Marjorie, *see* Hodder, Mrs, 135, 137
Diogenes, 256, 262
Dreams and Dream Interpretation, 24, 51, 55
Dream Psychology, 51, 56, 61-63, 116
Dreyfus, 73
Dunkirk, 141, 149
Dunlop, Miss Isa of Kelso, first wife of Sir William Robertson Nicoll and mother of Maurice, 4

Edwards, John, 278
Edwards, Mrs, *see* Lance, Miss Nancy
Elliott Smith, Professor, 57
Elliott, Dr, 246
Elliott, Mrs, 239-40
Entropy, 224
Epilepsy, 54
Expositor, The, 2

Farquhar-Buzzard, 57
Felce, Miss Winifred, 260
Flood, 216
Fludd, 117
Fourth Way, The, 95, 147-8
Fragments of an Unknown Teaching, 114, 260, 263
French, General, 167
Freud, Professor Sigmund, 23, 49, 52-55, 70, 128
Freudian system of psychology, 18
Furze, Dame Katherine, 70

Georgette, 17-18
Gloster, Peter, 125
Gloster, Mr and Mrs, 241
Goethe, 128
Gonville and Caius College, Cambridge, 11
Goodman, Laurie, 226, 238
Gordon, Miss Marjorie, 125
Gothic architecture, 39
Grandchild, 251
Great Amwell House, see Amwell
Gurdjieff, George Ivanovitch (1872-1950) expected in London, 71; the Institute opened, 72; 76, 77, 78, 79, 80; his methods of building, 81-83; work on vanity, 84; his theatre at the Institute, 85; as a carpenter, 86; buys a car, 86; decides to spend a night in Switzerland, 87, 88, 89; on associations, 90; exercises for developing attention, 91; decides to close the Institute, 92; prophecy regarding war, 132, 146; had often no external habitation for the Work, 147; interpretation of Crucifixion, 201; announcement that teaching could be published, 259; circular letter, 260; died, 260

Hartmann, M. de., 83, 85
Head, Henry, 57
Hitler, 73, 217-20
Hodder, Captain (Bill), 137, 208
Hodder, Mrs, 138, 144, 206, 208, 229
Hodder and Stoughton, publishers, 2, 26
Hoffer, Mrs, 128
Hoffman, Miss Maud, 16, 63, 64, 70, 74, 76, 80, 88, 278
Holmes, Miss Florence, 240
Horsley, Sir Victor, 44
Howarth, Mrs, 125
Humby, Miss, 241, 242, 248
Hypnotism, 23
Hysteria, 154

In Mesopotamia, 43, 45, 48, 61
In Search of the Miraculous, see Fragments of an Unknown Teaching

Institute, 72, 73; Miss Hoffman's impressions of 74-77; Christmas at, 84-85; rigorous conditions at 80-82; 88-92; aphorism from, 123
Ivanova, Olga, 79, 85

Jackson, Hughlings, 222
Jane, daughter of Dr and Mrs Nicoll, see Mounsey, Jane
Jarvis, Major, 243
Johnson, Dr, 27, 28, 155, 190, 206, 211, 244, 245
Ju-jitsu, taught by Mr Pagose, 126
Jung, Dr C. J., 18-20, 23, 24, 33, 50-54; at haunted cottage with Dr Nicoll, 63-66, 68, 69; compared with Socrates, 70, 71, 116; Essay on Synchronicity, 212, 213
Jung, Mrs, 68, 69

Kadleigh, George, 120
Kadloubovsky, Mme, 131
Keane, Miss, 143
Keane, Mrs, 229, 230
Kirkcaldy, Mrs, 10, 12, 32, 68, 191
Kitchener, 166, 167, 171
Knapp, 185
Knox, Mgr, 96
Kent, Duke of, 207

Labori, Maitre, 73
Lance, Miss Nancy, 133, 135, 137, 240
Lancet, The, 51, 55, 56
Landau, Rom, 263
Lawrence, D. H., 188
Living Time, 116, 117, 265, 266, 277
Lloyd George, 25, 33, 166, 177
Lodge, Sir Oliver, 59
Lord, Miss, 245
Lord Richard in the Pantry, 26
Lumsden, 2
Lydall, Miss C. M., 117, 120

Maclagan, Miss, 4
Maffett, Colonel, 131
Maffett, Mrs, 140
Mansfield, Katherine, 85, 86, 74, 77, 79, 81, 84
Mark, The, 134, 274

Maude, Cyril, 16
Mayor, Mrs Beatrice, 277
Mearns, Joe, 277
Miles, Mrs Elystan, 4, 6, 10, 14, 15, 21
  26, 30, 31, 38, 58, 64, 66
Miller, Dr Crichton, 21, 22, 23, 57
Minnie, Aunt (sister of Lady Robertson
  Nicoll), 9
Moore, Dr Gordon, 11, 12, 14, 21
Mounsey, Mrs Jane (neé Nicoll), 20,
  70, 73, 79-80, 87; illness at Institute,
  90, 91, 93, 96, 117, 120, 132, 135,
  137, 205
Mounsey, Mr John, 131, 135, 137, 141
  206
Movements, 80, 81, 82, 83, 87, 88, 125,
  126, 134
Moxon, Miss Selene, 118, 119, 135
Mullins, Claud, 21
Murry, John Middleton, 77-79, 85, 86

Napoleon, 154, 164, 169, 173, 182
Nellie, Aunt (sister of Lady Robertson
  Nicoll), 5
New Age, The, 71, 72
New Man, The, 198, 199, 261, 262, 263,
  265
New Model of the Universe, A, 114, 115
Ney, Miss Frances, 116, 117
Nicoll, Dr William Robertson (later
  Sir William), 2; his library, 6;
  methods of working, 7-8, 13; re-
  ceives knighthood, 14, 16; relationship with his son, 19, 21, 24-29;
  tastes and method of working, 27-28;
  work during 1914 war, 32-34, 37,
  47, 55, 57, 58; death, 87
Nicoll, Lady Robertson, marriage, 4;
  description of Maurice, 5-6, 20, 26,
  32, 35, 43, 58, 61
Nicoll, Dr Henry Maurice Dunlop,
  see Biographical Table, Intro., ix
Nicoll, Mrs, née Catherine Champion
  Jones, 65; first meeting with Maurice
  Nicoll, 67; marriage, 68; early life,
  69; birth of daughter, Jane, 70;
  attends Ouspensky's meetings, 71;
  life at the Institute, 80; present at
  death of Katherine Mansfield, 86;

return to London, 92; winter at The
  Old Manse, 93-94; Bay Tree Lodge,
  94; Alley Cottage, 96, 115; Lakes
  Farm, 117, 118; Tyeponds, 120, 122,
  124; daughter's wedding, 137; journey to Birdlip, 138, 139, 143-5;
  operation, 231; finds Great Amwell
  House, 240, 241; shock of Ous-
  pensky's death, 249; approached by
  members of Ouspensky's group,
  249; birth of grandchild, 251; teaches
  new group, 251; on Committee for
  private publication, 257; operation,
  276; recurrence of illness, 278
Nicoll, Jane (daughter of Maurice
  Nicoll), see Mounsey, Mrs Jane
Nicoll, Constance (sister of Maurice
  Nicoll), see Miles, Mrs Elystan
Nicoll, Mildred (stepsister of Maurice
  Nicoll), see Kirkcaldy, Mrs
Nicolson, Harold, 243
Nina, 78
Nineteenth Century, The, 55, 56
Nott, Mrs Rosemary, 125

Orage, A. R., 71, 72, 77, 85, 91, 92
Ostrovsky, Mme, 78
Ouspensky, Madame, 99, 100, 119
Ouspensky, P. D., lecturing at the
  Quest Society, 70, 71; his connection
  with Gurdjieff, 71-72; visit to the
  Institute, 80, 81; meetings, 84, 89;
  his group help with publication of
  A New Model of the Universe, his
  method of working on the New
  Testament, 95; at Alley Cottage, 96,
  97-105; authorizes Dr Nicoll to
  teach the System, 108-9, 114, 117; at
  Dr Nicoll's meetings, 127, 132; in-
  terpretation of Crucifixion, 201;
  died, 248; as a 'Cock of Wood', 249

Page, Walter, 'Life and Letters', 170,
  171
Pagose, 126
Parfit, Cyril, 122
Park, Miss Winifred, 241, 246
Parsons, Mrs, 125
Pelican Hotel, unfinished novel by Dr
  Nicoll, 25, 30, 128, 134, 137, 145

INDEX

Pettavel, John, 278
Pierpoint, Miss, 4, 5
Pinder, 82
Plato, 114, 116, 124
Pogson, Mrs, introduction to Dr Nicoll's meetings, 113-15; first conversation with Dr Nicoll, 115; visit to Dr Nicoll at Harley Street, 115; work on anthology, 115-16; building at Tyeponds, 121-2; begins secretarial work for Dr Nicoll, 127-8; gives English lessons to Freudian Psychologists from Vienna, 128; becomes Dr Nicoll's full-time secretary, 133; recollections of wartime life at Tyeponds, 135-6; first impressions of The Knapp, 139; secretarial work at The Knapp, 146, 198; collected material for Gospel papers, 199; experience of synchronicity, 212; moved to Quaremead, 227; organization of work at Quaremead, 228; visited Great Amwell House with Dr Nicoll, 237; moved to Great Amwell House, 238; visited Mr Bush to arrange for publication of the Commentaries, 257; corrected proofs of Commentaries, 258; father's death coincided with publication of In the East my Pleasure Lies, 264; accompanied Mrs Nicoll to Out of the Whirlwind in Westminster Abbey, 278; asked by Mrs Nicoll to write Dr Nicoll's biography, xiii
Pollard, Miss Catherine (see Nicoll, Lady), 4
Pollard, Joseph, 9, 11, 13
Powell, Miss, 135, 145
Priestley, J. B., 252
Pushti, 97, 119

Quest Society, 70

Reekie, Miss, 124
Regression, 50
Rheumatism, cause of, 107
Republic of Plato, 116
Riddell, Lord, 25, 116
Riddoch, Dr George, 56, 57
Riley, Peter, 132

Rivers, Dr, 56, 57
Royal Society, The, 56

Sandheim, Mrs, 124, 136, 241
Salzmann, Madame de, 263, 264
Salzmann, Mr, 79, 85, 86, 241
Saunders, Miss Edith, 243
Schrödinger, Erwin, 223-5
Sharp, Clifford, 71
Squire, W. Haddon, 125
Squire, David, 122
Stalker, Miss Marjorie, 125
Strand Magazine, 21
Streatfeild, Michael, 124, 240
Streatfeild, Mrs, 213, 247
Stuart, Vincent, 279
Swayne, Martin (pseudonym of Dr Nicoll), 21, 61
Syfret, Lady, 207
Syfret, Rear-Admiral, 207

Taylor, Mrs, 131
Tertium Organum, 115
Thompson, Edward, 151
Trotter, Wilfred, 221, 272
Tyeponds, 120-4; new house built, 125, 126; sudden order to leave, 137; under military occupation, 145

Ugley, 138
University College Preparatory School, Hampstead, 3

Wadham, Miss, 125, 133, 135, 138, 139, 143, 144
Walker, Kenneth, 11, 12, 14, 17, 56, 65, 66, 93 105, 119, 127, 132, 146, 216, 265, 271
Warre-Cornish, Mrs, 249
Wilding, Mrs, 278
Wilding, Miss Diana, 278
Williams, Dr Leonard, 67, 68, 69
Wilshin, Miss Sunday, 118, 119, 124, 136
Wilshin, Mr and Mrs, 227
Wordsworth, William, 184, 193
Wordsworth, Dorothy, 184, 193
Wynne, David, 278

Young, Dr James, 63, 64, 69, 72, 84, 85, 89

288

FOURTH WAY BOOKS publishes works that explain and expand the powerful psychological system originated by G.I. Gurdjieff. These books range from the very beginnings of the system to the most recent works in the field.

If you would like to find out about our forthcoming publications, mail in the Order Form/Mailing List Request on the back of this page. A description of one of our other titles follows:

Body Types
by Joel Friedlander
5½ x 8¼, 168 pages
Hardcover $19.95
Softcover $9.95

Learn how to recognize the physical and psychological characteristics of the seven archetypal Body Types. Using the powerful psychology of Gurdjieff and Ouspensky, explore the automatic thoughts, attitudes, motives and morality of each type. See yourself, your relationships and the people you know in an entirely new way.

Written in such an easily read style you will wish it were longer. Recommended. – The Unicorn.

ORDER FORM/MAILING LIST REQUEST

Please send me the following books:

Title	Quantity	Amount
Maurice Nicoll, A Portrait at 12.95	_____	_____
Body Types, hardcover at 19.95	_____	_____
Body Types, softcover at 9.95	_____	_____
Subtotal		_____
NY residents add tax:		_____
Shipping (see below)		_____
Total Enclosed		_____

Please include my name on your mailing list._____

Name_____

Address_____

City_____State_____Zip_____

Country_____ PostCode_____

Shipping Charges

U.S. Addresses:

Surface	$1.50 for the first book .50 each additional book Delivery: 10–21 days	Air	$3.50 for the first book 1.00 each additional book Delivery: 4–9 days

Foreign Addresses:*

Surface	$1.50 for the first book .50 each additional book Delivery: 2–14 weeks	Air	$5.00 for the first book 3.00 each additional book Delivery: 5–14 days

*Foreign Orders: *Maurice Nicoll, A Portrait* is available for shipment only to U.S. addresses. *Body Types:* Foreign orders payable in U.S. funds only.

Our Guarantee: If, for any reason, you are not satisfied with any book, return it in saleable condition within 30 days for a prompt and friendly cash refund.

To order, mail this Order Form
with your check or money
order to:

GLOBE PRESS BOOKS
P.O. BOX 2045-C
MADISON SQUARE STATION
NEW YORK, NY 10159.